Limited Scope
Legal Services

Unbundling and the Self-Help Client

STEPHANIE L. KIMBRO

ABA **LawPracticeManagementSection**
MARKETING • MANAGEMENT • TECHNOLOGY • FINANCE

Cover design by RIPE Creative, Inc.

Printed in the United States of America.

15 14 13 12   5 4 3 2 1

Library of Congress Cataloging-in-Publication Data

Kimbro, Stephanie L.
    Limited scope legal services: unbundling and the self-help client / Stephanie L. Kimbro.
        p. cm.
    Includes index.
    ISBN 978-1-61438-362-8
    1. Practice of law—United States. 2. Legal services—United States. I. Title.
    KF300.K59   2012
    340.0973—dc23

                                                                    2012005079

Dedication

TO MY PARENTS, MY husband, and my children for their patience and support.

Contents

About the Author

Stephanie Kimbro

Stephanie Kimbro, MA, JD, has operated a Web-based virtual law office in North Carolina since 2006 and delivers unbundled estate planning to clients online. She is the recipient of the 2009 ABA Keane Award for Excellence in eLawyering and has won the *Wilmington Parent Magazine* Family Favorite Attorney Award five years in a row for her virtual law office. Her book, *Virtual Law Practice: How to Deliver Legal Services Online,* was published by the ABA/LPM in October of 2010. She is also the cofounder of Virtual Law Office Technology, LLC (VLOTech), which was acquired by Total Attorneys in the fall of 2009.

In addition to her virtual law practice, Kimbro is a technology consultant who provides assistance to other legal professionals interested in the online delivery of legal services. Kimbro writes about the ethics and technology issues of delivering legal services online and is interested in the use of technology by legal professionals to increase access to justice in our country. She has presented continuing legal education (CLE) courses on a variety of topics for the ABA, ALI-ABA, and different state bar groups and law schools.

Kimbro serves on the advisory board of the International Legal Technology Standards Organization (ILTSO) and is a member of the ABA eLawyering Task Force, the Vice Chair of the ABA LPM's Ethics and Professional Responsibility Task Force, and a member of the North Carolina Bar Association (NCBA) Law Practice Management (LPM) Council and the NCBA Tech Advisory Committee.

Acknowledgments

I WOULD LIKE TO thank the Publishing Board and the publishing staff of the ABA's Law Practice Management Section, especially Timothy Johnson, Executive Editor, Denise Constantine, Production Manager, and Lindsay Dawson, Marketing Director.

I also would like to thank the individuals who took the time to review the manuscript. Art Garwin, Richard Granat, Will Hornsby, Timothy White, and Jim Ring all provided helpful feedback and guidance. Richard Granat provided invaluable feedback on the background of unbundling as well as the business and marketing implications for the future of legal service delivery. Jim Ring provided valuable guidance in understanding game-theoretic bargaining systems and other concepts found in the chapter on technology to unbundle legal services. I am grateful for their assistance.

Many attorneys over the years have developed and championed limited-scope representation legal services. In particular, the work of Sue Talia and Forest Mosten and the ABA Standing Committee on the Delivery of Legal Services, which maintains a Pro Se/Unbundling Resource Center, have provided valuable resources and experience to build on.

Thank you to the following individuals for providing guidance, whether by responding to my interview questions for the book or through their work on the advancement of limited-scope representation in our profession: Jared Correia, Ronald Staudt, Kenneth Adams, Richard Granat, David Bilinsky, Michael Mills, Darryl Mountain, Jim Ring, Camille Stell, Charley Moore, Lee Rosen, Kevin Chern, Brian Whalley, Susan Cartier-Liebel, Aaron Kelly, Michael Moradzadeh, Michael McMullan, Jr., Rania Combs, Susan Wakefield, John Skiba, and Gordon Firemark. Thank you to Total Attorneys for their support of my work and the freedom to explore the future of law practice management and the delivery of legal services.

Foreword

WE LIVE IN A "workaround" society. Whether it's an indifferent institution, an inflexible bureaucrat, or an unresponsive process, you and I run into system blockages every day that make it difficult for us to do our jobs or accomplish our goals.

In response to these obstacles, we come up with workarounds: detours, back-channels, and jury-rigged solutions that aren't especially efficient, but that at least deliver a solution we can live with. Workarounds are far from ideal, but in a complex society like ours, they get the job done.

There's really only one thing you do not want to be in a workaround society: the obstacle that's being worked around. It's my unhappy duty to advise lawyers that our noble profession now holds this ignoble position in the legal marketplace.

The signs should be clear enough. The volume of pro se litigation continues to set new records every year, most notably in family law. Do-it-yourself websites for contracts, wills and divorces keep multiplying. Nonlawyer service providers like LegalZoom and Rocket Lawyer boast millions of customers and millions of dollars in venture capital investment. Foreign lawyers and sophisticated software are surging onto our traditional business turf. These trends and others show every indication of continuing throughout this coming decade.

The legal market, despite what you might have heard, is strong and growing. But in many respects, it's growing with only minimal involvement or financial gain for lawyers. We're being worked around, because we're slower, less accessible and more expensive than clients are now willing or able to tolerate. Lawyers have long since become used to being unpopular, but today we're facing a worse prospect: being irrelevant.

We're losing the battle for legal clients; however, we haven't yet lost the war. A trustworthy, skilled and caring lawyer should be more than a match for any pseudo-advocate or upstart competitor, no matter how deep their pockets or complex their programming. The problem is that for the most part, we haven't even shown up at the battlefield. We might not even be aware there's a war on.

It's no longer enough for us to simply stand in the legal marketplace and announce "The lawyer is here!", and await with dignified satisfaction the resulting flood of grateful clients. Whatever the merits of lawyers' traditional way of doing business—and let's be honest, they were considerable, back in the day—it's no longer effective. More clients are choosing to work *around* us rather than *with* us. We need to figure out why, and respond—fast.

One of the easiest, simplest and most beneficial responses we can make to these new market forces is to adopt the practice of limited scope retainers—more colloquially, unbundling. Stephanie Kimbro's important and essential book will tell you exactly why and how to do that.

Lawyers have traditionally cast their services in extreme terms: do everything for the client or do nothing at all. Common sense and market realities, however, both tell us that the vast territory between these two extremes is fertile ground for experiments in new delivery models. Why not try an innovative, collaborative approach that renders benefits to both buyer and seller?

Unbundling obviously offers advantages to clients, starting with a reduction in the price of fees paid to a lawyer and an increase in the predictability of those fees. But there's something else drawing clients to this option: a more equitable allocation of power. On the traditional lawyer-client journey, the client's job is forever to be a passenger; in an unbundled relationship, by contrast, the steering wheel is shared. The resulting restoration of confidence and dignity for clients should not be underestimated or undervalued.

Equally, however, unbundling offers advantages to lawyers. Among the clearest are the acquisition of previously unprofitable work and the availability of more time to devote to other client projects. Significantly, lawyers also benefit from the clear delineation of expectations. A limited scope retainer means exactly that: the explicit identification of what the lawyer will, and will not, do for the client. Few standard retainer agreements include that sort of definitive demarcation of duties; every unbundled retainer agreement must.

Perhaps most importantly, however, unbundling has the immensely positive effect of removing from lawyers our self-imposed burden of omnipotence. Our intense dislike of risk and our fervent striving for control has left us vulnerable to taking on more responsibility for our clients' outcomes than we often should. The modern view of clients—one they share themselves—emphasizes partnership over patronization, collaboration over command-and-control. Many lawyer-client relationships still fit well within the traditional model; but many more do not, and they need a better option. Limited scope retainers make for a very good start.

How do you escape the workaround trap? You figure out which of your actions and attitudes are causing friction and creating blockages in the system. Then you work hard to eliminate those obstacles and redirect traffic so that it flows back through you, not around you.

Unbundling won't solve every challenge facing the legal profession, but it can solve more than many lawyers think. Turn the page to start finding out what it could do for your own practice.

Jordan Furlong
Partner, Edge International
Ottawa, January 2012

CHAPTER ONE

Introduction

WE LIVE IN A do-it-yourself (DIY) society where the public is empowered through the use of the Internet in ways that it never has been before. Consumers are comfortable going online to handle business and professional transactions. They shop, conduct banking and investing, earn degrees, and communicate with family and friends over the Internet, but they also have rating and review websites and family and friend online recommendations at their fingertips before making any purchasing decisions. The public has become used to controlling online interactions, and many individuals see the benefit and convenience of handling business on their own time after having shopped around online to find what they perceive to be the best option available. Even when a consumer chooses to visit a shop or professional in person rather than online, chances are that he or she has used an online resource to either locate and/or review his or her choice ahead of time. The empowered consumer also understands that when a product or service has a DIY component, it tends to be more affordable. This is seen as an acceptable trade-off for doing a little or a lot of the footwork. In the current economy, many average-income individuals are more than willing to do the extra work to save money on their legal needs. The legal profession is not immune from the impact of these changes in consumer behavior.

Several major disruptors have begun to take greater hold on our profession, changing not only the way we must practice law but the expectations and demands of the public we serve.[1] Some of these disruptors are

---

[1] *See generally* Richard Susskind's description of disruptors in the legal industry in his book, *The End of Lawyers? Rethinking the Nature of Legal Services,* Oxford Univ. Press, 2008, *available at* **http://www.susskind.com/endoflawyers.html** (last accessed Oct. 30, 2011).

technology-based, such as document assembly and automation, the growth of e-commerce, the spread of online legal service providers, and a general digital connectivity that ignores geographic boundaries and enables perpetual sharing of information. Other disruptors are more philosophical or are based on changes to the underlying business models in the marketplace rather than on technology. These include the increasing accessibility of legal information, the growth of open-sourced and multidisciplinary legal education, a sense of duty to resolve disputes while keeping legal costs minimal, outsourcing of legal work, globalization of law firms, and the collaboration of professionals within and outside the legal profession across previously tight-knit industries.

These changes in the marketplace may not actually mean that the quality of the services generated have greatly improved. Rather, the increased convenience, accessibility, and self-help capabilities created by these disruptors have irrevocably changed consumer concepts of the value of commodities and services.[2] This will require lawyers to rethink the value they place on the services they deliver to clients and find ways to innovate that will meet the new consumer's concept of the value of legal services.[3] This is leading to a renewed interest in and need for the unbundling of legal services.

For at least the past five years, online legal service companies, such as LegalZoom, and other disruptors in the legal services marketplace have begun to meet this need and have educated the public about unbundled legal services. Consumers fill out questionnaires and purchase automated legal forms for sale online that they then must be responsible for executing and filing at the courthouse. Self-help legal form kits also are for sale at most office-supply stores. Other consumers make the dangerous choice to cut and paste together legal forms from samples they have found online on various free legal resource websites after running Google or

---

[2] The change in value proposition has even affected nonlawyer legal service providers. *See, e.g.,* WethePeople.com, a franchise that provides unbundled document preparation services to customers through storefronts in several states. The company filed for Chapter 11 bankruptcy in 2010 following a decrease in revenue perhaps caused by the movement toward more online DIY legal services. *We the Pauper,* A.B.A. J., May, 2, 2010, *available at* **http://www.abajournal.com/ magazine/article/we_the_pauper/** (last accessed Oct. 30, 2011).

[3] "As more and more industries fracture, many traditional companies will find themselves cut off from their customer base. Just to reach their markets, they will have to compete or cooperate with an increasingly powerful group of infomediaries. To survive, traditional companies might have no choice but to unbundle themselves and make a definite decision about which business to focus on. . . ." John Hagel III & Marc Singer, THE MCKINSEY QUARTERLY, 2000, No. 3, pp. 148–61. *See also* JOHN HAGEL III & MARC SINGER, NET WORTH: SHAPING MARKETS WHEN CUSTOMERS MAKE THE RULES (Harvard Business School Press, 1999).

other search engine requests to find free legal resources. Attempting to counter this dangerous self-help, cut-and-paste trend, some nonprofits and court systems have taken steps to create self-help centers and to work with private practitioners who volunteer in court-sponsored limited services programs. However, these resources are not available for all individuals and may pertain to assistance only in certain areas of the law.

While some law firms have provided unbundled legal services for years, it is not a practice that private practitioners have widely embraced. Some nonprofit legal-aid organizations still carry reservations about unbundling based on the philosophy that everyone is entitled to full-service representation, whether or not that ideal will ever come to pass and despite the growing number of pro se litigants flooding the court systems. Private practitioners, if aware of how to unbundle, may not see how to integrate it into their practice in a way that would be cost-effective, either with technology or alternative forms of billing, such as value or fixed fee billing methods. They also may believe there are too many malpractice risks for the private practitioner in limited-scope representation and additional administrative burdens to make sure this type of representation is handled correctly. Guidelines and best practices for alternative forms of delivering legal services, such as providing limited-scope assistance, are rarely taught in law schools.

From the perspective of the private practitioner, who is also a business owner attempting to survive in a rapidly changing and competitive legal marketplace, there is opportunity for both financial and intrinsic value by helping to fill this gap in access to justice with unbundling. Lawyers may provide limited-scope representation to serve a significant segment of the population in need of basic legal services in ways that are cost-effective and beneficial for their law practices. For example, adding unbundled legal services to a traditional law firm structure may be used to market a law practice to an entirely new client base and give the firm a competitive advantage by tapping into the market for DIY legal services. Lawyers also may provide pro and "low" bono unbundled services through the use of technology that streamlines the process, making it more efficient and cost-effective to donate their time and expertise.

The number of pro se individuals in the United States continues to rise steadily along with increasing numbers of individuals going online to seek out unbundled legal services from nonattorney companies.[4] Recog-

---

[4]*See generally* John Broderick, Jr. & Ronald M. George, *A Nation of Do-It-Yourself Lawyers*, N.Y. TIMES, Jan. 2, 2010.

nizing unbundling as a solution, more than 42 states have either adopted the ABA Model Rule 1.2(c) permitting unbundling of legal services or a similar rule. This profession needs to renew its enthusiasm for unbundling by private practitioners. The goal of this book is to provide lawyers and law firms with a background in different forms of limited-scope representation and with ways that this delivery method may be integrated into a law practice. We will discuss ethics issues and best practices for unbundling, but also explore popular and emerging technology used in the unbundling process, as well as how to successfully market unbundled services. Throughout the book are contributions from individuals with expertise on unbundling, law practice management, technology, and marketing. The appendix contains samples, checklists, and further resources. The author hopes some of the ideas in this book will assist practitioners with the skills they need to adapt to the changes in the legal marketplace and help nudge the legal profession to the next evolution of legal service delivery.

What Is Unbundling?

Unbundling legal services, also termed limited-scope services, a la carte legal services, discrete task representation, or disaggregated legal services, is a form of delivering legal services in which the lawyer breaks down the tasks associated with a legal matter and provides representation to the client only pertaining to a clearly defined portion of the client's legal needs. The client accepts the responsibility for doing the footwork for the remainder of the legal matter until reaching the desired resolution.

A few examples of unbundled legal services include:

- Ghostwriting
- Drafting pleadings, briefs, declarations, or orders
- Document review
- Conducting legal research
- Negotiating
- Making limited appearances
- Advising on court procedures and courtroom behavior
- Coaching on strategy or role playing
- Preparing exhibits

- Alternative dispute resolution
- Online dispute resolution
- Organizing discovery materials
- Drafting contracts and agreements
- Providing legal guidance or opinions
- Providing direction to resources such as local and state rules
- "Collaborative lawyering"

Revised in 2002, ABA Model Rule 1.2(c), titled "Scope of Representation," formally allows for the unbundling of legal services by stating "(c) [a] lawyer may limit the scope of the representation if the limitation is reasonable under the circumstances and the client gives informed consent."[5] This rule has been either adopted or modified by more than 42 states since its addition to the Model Rules.[6] A full list of state bars that have added this rule with the links to online copies can be found on the ABA's Standing Committee of the Delivery of Legal Services' Pro Se/Unbundling resource page.[7] Some states have modified Rule 1.2(c) to limit unbundling to only noncriminal law matters. See the Appendix for a list of state-by-state adoption of this rule and Chapter Five for a discussion about unbundling in criminal law matters.

---

[5] ABA MODEL RULE 1.2(c), *available at* **http://www.americanbar.org/groups/professional_ responsibility/publications/model_rules_of_professional_conduct/rule_1_2_scope_of_ representation_allocation_of_authority_between_client_lawyer.html** (last accessed Dec. 28, 2010). The pre-2002 wording of this rule read "[a] lawyer may limit the objectives of the representation if the client consents after consultation." Another rule that comes into play in unbundling is Model Rule 6.5, "Nonprofit and Court-Annexed Limited Legal Services Programs." This rule provides that "(a) A lawyer who, under the auspices of a program sponsored by a non-profit organization or court, provides short-term limited legal services to a client without expectation by either the lawyer or the client that the lawyer will provide continuing representation in the matter: (1) is subject to Rules 1.7 and 1.9(a) only if the lawyer knows that the representation of the client involves a conflict of interest; and (2) is subject to Rule 1.10 only if the lawyer knows that another lawyer associated with the lawyer in a law firm is disqualified by Rule 1.7 or 1.9(a) with respect to the matter." For the purposes of this book, we will focus on Rule 1.2(c).

[6] For an in-depth discussion of the different states' adoptions and modifications to Model Rule 1.2(c), see the Standing Committee's White Paper, "An Analysis of Rules that Enable Lawyers to Serve Pro Se Litigants," at **http://apps.americanbar.org/legalservices/delivery/downloads/ prose_white_paper.pdf** (accessed Dec. 12, 2011). *See also* ABA/BNA LAWYER'S MANUAL ON PROFESSIONAL CONDUCT, SCOPE OF RELATIONSHIP PRACTICE GUIDE, at 31:303. The following states made significant changes to Model Rule 1.2(c) upon adoption: Florida, Iowa, Maine, Missouri, and Wyoming.

[7] ABA Standing Committee on the Delivery of Legal Services, Pro Se/Unbundling Resource Page with links to the state bars that have adopted or modified Model Rule 1.2(c), **http://www .americanbar.org/groups/delivery_legal_services/resources/pro_se_unbundling_resource_ center/court_rules.html** (last accessed Dec. 28, 2010).

In 2007, the ABA published Formal Opinion 07-446, which permits ghost-writing.[8] This opinion stated that an attorney could provide limited assistance to a pro se litigant by helping him or her prepare written materials without disclosing the lawyer's involvement in the preparation to the court. State bars have addressed ghostwriting in different ways, which is discussed in more detail in Chapter Five.

Most law firms may fit unbundling into the practice areas and services that it currently offers. However, certain practice areas do not lend themselves well to unbundling. These might include criminal law, tax law, complex child-custody matters, or any practice where the client's case requires continuous legal representation from start to finish to ensure the best outcome for the client. Transaction-based or document-heavy practice areas, such as business law, estate planning, intellectual property, immigration law, and family law, work well for a firm wanting to devote a portion of its practice to unbundling legal services. Even firms whose practices are litigation-based, however, may find ways to offer unbundled services to either existing, full-service clients or to a new base of pro se litigants seeking limited-scope representation. In this book, we will explore various methods of delivering unbundled legal services and discuss procedures and best practices for ensuring ethical implementation of these services in a law practice.

Brief Background

Unbundling and self-representation are not new phenomena. Limiting the scope of legal representation has been around in one form or another and was recognized by courts long before the drafting of the ABA Model Rule 1.2 (c).[9] Unbundling is closely linked to the right to self-representation, which goes back to the Judiciary Act of 1789 when Congress first recognized the right.[10] Self-representation is linked to access to the courts, which is grounded in the U.S. Constitutional rights found in the First

---

[8]ABA Standing Comm. on Ethics and Prof'l Resp., Formal Op. 07-446, "Undisclosed Legal Assistance to Pro Se Litigants" (issued May 5, 2007), *available at* **http://www.abanet.org/legalservices/delivery/downloads/aba_07_446_2007.pdf** (accessed Dec. 28, 2010). The ABA Model Rule does not require that the lawyer reveal that he or she has provided assistance to the pro se litigant.

[9]*See, e.g.,* some of the earlier court cases providing for limited legal representation: Delta Equip. & Constr. Co. v. Royal Indemnity Co., 186 So. 2d 454 (La. Ct. App. 1966); Grand Isle Campsites v. Cheek, 249 So. 2d 268 (La. Ct. App. 1971), *modified,* 262 So. 2d 350 (La. 1972); Young v. Bridwell, 437 P.2d 686 (Utah 1968).

[10]*See* 28 U.S.C. § 1654 (1994) at **http://www.law.cornell.edu/uscode/usc_sec_28_00001654----000-.html** (last accessed Oct. 26, 2011).

Amendment,[11] Privileges and Immunities clause,[12] and Due Process clauses in the Fifth, Fourteenth, and Sixth Amendments.[13]

We see the increase in the number of self-represented individuals in our court systems. Why don't we see an equal increase in the number of lawyers unbundling legal services to guide these individuals through the justice system? One answer is that for the states to formally accept unbundled legal services as an alternative or complementary form of delivering legal services requires a clearer definition of what constitutes the "practice of law." The increase in the number of legal service providers and companies delivering services to the public without the guidance of a licensed attorney casts a cloud over unbundling. To this day, many in the legal profession associate unbundling with low-quality assistance offered by for-profit company providers and the claims of unauthorized practice of law that such services have raised.

Claims of unauthorized practice of law began to increase with the popularity of companies providing limited legal services to the public across the United States, including nonlawyer documents preparation services. Without a lawyer reviewing the legal work provided to the customer, this activity might be considered the unauthorized practice of law by most states' statutes. The states had not readdressed the issue of what constitutes the unauthorized practice of law since before Internet-based technology was able to facilitate the online delivery of legal services. Definitions of "practice of law" were out of date. In the meantime, unauthorized practice of law statutes were and still are used to prevent other industries, such as real estate, banking or insurance adjustors, from providing services that too closely mirror services provided by legal professionals. States remain reluctant to bring claims of unauthorized practice of law against nonlawyer document preparation services for fear that these statutes will be challenged on constitutional and anti-trust grounds. Accordingly, companies providing these services are able to step in to fill the void that legal professionals have not filled and provide online limited scope legal assistance to the public without too much fear of regulation or retaliation. At one point the ABA attempted to address these new concerns with unauthorized practice of law by re-examining the model definition of the practice of law.

---

[11]*See, e.g.,* Eastern R.R. Presidents Conf. v. Noerr Motor Freight, Inc., 365 U.S. 127, 138 (1961) and Cal. Transport Co. v. Trucking Unltd., 404 U.S. 508, 513 (1972).

[12]*See* U.S. Constitution Art 4, § 2; *see generally* Corfield v. Coryell, 6 F. Cas. 546, 551-552, No. 3, 230 (1823) and Chambers v. Baltimore & Ohio Ry. Co., 207 U.S. 142 (1907).

[13]*See, e.g.,* Mullane v. Central Hanover Bank & Trust Co., 339 U.S. 306, 313 (1950); Logan v. Zimmerman Brush Co., 455 U.S. 422, 428 (U.S. 1982); Boddie v. Connecticut, 401 U.S. 371 (1971); and Faretta v. California, 422 U.S. 806 (1975).

In 2002, the ABA created a Task Force on the Model Definition of the Practice of Law.[14] This task force's role was to reevaluate the definition of "practice" in light of the changing legal landscape and also to focus on the unauthorized practice of law by nonlicensed individuals, which included taking a look at legal service companies providing unbundled legal forms and documents to clients without attorney review.[15] During the course of its review, the Task Force received a letter from the Federal Trade Commission urging the ABA not to adopt a revised definition of the practice of law that was too broad or that might constrain competition between lawyers and nonlawyer legal service providers which they felt would raise costs for consumers and limit their choices.[16] As a result of the study, the task force did not recommend a single model definition but rather recommended that every state and jurisdiction adopt a definition of the practice of law.[17] However, without uniformity in the definition of "practice of law," enforcement of regulations that pertain to multijurisdictional law practice and unauthorized practice of law remains difficult across the country. Accordingly, the popularity of nonlawyer legal service providers will continue to increase creating additional competition for the legal profession unless it is able to adapt to changes in consumer demand for legal services and increase its adoption of limited scope representation.

---

[14]Lish Witson, *Report of the ABA Task Force on the Model Definition of the Practice of Law* (2003), *available at* **http://www.americanbar.org/content/dam/aba/migrated/cpr/model-def/taskforce_ rpt_803.authcheckdam.pdf** (last accessed Oct. 26, 2011).

[15]*Id.* at 1, 13. From the report:

> Many jurisdictions have left the determination as to what constitutes the practice of law to a case-by-case analysis. As a result, there are an increasing number of situations where non-lawyers, or lawyers licensed in a different jurisdiction, are providing services that are difficult to categorize under current state authority as being, or not being, the delivery of services that are included within the definition of the practice of law. The adoption of a definition of the practice of law is a necessary step in protecting the public from unqualified service providers and in eliminating qualified providers' uncertainty about the propriety of their conduct in any particular jurisdiction.

Separately, different states have filed complaints against companies offering unbundled legal services to members of the public without the involvement of a licensed professional in that state's jurisdiction, citing unauthorized practice of law. *See, e.g.*, the 2010 settlement agreement entered into by LegalZoom and the Washington State Attorney General's Office, *available at* **http://www.atg.wa.gov/pressrelease.aspx?&id=26466**, as well as complaints in North Carolina and Missouri, *available at* **http://ipwatchdog.com/2010/02/09/legalzoom-sued-in-class-action-for-unauthorized-law-practice/id=8816/** (last accessed Oct. 26, 2011).

[16]Letter from the Federal Trade Commission and the Department of Justice to the ABA Task Force on the Model Definition of the Practice of Law, dated December 20, 2002.

[17]ABA TASK FORCE ON THE MODEL DEFINITION OF THE PRACTICE OF LAW, RECOMMENDATION OF THE TASK FORCE ON THE MODEL DEFINITION OF THE PRACTICE OF LAW, **http://www.americanbar.org/content/ dam/aba/migrated/cpr/model-def/recomm.authcheckdam.pdf** (last accessed Oct. 26, 2011).

Perhaps in recognition of this, when the ABA's House of Delegates adopted several revisions to the Model Rules of Professional Conduct in 2002, they included provisions that support limited-scope representation. So far, 14 states have adopted the model rule and 29 have adopted a similar but modified version.[18] See the Appendix at end of this book for a list of state bars that adopted or modified Model Rule 1.2(c) supporting unbundled legal services.

In 2003, the ABA's Section of Litigation published its *Handbook on Limited Scope Assistance, a Report of the Modest Means Task Force.*[19] This handbook provides an extensive overview of the practice of unbundling legal services for lawyers, judges, legal-aid organizations, and others in the legal profession. The ABA's Standing Committee on the Delivery of Legal Services also maintains a website with additional resources related to the unbundling of legal services.[20] In November of 2009, this committee published its white paper, "An Analysis of Rules that Enable Lawyers to Serve Pro Se Litigants." This white paper studies the ways that different states have constructed their rules of professional conduct or other rules and laws to enable lawyers to provide limited-scope services to pro se individuals. The white paper is intended for use by policymakers but is also good background reading for lawyers interested in understanding the national status of unbundling practices.

More recently, in October of 2011, the American Bar Foundation released a report mapping the civil justice infrastructure, which includes a look at how services are unbundled across the states.[21] The report states, "[t]he 'unbundling' of legal services has opened up opportunities for innovations in both fully subsidized and market-based delivery models." The authors of the report specifically studied limited-scope representation because "such services are an important element of how civil legal assistance is currently delivered and are often suggested as one way of making market-based civil legal services more affordable to the public."[22]

---

[18] Arthur F. Greenbaum, *Multijurisdictional Practice and the Influence of Model Rule of Professional Conduct 5.5—An Interim Assessment*, 43 AKRON L. REV. 729, 735 (2010).

[19] ABA's Section of Litigation published its *Report of the Modest Means Task Force Handbook on Limited Scope Assistance* (2003), *available at* **http://apps.americanbar.org/litigation/taskforces/ modest/report.pdf** (last accessed Oct. 26, 2011).

[20] ABA Standing Committee for the Delivery of Legal Services website, **http://www.americanbar .org/groups/delivery_legal_services.html** (last accessed Oct. 26, 2011).

[21] REBECCA L. SANDEFUR & AARON C. SMITH, ACCESS ACROSS AMERICA: FIRST REPORT OF THE CIVIL JUSTICE INFRASTRUCTURE MAPPING PROJECT, Oct. 7, 2011, American Bar Found. *available at* **http://www .americanbarfoundation.org/uploads/cms/documents/access_across_america_first_report_ of_the_civil_justice_infrastructure_mapping_project.pdf** (last accessed Oct. 26, 2011).

[22] *Id.* at 27.

Reasons why some members of the public seek unbundled legal services include:

1. They like to control their legal matters and have DIY personalities.

2. They cannot afford to pay for full legal representation.

3. They want the flexibility and convenience that unbundling may give them.

4. They would benefit from alternative fee arrangements, such as the fixed fees and value billing that can accompany unbundled services.

5. They are less intimidated with limited interaction with lawyers than they would be in traditional, full-service law firms or they may be more comfortable with online DIY services using the Internet to communicate and accomplish their business needs rather than making appointments at traditional law offices.

6. They live in remote areas or for other reasons do not have the means to travel to larger cities to visit physical law offices multiple times as often is required with full-service representation.

Recent Developments in Unbundling in Canada

♦ The Canadian Bar Association published a report in August of 2000 entitled "The Future of the Legal Profession: The Challenge of Change," which addressed unbundling.[23]

♦ The Law Society of British Columbia conducted a study and issued a report in April of 2008 entitled "Report Of The Unbundling Of Legal Services Task Force—Limited Retainers: Professionalism And Practice," which recommended methods and procedures for unbundling.[24]

♦ The Law Society of Alberta and the Nova Scotia Barristers' Society have included unbundling in some format in their rules or codes of professional conduct.[25]

---

[23] *See* "The Future of the Legal Profession: The Challenge of Change," a report of the Young Lawyers Conference, at **http://www.cba.org/cba/news/pdf/future.pdf** (last accessed Oct. 22, 2011).

[24] *See* "Report of the Unbundling of Legal Services Task Force—Limited Retainers: Professionalism And Practice," at **http://www.lawsociety.bc.ca/docs/publications/reports/LimitedRetainers_2008.pdf**.

[25] *See* the Law Society of Alberta's Website, "Access to Justice: Alternate Delivery of Legal Services," at **http://www.lawsociety.ab.ca/about_us/initiatives/initiatives_a2j.aspx** (last accessed Oct. 22, 2011) and Nova Scotia Barristers' Society Access to Justice Working Group, at **http://www.nsbs.org/documents/general/Committees/2011-09-20_AccessToJusticeWGWorkplan.pdf** (last accessed Oct. 22, 2011).

♦ The Law Society of Upper Canada at the convocation's September, 2011, meeting approved amendments to the Rules of Professional Conduct and the *Paralegal Rules of Conduct* regarding providing work under "limited-scope retainers," another term for unbundled legal services.[26] The amendments require written consent from the client for the limited-scope of representation. A working group also was formed to begin discussions with other legal organizations and entities to identify ways to facilitate procedures for unbundling in litigation.

Increasing Access to Justice

Adding limited-scope services to a law practice has the potential to provide a new source of client revenue for a law firm, especially with the untapped market potential for this form of delivery. Unbundling also provides a significant benefit to the public. The ABA and most state bars acknowledge that unbundling legal services is one important key to chip away at our nation's access to justice problem.[27] As our court systems continue to be overburdened with pro se individuals, expecting the legal profession to come up with a full-service representation solution for each individual is a pipe dream.

The unfortunate truth is that in this down economy many individuals who need legal assistance are either postponing what they can, are going into the courthouse alone without any guidance, or are going online to cut and paste together their own legal documents. All these reactions to legal needs are unacceptable solutions.

There is little chance that those involved in maintaining the complicated and archaic processes in the judicial system are going to become motivated to simplify the process for the benefit of our citizens any time soon. Instead, limited-scope representation provides the pro se individual with a more affordable option of receiving assistance with his or her legal need rather than making a go of it completely alone. Legal professionals have

---

[26] *See* "Unbundling" of Legal Services and Limited Legal Representation: Background Information and Proposed Amendments to Professional Conduct Rules, published by the Law Society of Upper Canada, Sept. 2011, *available at* **http://www.lsuc.ca/WorkArea/DownloadAsset.aspx? id=2147483764** (last accessed Oct. 22, 2011).

[27] *See* the ABA Standing Committee on the Delivery of Legal Services' Pro Se/Unbundling Resource Page, **http://www.americanbar.org/groups/delivery_legal_services/resources.html** (last accessed Dec. 12, 2011).

an opportunity to meet a critical public need by considering adding some form of unbundled services to their law practices. However, many individuals in the public are not aware that limited-scope services are an alternative to full service or no service.[28]

For attorneys who devote a percentage of their practice to providing pro bono and "low" bono services, unbundling is a great opportunity to assist more individuals by streamlining and possibly using technology to aid in the unbundling process. The increase of specialization in law firms over the past 10 years also has made it more difficult for many private law firms to fit full-service pro bono work into their practices. This is particularly true with solo and small firm attorneys who may want to provide these services but cannot figure out how to do so in a cost-effective manner while trying to keep their own practices afloat in a crowded legal marketplace. Setting up a procedure and organizing a system that employs technology for unbundling specific legal matters may give the private practitioner greater flexibility to provide pro bono and low bono work.

Regarding the nonprofit sector, legal-services organizations need to recognize unbundling as an alternative to full-service representation where appropriate. Legal-aid entities might adopt better procedures for referring potential limited-scope clients to private practitioners who are able to provide these services either pro bono or for discounted legal fees. Some nonprofit organizations already have created wonderful tools using technology that allow individuals seeking unbundled legal services to guide and navigate themselves through the legal system.[29] These two areas of the legal profession could find ways to use technology to merge interests for the benefit of the public. For a discussion of the possibilities, see Chapter Eight. Both private practitioners and nonprofit legal-aid entities should work together to add limited-scope services to their training, routines, and procedures for this form of legal-services delivery to make a dent in the nation's lack of access to justice.

---

[28]The Access Across America report commissioned by the American Bar Foundation stated that "[a] 2010 survey of Americans commissioned by the American Bar Association found that, while most people were unfamiliar with limited-scope representation, many found the idea attractive once it was explained to them." REBECCA L. SANDEFUR & AARON C. SMYTH, ACCESS ACROSS AMERICA: FIRST REPORT OF THE CIVIL JUSTICE INFRASTRUCTURE MAPPING PROJECT, page 28, Oct. 7, 2011, American Bar Foundation at **http://www.americanbarfoundation.org/uploads/cms/documents/access_across_america_first_report_of_the_civil_justice_infrastructure_mapping_project.pdf** (last accessed Oct. 26, 2011).
[29]*See* Access to Justice Author (A2J) Guided Interviews, **http://www.kentlaw.edu/cajt/A2JAuthor.html** (accessed Dec. 28, 2010).

Critics of Unbundling

As with any business concept that falls outside of mainstream law practice management, there are critics of unbundled legal services. One criticism questions the intelligence and capabilities of the client to follow instructions and to complete the legal matters on his or her own even with the guidance of the attorney. Another criticism is that the clients who request DIY legal services are not really individuals who cannot afford an attorney; they just want to find a cheap way out of paying a law firm and see unbundling as a way to avoid paying an attorney's fees. These critics worry that the limited-scope client will not follow the attorney's advice and will attempt to pick and choose the services the client thinks he or she needs without the benefit of an attorney's experience and legal education.

Another concern is the success rate that a self-help individual has after receiving limited-scope representation. The client empowered with legal guidance, the correct legal forms, and instructions for proceeding may have all the necessary pieces to complete a legal matter, but not the additional skills, such as the ability to comply with deadlines, basic reading and writing skills, or just the self-motivation to follow through with the instructions the lawyer has provided on termination of the limited-scope representation.[30] Other factors, such as the client's physical and mental health, may play a part in the ability to proceed on his or her own. While an unbundling lawyer may conduct a thorough client intake process to attempt to determine whether the client will be able to handle the completion of the legal matter after arming the client with the requested limited-scope services, it may not be possible for the lawyer to always make an accurate judgment call based on the limited amount of time spent with the prospective client.

But the primary criticism of unbundled legal services seems to be that the practice of unbundling leads to the "commoditization of the law" and more emphasis on the profession as a "business." If you hold this belief, I regret to inform you that this ship has long since left the port. Like any other service in almost every other profession, the work that attorneys do can be broken down into a packageable product that is delivered to a paying consumer. Basic laws of supply and demand dictate that as the public

---

[30]See a study conducted in 1996 at the Maryland School of Law Legal Clinic in part to measure the success of having the law students provide pro se litigants with limited-scope assistance. Michael Millemann, Natalie Gilfrich & Richard Granat, *Rethinking the Full-Service Representation Model: A Maryland Experiment*, 30 Clearinghouse Rev. 1178 (1997).

was provided with alternative and more affordable legal services in the form of legal document kits from office-supply stores and online DIY legal software kits, this trend would turn into a market need for a considerable percentage of the public.

There will always be the need for the traditional law firm structure and perhaps even the billable hour pricing model with certain clients and cases. However, the public's demand for changes in the delivery of legal services has created other forms of alternative services, many that provide legal assistance without an attorney's involvement at all. Unbundling is not the source of this change. Throughout this book we will cover the risks and benefits of different forms of unbundling by private practitioners and concerns about ethical unbundling will be addressed throughout. Hopefully, legal practitioners will find a way to balance the limited-scope delivery method with full-service representation in a way that best serves their clients and the practice areas they work in. Unbundling should be viewed as a way for attorneys to take control over changes in the legal marketplace and to meet a significant consumer need for access to justice by adapting the law practice business model.

> "Unbundled legal services will be a mainstay of many a solo practitioner and it will prove essential to learn how to ethically and responsibly unbundle. . . . Lawyers have argued if the courts embrace this type of delivery of services it undermines the need for a lawyer. I beg to differ. A lawyer's value lies in their ability to counsel. Effective counseling can convert a do-it-yourself-er into a paying client. The foresightedness to offer these services makes you more attractive to those on the fence."[31]
>
> —Susan Cartier Liebel, founder of Solo Practice University

Business Lessons on Unbundling from Other Industries

The economy does not exist in a bubble and neither should legal professionals. There are lessons to be learned from looking at ways that other industries have unbundled their services to create new or improved markets that adapted to changes in the global economy and the way consumers exercise their purchasing power.

---

[31]Susan Cartier Liebel, "Have We Become a Nation of Do-It-Yourself Lawyers?" Solo Practice University blog, **http://solopracticeuniversity.com/2010/01/04/have-we-become-a-nation-of-do-it-yourself-lawyers/**, Jan. 4, 2010 (last accessed Nov. 2, 2011).

The Music Industry

More than a few people in the music industry initially questioned the unbundling of music. Traditionally, a music producer would bundle a musician's less popular recordings with the one or two singles that were commercially popular and charge a higher fee for the entire catalog of records on a CD. When iTunes presented the concept of allowing the consumer to pick and choose whichever songs he or she wanted from the hits and the not-so-popular songs, it revolutionized the way that music is purchased. Critics had to admit that it did not culminate in the downfall of the music industry or result in decreased sales. Instead, unbundling songs at a lower cost per purchase allowed the consumer to learn about the artists and their music offerings without making a large up-front investment in an entire album. If consumers liked the services, they would come back for the rest of the album, and the full album could always be downloaded from the iTunes store for the customers that wanted the entire recording.

The Airlines

Remember the days when you purchased an airline ticket and the cost included more than just a seat on the plane? The airlines began unbundling their services around 2010. Customers who want to have their bags checked or prefer choice seating must pay extra fees. Travel insurance is another add-on. Charging only the base fee for the seat and then selling add-ons has resulted in increased profits for the airlines. While many customers see this form of unbundling as not actually resulting in lower costs but tacking on additional fees, others, including the airlines, see it as a way for customers to not have to pay for something they do not need.

The Newspapers

Newspapers are part of another industry in which the Internet has changed the way that its product is purchased and consumed. A newspaper or other publication is a bundled product. Most consumers do not read through an entire newspaper but pick and choose the articles that interest them. Rather than read through a printed magazine produced by a single publisher and inevitably containing a number articles and advertisements that may not be of interest to the purchaser, readers may now turn to multiple blogs and subscribe to those with articles that meet their more narrow interests. This more narrow focus through unbundling also works to the benefit of advertisers who now have a better chance of spreading their message to a more tailored audience. Until the growth of online media, the reader paid a single price for the entire bundled product even if half of it went unread. Now, the consumer is able to pick and choose the articles that are read and pay a price for access to the entire publication's site as a subscriber or purchase single copies of an article or even access articles in an archive for individual purchase. The Internet has provided more choices to the consumer about where he or she receives the news. To keep its readers from getting their news from the growing number of free suppliers of media, such as news sites and blogs written by journalists, the newspapers have unbundled their services in order to survive.

Wireless Providers

Wireless and Internet providers are notorious for pushing their bundled packages as part of a marketing strategy to offer a variety of choice and payment plans to their customers. These packages of bundled services are broken down for the consumers as separate prices if they choose to purchase one or two services or all together for supposedly less expensive monthly costs. The different unbundled and bundled services advertised as a la carte services of the company's primary product, their mobile devices and hardware add-ons, allows them to compete with each other on price and services. The concept of bundling packages gives them the opportunity to sell additional services that the consumer might not have known about or planned on obtaining when shopping for a cell phone.

Lessons from Intuit and the Unbundling of Small Business and Personal Finance Services

The story of Intuit and its ingenious methods of unbundling serve as an excellent example for the legal industry.[32] Intuit's Quicken software, used by its customers for personal finance, became a huge success for the company. Building on the brand that it established from selling its Quicken product, Intuit was able to lead existing customers to its website where it provides links to its other products and services that the customers using its financial software might be interested in, such as financial consulting, investing, mortgages, banking, credit cards, as well as access to online brokers and other educational content from Intuit. Intuit for small business has created a website that provides everything a small business might need and all in an unbundled format so that it provides visitors to the site with a variety of options and prices. Law firms may not be permitted to collect cookies and other user information from the visitors to its website for the purposes of identifying and targeting future needs. However, the

---

[32]See Intuit at **http://www.intuit.com/**, last accessed November 3, 2011.

lawyer may predict prospective client's interests based on website analytics and design the site content to appeal to these areas and to provide unbundled services that fill a variety of legal needs that clients may have. It is important to note that with the Intuit example comes the possibility that Intuit or other companies taking this unbundling approach to small business may easily become the next nonlawyer legal service provider adding legal documents and services to its list of unbundled products. For more discussion about the "branded network concept" of marketing legal services, see Chapter Eight. Studying the techniques and strategies of an unbundling company such as Intuit is simply keeping an eye on an emerging business competitor.[33]

Thinking About Restructuring Your Business to Unbundle?

A successful lawyer knows that the legal profession may play by its own set of rules and regulations, but it is not sitting in an isolated bubble. From time to time, it is good to take a multidisciplinary approach to reevaluating the strengths and weaknesses of a law practice by thinking more like a business owner than a trained lawyer. Answers to the basic questions that follow will differ for every law firm depending on the stage it is at now and its willingness to think outside of the box about how the firm delivers legal services, how it defines the practice of law, and how it operates its business to be competitive and to maximize profitability.

1. What is the true value of the legal services that the firm provides to clients? In the services offered, the value to the customer is

   _____.

2. What current compromises does the firm make between the quality of legal services delivered and the firm's ability to provide good customer service and affordable legal fees? Are there situations where the firm could increase customer service and improve communication and affordability without having to compromise on the quality of the legal services delivered?

---

[33]"The value chains of scores of other industries will become ripe for unbundling. The logic is most compelling—and therefore likely to strike soonest—in information businesses where the cost of physical distribution is high: newspapers, ticket sales, insurance, financial information, scientific publishing, software, and of course encyclopedias. But in any business whose physical value chain has been compromised for the sake of delivering information, there is an opportunity to unbundle the two, creating a separate information business and allowing (or compelling) the physical one to be streamlined. All it will take to deconstruct a business is a competitor that focuses on the vulnerable sliver of information in its value chain." from "Strategy and the New Economics of Information" by Evans, Philip B. and Wurster, Thomas S., *Harvard Business Review* (September 1997).

3. What processes does the firm conduct with the client that could be unbundled? Consider more than just the standard handling of legal cases for clients and think about a holistic approach to the business, such as evaluating other client support or services the firm could provide that would make the client's experience more positive.

4. In any of these processes of interacting with the client, are there ways that the operations involving information and tangible data might be streamlined either through using technology or re-creating new systems of organization and delivery?

5. To facilitate this, are there any new roles that may need to be created within the law firm? How might the firm fill that position or gain the necessary skills, or could part of the process be outsourced?

6. Would any of these new areas of focus in the business become liabilities instead of assets, and how would the firm prepare for that possibility and balance the risk?

A Team-Based Approach to Unbundling

Some legal work will not continue to support the high fees that lawyers have charged for it in the past. Therefore, many law firms will have to change their approaches, especially if they are attempting to be the one-stop shops for all their clients' needs. Learning to use outsourcing and a team-based approach in the process of delivering unbundled services will be important to make this model efficient.

Outsourcing certain unbundled services to nonlawyers, such as document creation, the client intake process, or the discovery preparation, might be one cost-effective solution to adding unbundled services to the menu of firm offerings. This book cannot cover all the ethics and best practices for outsourcing. However, consider how a firm might think outside of its own available resources and look at the potential ability to retain nonlawyer assistance and collaborate with legal process outsourcing companies to create new unbundling options.[34]

---

[34] *See, e.g.,* Seyfarth Shaw, LLP, an International firm that takes a team-based approach to delivering services and focuses the firm's strategy on "the application of structured team-based collaboration—internally and client facing—to deliver value," at **http://www.seyfarth.com/index.cfm/ fuseaction/firm_overview.six_sigma_approach/six_sigma_approach.cfm** (last accessed Nov. 3, 2011).

For example, imagine a firm that outsources a project to a trusted provider for preparation and then the lawyer spends only the time reviewing the nonlawyer's work before delivering it to the client as an unbundled service. The client has been charged a fixed fee for the work and the outsourcing provider has been compensated based on an agreement to handle transactions for the firm on a project basis. Imagine the law firm that enters into a relationship with the in-house counsel of a company and becomes the provider of unbundled legal services to that company's legal team. But see the *Qualcom* case study in Chapter Eight. Legal document assistants (formerly called independent paralegals), virtual paralegals, legal process outsourcing providers, and other nonlawyers could be used in collaboration with the unbundling law firm to systematize the unbundling process so that it remains cost-effective both for the clients and for the firm to implement.

CHAPTER TWO

Ethics of Unbundling

THE SLOW ADOPTION OF limited-scope representation by the American legal profession is largely a result of lawyers' concerns with the ethics risks associated with unbundling. For the practitioner wanting to unbundle legal services, he or she must make the careful determination on a case-by-case basis whether the prospective client's legal needs may be handled unbundled or whether the matter requires full-service representation. *Unbundling is not appropriate for every legal need or for every client.*

This chapter will discuss the existing rules of professional conduct that relate to unbundling and help the lawyer navigate through the ethics issues that may arise in handling limited-scope representation.

Competent Representation: What Is "Reasonable"?

The requirement that clients be provided with "competent" representation is covered in Model Rule 1.1.[1] The rule states: "A lawyer shall provide competent representation to a client. Competent representation requires the legal knowledge, skill, thoroughness and preparation reasonably necessary for the representation."

The attorney also must determine if the limited-scope representation is "reasonable" as required by Model Rule 1.2(c). The meaning of "reasonable" can be derived from a number of court cases where the court found

---

[1] ABA MODEL RULES OF PROF'L CONDUCT Rule 1.1 (2009).

limited-scope representation to be acceptable when the client's rights and interests were not harmed from the practice and when the attorney was not committing any ethics violations from his or her limited representation of the client's matter.[2]

A lawyer should not attempt to provide unbundled legal services in an area of the law in which the lawyer is not experienced. Although the representation may be limited to drafting a single legal document, assisting with part of the discovery process, or making a limited hearing appearance, it is necessary for the attorney handling the limited-scope case to understand the entire case in full. That attorney should be able to provide the client with the instruction and guidance needed to complete his or her legal needs following the firm's limited representation. The attorney must be able to explain to the client any of the potential issues that may come up as the case proceeds, identify collateral issues, and make sure that the client understands that the firm is not going to be handling certain portions of the case.

Unfortunately, some prospective unbundling clients may believe that because they are requesting limited-scope representation, the lawyer will do less to uncover malicious intent or fraud as he or she might in a full-service case. This is simply not true, but the firm should protect itself from the risk of a client seeking unbundled services to commit fraud. It should go without saying that a lawyer should not file or assert frivolous pleadings on behalf of an unbundled client. If the firm detects during the client intake process that the client's claims are frivolous or the client's desire to start litigation is merely malicious rather than based on valid claims, the law firm should decline to represent the client and put this rejection in writing with a copy for the individual as well as for the firm's records.[3] Likewise, if the firm becomes aware that the matter it is being requested to handle is related to an illegal or fraudulent matter, the firm should decline the limited-scope representation. This rejection of the unbundled matter also should be recorded in writing.[4]

The attorney should have experience in the practice areas in which he or she is unbundling legal services. The limited-scope representation always

---

[2]*See, e.g., Greenwich v. Markhoff*, 650 N.Y.S.2d 704 (App. Div. 1996); Parents Against Drunk Drivers v. Graystone Pines Homeowners' Ass'n, 789 P.2d 52 (Utah Ct. App. 1990); and Hartford Accident & Indemnity Co. v. Foster, 528 So. 2d 255 (Miss. 1988).

[3]*See* ABA MODEL RULE 1.16, "Declining or Terminating Representation."

[4]*Id.*

must be competent and diligent. Limited-scope representation does not mean that the attorney's advocacy for the client's legal matter should be less than it would be for a full-service client.[5]

Defining the Scope of Representation and Informed Client Consent

One of the most important components for unbundling is clearly defining the scope of representation for the client.[6] Rule 1.2(c) requires that "the client gives informed consent" to the limited scope.[7] Informed consent does not necessarily have to be written consent from the client under the rules of most states. Technically, under this rule, a client could consent to the limited scope in a phone conversation or during a web conference. However, some states have added written informed consent to their version of Rule 1.2(c). The client needs to understand the nature of the limited-scope representation from the beginning of the attorney/client relationship.[8] Without this clarity, the client may misunderstand the scope of services that the attorney is providing and carry false expectations. Drafting a well-crafted limited-scope engagement agreement helps to ensure that the client is informed about the scope of representation and also provides a record of the client's consent to that representation. Some malpractice insurance carriers also may request a copy of the firm's limited-scope engagement agreement prior to evaluating a policy for cov-

---

[5]To quote unbundling pioneer M. Sue Talia, "Limited-scope representation is not a second-rate service, and is not limited liability. It is limited only in scope, and the standard of care for an attorney performing limited-scope services is precisely the same as if those services were being provided in full-service context." "Roadmap for Implementing a Successful Unbundling Program," (2005) at **http://www.ajs.org/prose/South%20Central%20Notebook%20Contents/Tab%206/Roadmap%20for%20Implementing.pdf** (last accessed Oct. 29, 2011).

[6]Some states require a formal writing or standardized form that lays out the limited-scope representation for the client. *See* Fla. R. 4-1.2(c); Mo. R. 4-1.2(c); Iowa R. 32:1.2(c); Wyo. R. 1.2(c); and Me. R. 3.4(i).

[7]ABA MODEL RULE 1.2(c), *available at* **http://www.americanbar.org/groups/professional_responsibility/publications/model_rules_of_professional_conduct/rule_1_2_scope_of_representation_allocation_of_authority_between_client_lawyer.html** (last accessed Nov. 14, 2011).

[8]*See generally* MODEL RULE 1.2, Scope of Representation; *see, e.g.,* the following cases where the client was required to consent to the clearly defined limitations of the representation provided by the attorney: Indianapolis Podiatry PC v. Efroymson, 720 N.E.2d 376 (Ind. Ct. App.1999); *In re* Bancroft, 204 B.R. 548 (Bankr. C.D. Ill. 1997); Johnson v. Freemont County Bd. of Comm'rs, 85 F.3d 489 (10th Cir. 1996).

erage of a law practice that unbundles. Accordingly, the best practice for any law firm unbundling would be to use a limited-scope agreement as part of the process of delivering unbundled legal services.

Limited-scope agreements should clearly define the nature of the services being provided by the firm to the client. If the firm is using technology to deliver unbundled services online, the agreement needs to explain the use of the technology and how the client can expect to receive services in digital format and communicate with the firm online. It may be possible for the attorney to draft a standard limited-scope agreement for each type of unbundling service that the firm provides. However, in most cases, it may be necessary for the attorney to tweak the agreement on a case-by-case basis to ensure that the scope is appropriately limited to the client's unique legal needs. In addition, to avoid misleading the client, the agreement should be written in plain language rather than legalese. See an example of a limited-scope engagement agreement in the Appendix. Regarding the creation of the limited-scope engagement agreement, Beverly Michaelis, lawyer and practice manager adviser with the Oregon State Bar Professional Liability Fund, states "[i]n general, avoid having clients sign on the spot. Give them an opportunity to take your engagement letter home, review it thoroughly, and call with any questions. This will protect you against later claims of duress or lack of informed consent."[9]

Another concern in defining the scope of representation is that the prospective unbundled client may not understand the difference between full-service representation and unbundled services. Most clients are focused on the end result of the legal services, the completion of their legal needs, and do not have a good understanding of the work involved in getting there. To ensure that the client fully grasps the limited-scope of the representation, the attorney may want to consider providing the client with a handout that lists the steps typically involved in the process of the case. This handout might compare the full-service representation to the limited-scope services that the client will be receiving from the attorney.

In the agreement or in an attachment to the agreement, the clients must be made aware of the risks that may be involved in their cases by

---

[9]Beverly Michaelis, *Unbundling in the 21st Century: How to Reduce Malpractice Exposure While Meeting Client Needs*, Ore. State Bar Bulletin, Aug./Sept. 2010, *available at* **https://www.osbar.org/publications/bulletin/10augsep/practice.html** (last accessed Nov. 14, 2011).

not choosing full-service representation and must receive help in doing a risk/benefit analysis for this decision. See the Appendix for "Additional Questions for the Unbundled Client Intake Process" to help clients make this decision. List exactly what services will not be provided to the client as well as listing the client's responsibilities. Providing this education to the client as part of the limited-scope engagement process helps to ensure there will be no misunderstandings or false expectations as the case proceeds.

In some cases, the attorney may want to limit his or her interaction with the client to methods of communication that keep the practice of unbundling efficient for the firm. For example, the attorney may desire to meet with a client only once in person and handle the remainder of the communication online through either secure e-mail or a client portal where the client has access to his or her case file online. It is important that the client understands this restriction on communication as part of the limited-scope representation and that he or she does not have the mistaken expectation of being able to schedule multiple in-person office meetings or phone calls with the attorney during the course of the limited-scope representation.

After the client has signed the limited-scope agreement, the firm must be careful to adhere to the agreed-on scope of the services. Even if it may be tempting to start working on the next step in the client's case, the attorney should not extend the firm's work into the tasks that it agreed would be the client's responsibility. For example, if the firm agreed to provide a limited appearance at a hearing to address a specific issue that the client needed assistance with, the attorney present at that limited appearance must resist speaking outside of the scope of what the firm had agreed to cover. The attorney at that hearing must allow the client to represent himself or herself in the portions that the client agreed to handle. Furthermore, if the firm will be handling limited court appearances for unbundled cases, make sure that the court in the firm's jurisdiction will allow the attorney to withdraw after that limited appearance. The court may not be aware of the limited-scope agreement or may not choose to honor it. See Chapter Five for a discussion of limited appearances.

Some traditional law firms that have added unbundling to their practices have found that a number of their unbundling clients end up becoming full-service clients after the firm has provided a limited portion of the work for their cases. After clients see the work the firm has done, have received an education on the complexity of their cases, and understand the responsibilities they will have, some clients may decide to turn over their entire matters to the firm. If the scope of the original limited services agreement changes, the firm must discuss this with the client first and put the terms for the expanded representation, whether full-service or additional unbundled work, into a new agreement so that the change in scope is clear and on record.

CHAPTER THREE

Best Practices for Unbundling

ONCE THE LAWYER IS familiar with the rules of professional responsibility that govern unbundled practice, he or she must establish procedures and best practices for unbundling that will minimize risk. These best practices also may benefit the firm by streamlining the unbundled work and keeping it cost-effective to offer as an alternative form of legal service delivery.

Case Study
Jared Correia, Esq.

Jared Correia, Esq., is Law Practice Management Advisor at the Massachusetts Law Office Management Assistance Program (LOMAP).[1] Prior to joining LOMAP, he was the Publications Attorney for the Massachusetts Bar Association (MBA). He was the first Publications Attorney for the MBA and established the continuing legal education publication protocols and standards. Correia writes for the Mass LOMAP blog at http://www.masslomap.blogspot.com/ and produces Legal ToolKit podcasts on LegalTalkNetwork.

1. Do you have any tips for attorneys to help them determine whether a case may be unbundled or needs full-service representation?

. . . the obvious, baseline consideration is whether there are discrete tasks to be effectively unbundled. Many new attorneys, for example, rush

---

[1]Massachusetts Law Office Management Assistance Program at **http://www.masslomap.org/**, last accessed November 15, 2011.

headlong into taking cases without really thinking about what the work will entail. With unbundled cases, it is essential to have a solid idea of the segments of the case, and of how each segment is likely to progress. This will inform everything that happens moving forward, for the entirety of the limited representation. If a new lawyer is not as knowledgeable respecting the progress of particular sorts of matters, it is likely necessary to engage a mentor(s) or to gain experience, perhaps through volunteering first.

2. How would you advise attorneys to respond to critics of unbundling or accusations from other professionals that their unbundling work is "commoditizing" the practice of law?

The horse is out of the barn with respect to this issue. While the practice of law is not a commodity, lawyers are always trading in commodities— discrete sets of services. A simple will is a commodity, and so is an estate planning package. An easement is a commodity; a real estate closing is a commodity. There is nothing evident in unbundling that changes the basic character of the practice of law; it is merely the outgrowth of thinking about service packets in different ways. In an administrative Republic, like ours, with ever more complex rules and regulations, it makes sense that discrete issues would be addressed on a one-off basis, and that specialties would shrink.

3. What role do you think unbundling will take in the legal profession in the future?

Unbundling is likely the substantive future of the legal profession. The complexity of discrete legal issues continues to increase in an administrative state, and it makes sense that attorneys will want to address small(er) areas, in which they are subject matters experts, as opposed to measuring themselves against wider-ranging cases. Cost is the driving force of nearly everything in a capitalist society, and it is no different when it comes to the increasing popularity of unbundling legal services. Attorneys can focus on more discrete matters, and so spend less time and money researching outside of their expertise. It also serves as a hedge against malpractice in cases where lawyers get caught overreaching their acumen. Clients are seeking price certainty; and it is easier to determine pricing in unbundled service provision, if for no other reason than that, in those cases, lawyers are dealing with a closed universe. While attorneys gripe about companies like LegalZoom, the fact of the matter is that modern technology and unbundling, two tenets on which LegalZoom is built, make it possible to charge lower rates for systematized services. Lawyers should take this as a cue to the future direction of their profession and become proactive in advancing to that future, rather than expressing continued disappointment over market trends that they can better control.

4. Do you have any best practices or suggestions for attorneys wishing to minimize the risk of malpractice when unbundling services?

Apply an airtight, client-specific fee agreement. Gather samples from mentors and colleagues to help develop same.

Client Intake

Establishing a client intake process and procedures for working with limited-scope clients is the first step to integrating unbundling into a law firm. In many cases, the law firm may use some of its existing client intake forms or worksheets to collect the information from the prospective unbundled client.

Following are some additional factors to consider in determining whether the case may be unbundled or if it requires full-service representation:

- ♦ The complexity of the matter: How much litigation is involved or is it a more clear-cut case? Has the client worked with another attorney before on the matter before seeking out limited-scope assistance?

- ♦ Is there some urgency to the case? Is the client contacting the lawyer with the matter as a last-minute emergency? Will the law firm be required to complete the work within a time frame that is feasible without the risk of providing services that are not competent?

- ♦ The client's personality: Will this client be able to handle the remainder of the case following the firm's instructions and guidance? Does the client have the necessary education level to complete the task?

- ♦ Would it be in the client's best interests in this particular circumstance if the representation were consistent from start to finish? For example, in a complex child-custody matter or a criminal-defense case, the client's best interests would most likely be served through continuous and consistent representation rather than unbundling.[2]

♦ Does the client take instruction well?

♦ Is the client going to be comfortable communicating with the firm using the methods that the firm has set up for limited-scope cases, such as a virtual law office or web conferencing, rather than in-person office visits?

♦ Will the client consent to the limited representation?

When determining the ability of the firm to handle the unbundled legal matter, the attorney must ask thorough questions of the client during the initial client intake process to identify any potential collateral issues that the client may not have brought up or even be aware of as potential issues. This also includes identifying all the parties that might be involved in the matter. Identifying any collateral issues during this process and making sure that these are included in the limited-scope agreement may limit the risk of malpractice claims from a client who may not understand the firm's lack of representation regarding unexpected collateral issues that may arise further down the road in the process of completing his or her legal needs. If found, these potential collateral issues should be included in the list of the client's responsibilities if the firm does not intend to provide representation on these matters in the event they arise.

Check for Conflicts

Attorneys who provide unbundled legal services may work with a larger quantity of clients for shorter periods of time than does a traditional firm. Often, to make the practice of unbundling profitable for a law firm, it is necessary to generate a higher quantity of prospective clients through leads from attorney referral services, directories, or other marketing strategies. Chapter Eight, "Marketing Unbundled Legal Services," covers this in more detail. The firm will need a thorough system in place for checking for potential conflicts of interest with prospective limited-scope clients and full-service clients.

---

[2]*See, e.g., In re* Egwim, 291 B.R. 559 (Bankr. N.D. Ga. 2003) and *In re* Castorena, 270 B.R. 504 (Bankr. D. Idaho 2001). In some states, the courts are still considering whether or not unbundling or limited appearance may be allowed for certain matters, such as criminal defense cases.

Conflicts checks can be tricky with certain unbundled matters because the lawyer may not be starting on the case from the beginning of the process. For example, if the lawyer has been retained to provide coaching, strategy, or other trial-preparation services, he or she may not be familiar with all the parties involved in the case before he or she was retained. Accordingly, the lawyer must be especially careful to inquire about all the potential parties involved in the legal matter through the initial client intake process and before determining whether to provide limited-scope services to the client.

It also is necessary to keep good records of prospective clients that the firm refused to represent. Maintaining records of prospective clients that have been declined unbundled services is easiest in digital format. A firm may choose from many available solutions to meet this need, from importing contacts and recording new clients in a virtual law office application to using a cloud-based customer relations manager (CRM) program. The key is for the firm to find a reliable and consistent method of making the conflicts check a critical step with each prospective unbundling case.

Educate Your Client with Checklists and Instructions

Because limited-scope clients will be handling a majority of their legal needs for themselves after you have provided a portion of the work, most of these individuals need guidance to complete the matter. The attorney should be responsible for explaining to the client how the typical legal process works and what the client will need to follow through to the end. For example, with a no-contest divorce, the client should be given a chronology that explains what documents are filed and where, how long the waiting period typically will be, when there are hearings, what the client will have to provide at hearings, and so on through to the end of a typical no-contest divorce. The client thus has a better understanding of how the limited-scope representation will assist him or her in accomplishing the goals and is better prepared to handle the footwork.

When the attorney completes the agreed-on unbundled task, he or she should provide the client with detailed instructions for completing the remainder of the matter. This document should contain the caveat that the instructions are for a typical case and that the attorney can make no guarantees of any outcomes or changes in this procedure that may occur as a result of the client, court, or opposing parties' actions or omissions. Using a checklist format for the instructions may be the easiest way for the client to follow through after the attorney has handed over the work. Placing these instructions online for the client in a secure digital case file ensures that the client can access that information 24/7 and refer back to it throughout the case.

Keep Records of Your Interactions with the Client

A law firm that is unbundling should keep good records of its interactions with limited-scope clients from the beginning of their contact with the firm. Unbundling clients in particular may be more likely to contact the attorney after the services are complete to ask follow-up questions or to request additional services beyond the scope of the initial engagement agreement. To avoid malpractice claims, the attorney should record each of these conversations for the client's file and be careful to record when the client was provided with documents and instructions. Copies of all checklists, instructions, and detailed information given to the client should be kept in this file with the date each was provided.

Using technology, such as providing the client with a client portal and online case file access, may facilitate this process because it allows the client to contact the attorney with additional questions while also recording that conversation for future reference. When the DIY client doesn't take instruction well, this record may serve to protect the law firm from claims that it did not provide adequate or prompt communication or the promised level of representation.

Explaining Unbundled Services to Full-Service Clients

When a full-service law firm adds unbundling to its list of services, there may be some question by its full-service clients regarding the level of service and pricing that is provided to limited-scope clients. For example, if the firm operates a virtual law office where "packaged" or fixed fee services are offered for unbundled matters online, the firm website may include sample fixed fee prices and an explanation of the unbundled services. Full-service clients may review this material. The firm should have a planned response to full-service clients who may question the lower fees or value billing arrangements offered to unbundled clients if the law firm does not provide similar billing options to its full-service clients. This might include the same handout that the firm provides to unbundled clients providing a comparison of the firm's work process for full-service versus limited-scope representation on specific cases.

The firm also may choose to provide its full-service clients with unbundled legal services pertaining to matters outside their primary legal need. For example, a firm that handles real estate transactions also may agree to draft the estate-planning documents for a client who needs updated documents after purchasing a new home and moving to a new state. A separate limited-scope engagement agreement should be executed with the existing full-service client to ensure that the client understands the scope of this unbundled work as separate from his or her full-service matter. This will protect the firm in the event that the client assumes that the billing methods and other terms of the representation used for the unbundled matter will carry over to the full-service case. However, a truly progressive firm will realize that offering its full-service clients similar billing options to those of its unbundled clients creates greater customer loyalty and trust. See Chapter Four for a discussion of fixed fees and value billing.

Malpractice Insurance: Making Sure Unbundled Services Are Covered

Limited-scope representation does not mean limited malpractice liability risk. Attorneys who unbundle legal services need to be extra careful to record each step of the delivery process. Most standard malpractice insurance policies cover unbundling. However, the carrier may wish to review the firm's limited-scope agreement and ensure that there is a solid process in place for the firm to ensure that there is informed client consent and acceptance of the limited-scope of representation. If the firm will be using technology to provide unbundled legal services, such as the use of software as a service (SaaS) applications or other third-party hosting of law office data, the firm may want to check with its insurance carrier regarding any exclusion in its policy that may relate to this aspect of the delivery process.

Consumers do not realize that using a lawyer instead of a free DIY service or online legal services companies is a form of insurance for themselves. The lawyer can be sued for malpractice if something he or she provided to the client has a negative result because of the lawyer's actions, while these other services offer no protection from their own negligence or lack of competence in a particular area of law. Pointing this out to prospective clients might be one way to help them understand the value of the law firm's services.

Case Study
Lawyers Mutual Liability Insurance Company of North Carolina—
http://www.lawyersmutualnc.com/"www.lawyersmutualnc.com

Lawyers Mutual provides continuous financial protection from professional liability to more than 8000 North Carolina lawyers. The company has published a set of risk management handouts on its website including one that discusses the unbundling of legal services.

1. Are you seeing more of your insureds unbundling or asking questions about the risks associated with unbundling and how it affects their practices?

We have not seen a meaningful increase in insureds asking about unbundling of legal services. We occasionally get questions about how to deal with practical issues related to unbundling, but the attorneys asking the question don't usually phrase it as such. Rather, they say they are handling this or that piece of a legal representation and they want to know how to best protect themselves in the limited engagement. Our advice includes documenting the scope of representation through the use of client engagement letters and fee agreements, both of which may need to be revised if the scope of the representation changes.

These issues come up frequently in family law practices; separation agreements and prenuptial agreements in particular. We have also received inquiries from collaborative lawyers and family law mediators who agree to take on drafting duties to effectuate the settlement reached by the parties through mediation.

The question also presents from real estate practitioners, who now are frequently asked to provide limited services associated with a purchase closing or refinance. Frequently the closing ceremony and disbursement of funds are being handled by other law offices or title insurance agents and the attorney is retained to certify title or prepare deeds and related documents only.

At our 2010 CLE programs, we discussed unbundled legal services in the context of client relationships and we guided insureds to the unbundled handout on our website which includes among other items best practices for unbundling legal services and a sample limited scope engagement agreement letter.

During our 2011 CLE programs, we discussed unbundled legal services in the context of emerging ethics and legal issues. We asked attendees whether they were experiencing more client requests for unbundled services. A small percentage of attorneys responded affirmatively, although many anticipated this would probably change in the future. Audience feedback also confirmed that unbundling has been part of many practices for a significant period of time, but not specifically referred to as unbundling.

> **2.** How insurers think about unbundling and what, if any, are the changes that might be in a policy or the approval process for a firm that unbundles?

There is an argument to be made that if an attorney specializes in an area of practice, using forms, checklists and best practices and handling matters consistently, the practice may be a better risk (present less exposure to loss) than a general practice. That being said, major concerns relative to unbundled service include miscommunication, unmet expectations and unmet or undefined legal needs. At Lawyers Mutual, we plan to continue to look at our claims history, which will guide us on how we assess the exposure and price policies. However, from a risk management perspective we do believe that it is possible to provide unbundled services in a way that does not significantly increase an attorney's exposure. In these situations it is critical that the attorney have a limited scope engagement agreement. It is also equally as important to thoroughly document throughout the course of the representation. Interestingly, utilization of a detailed engagement letter and thorough documentation is advice we provide all insureds, irrespective of whether they are unbundling.

> **3.** Do you require that the insured provide a sample limited scope engagement agreement to verify that they follow this best practice?

In our underwriting department, we are asking about and strongly recommending the use of engagement letters in certain areas of practice to define the scope of representation. However, we do not ask firms to identify whether they unbundle, so we do not have a requirement that they provide us with a sample engagement agreement in that context. As a company, we have been discussing the exposure presented by unbundling and ensuring that we provide relevant guidance to insureds. We are also analyzing claims for case studies to develop policies if we need to change our underwriting practices such as to include questions on the application about the percentage of work performed as a result of unbundling.

4. How might the policies differ, if they do?

Right now we are not underwriting differently for firms that offer unbundled services. Even if we were to do so, we would not anticipate offering a different policy. Any differences in exposure which may exist would most likely be reflected in the premium charged.

5. Have you seen many malpractice claims associated with the practice of unbundling?

We have seen claims that arise because the scope of the representation was not well-defined. The attorneys and clients had differing ideas about scope. Rarely have we specifically identified those types of claims as an unbundling issue. However, we fully expect that to change as the client awareness of unbundling increases. We also expect that new lawyers will begin to practice in different ways than today's full service lawyers (we are beginning to see evidence of this) and we expect they will be looking for more resources to help them deal with issues such as unbundled services.

A case study can be drawn from one of our claims. One of our insureds was hit with a $1.4 million dollar verdict (that was ultimately reversed) based on an error the attorney made in filing a financing statement on behalf of a client. The client and his financial associate had worked out a deal and only wanted our insured to make sure the deal was done "legally." When the deal went bad, the client went looking for someone to sue. Our insured had volunteered to file the financing statement and as it was allegedly defective, he became a target.

Termination Letter

After completing the limited-scope of services for the client, the lawyer should send the client a termination letter or some form of written confirmation that the lawyer has fulfilled the scope of services that originally were set out in the limited-scope agreement. This serves two purposes: (1) to protect the lawyer from the client's claim that he or she believed a next step in the legal matter was up to the lawyer or firm to complete, and (2) to protect the client by reminding him or her of the responsibility to complete the legal matter from that point. Termination letters might include an attached checklist, time line, or strategy for the client to follow. The law firm also might want to attach this confirmation to the final invoice for the unbundled legal services. A copy of the termination letter, whether it is in paper or digital format, should be kept in the archived file for the client. A lawyer's malpractice insurance carrier also may ask to see a copy of the termination letter along with the limited-scope agreement. Therefore, before a law firm begins to offer unbundled services, drafting a standard termination letter or notice should be part of the planning process.

Good Customer Service

DIY clients research their options ahead of time. Most expect a level of service and respect from the business that they choose to patronize. If these individuals select your law firm over a generic online legal services company, they will take note when the firm goes above and beyond in providing educational content, checklists, and guidance for them to handle the remainder of their legal matters. Maintaining good communication with clients at all stages in the relationship and unbundling process is important to guarantee their satisfaction with the unbundled services. Implement tools, such as client portals, to keep the clients in the loop about the status of their matters and to record your communications for their later reference.

Setting up technology to automate reminders and streamline the unbundling process for specific matters makes customer service much easier for the law firm. Virtual assistants and paralegals may be added to the practice to handle some of the relationship-building aspects of the practice, such as making sure that the clients possess all the necessary instructions and handouts that relate to their legal matters or for following up to give clients gentle reminders of deadlines they are responsible for meeting. In some cases, the firm may provide its virtual assistants or paralegals with online access to the clients' case files and the firm's online backend law office.

Finally, when the limited scope of the representation for the client has been completed, the firm should check back with the client to make sure he or she was able to complete the legal matter. Good customer service practices help build the firm's reputation for quality legal services and also may prevent malpractice claims against the firm's members.

CHAPTER FOUR

Fixed Fee or
Value Billing

UNBUNDLING IS AN IDEAL opportunity to provide alternative fee arrangements to clients, in particular, fixed fee or value billing.[1] Payment plans that spread out the cost of the unbundled services also may be popular with clients and serve as another marketing point for the unbundling practice. Fixed fee billing also may help the client budget for his or her legal services and understand the limited scope of the arrangement. There is a difference between value billing and fixed fees, but both may be implemented in some form in an unbundling practice.

Value billing focuses on the client's financial situation and needs rather than on the firm's expected revenue generation.[2] The value is in the final work provided to the client rather than in the number of hours it takes attorneys and assistants at the firm to complete the project. Really, the term should be "value pricing" rather than value billing because the value of the unbundled project or each phase of the project is determined ahead of time rather than at the completion of the unbundled project after the time and resources have been calculated.

A firm could charge a combination of a fixed fee with a billable hour component depending on the scope of the project, and this billing method could be couched as value billing if the firm seeks the client's input

---

[1] A good resource for information about alternative billing practices, including fixed-fee and value billing, is MARK ROBERTSON & JAMES A. CALLOWAY, WINNING ALTERNATIVES TO THE BILLABLE HOUR, ABA Publishing (June 23, 2008).

[2] For an example of a law firm that has been a pioneer in value billing, *see* Valorem Law Group, a Chicago-based firm focused on business litigation, at **http://www.valoremlaw.com/** (last accessed on Oct. 29, 2011).

regarding the expected value of the firm's services. The creation of the billing method itself may be value billing through this process of working with the client to determine the value of the lawyer's services. With unbundled services, this value may be more easy to discern because the limited scope of the work must be so clearly defined ahead of time with the role and responsibilities of the lawyer written out in the limited-scope engagement agreement. It may be easier to include value billing in this initial process of setting the scope of unbundling. For example, as the lawyer is explaining to the prospective client the difference between a full-service representation on a matter and the limited scope, he or she may have a conversation about the value of the work the lawyer will be providing by accomplishing specific tasks on the project's checklist. Some firms have even experimented with asking their clients ahead of time what the client expects to pay for services, allowing the clients to set the legal fees based on their needs and what they think the value of the lawyer's experience and services are worth.

On the other hand, fixed fees may be set by the attorney at the firm ahead of even working with a client based on the average time and resources spent in handling a particular unbundled project. It also may be desirable to created fixed fees for each stage of the unbundling process. As a different milestone in the unbundling work is completed, then the lawyer and client come together again to determine the billing method and amount for the next part of the process. This method may appeal more to the litigator who is unbundling because of all the collateral issues that may not be discoverable at the beginning of the representation due to outcomes at hearings and trials that involve the actions of outside parties to the limited-scope engagement agreement.

Both fixed fee and value billing may require that the attorney experiment to develop the correct formula for particular unbundled projects. One method of doing this might be to calculate an entire unbundled project from start to finish for a client in billable hours. Take this final amount from several similar projects and come up with an average amount. Some fixed fee cases will take more time and resources than expected, but some cases will be completed faster than expected. Most lawyers who unbundle their services on fixed fees have found the difference balances out at the end of the month and does not harm the revenue flow for their business.

Another option to offer clients is a prepaid legal service plan that provides them with unbundled legal services from the law firm over the course of a year or other time period for a fixed fee. A plan could be set up that provides the client with access to legal forms, limited guidance, or occasional consultations, all based on a monthly fee that either the lawyer or client sets and both agree on. The monthly fee might provide access to legal assistance and guidance in unbundled format while any additional unbundled work would require a new limited-scope engagement agreement that covers more work outside of the fixed offerings. This would be easiest to provide through a law firm website and secure client portal where the law firm maintains a wealth of legal education, forms, web-based tools, one-hour-a-month consultations by telephone or real-time chat, or other materials and resources with access limited to clients who have selected the prepaid legal service plan option.

This may provide the law firm with a fixed-income stream from plan members, but also may lead to additional unbundling or even full-service representation when the client realizes through the self-help materials that he or she would prefer the additional guidance of the lawyer. With both the initiation of the prepaid legal service plan and any additional unbundling work, the law firm would need to obtain additional limited-scope engagement agreements, but these might be accomplished through clickwrap agreements for any web-based form of access and/or a more traditional, written limited-scope agreement. The prepaid legal service plan could be in the form of a fixed fee and any additional work could be value billed based on what the client feels is the value of that additional representation beyond the prepaid legal service.[3]

An unbundling attorney also must consider that the prospective client is shopping around before visiting the firm's website or office. The prospective client is empowered through searches on the Internet to know how much other attorneys as well as nonlawyer online legal services charge for certain unbundled work. Services such as AttorneyFee.com allow lawyers themselves to post their fees for legal services so that prospective clients may shop for representation based on cost.[4] When estimating fixed fees or value billing, the lawyer should check out their competitors, both lawyer and nonlawyer, to find out what expectations their clients may bring to the table.

---

[3]For additional information about prepaid legal services, see the resources of the American Prepaid Legal Services Institute, at **http://www.aplsi.org/**, last accessed December 13, 2011.
[4]AttorneyFee.com at **http://www.attorneyfee.com/**, last accessed November 15, 2011.

The increase in information on the Internet about lawyer fees and the cost of legal services leads to another concern regarding fixed fee billing: The average consumer may not understand the value of a licensed professional providing unbundled work over that of an online legal services company. Consumers also may not understand that more than just time goes into the creation of a legal fee and that the experience of the lawyer, geographic location, and other factors go into forming what one lawyer charges over the other. When explaining pricing models to clients, it might be a good idea to combat this misinformation up front by providing a comparison chart or written explanation of the value of a licensed professional versus a legal document assistant or a paralegal-created legal form. This is more of an issue for transactional unbundled work than it is for other forms of unbundling where there is not so much competition from nonlicensed legal service providers.

Another possible way to help the client understand that the lawyer is sincere about providing him or her with options for the billing method that best meets the client's needs is to provide that "satisfaction in service is guaranteed." While this may seem like a risk to some lawyers, it may go a long way to combating the public's distrust of lawyers and their billing practices. Lawyers cannot guarantee the results of their work, but they can provide statements that if the clients are unsatisfied with the work, that the clients will receive refunds. Depending on the lawyer's client base and practice area, it may not be desirable to provide this form of guarantee. However, if this can be presented on the lawyer's website, it may provide an additional level of trust that prompts the prospective client to make that initial contact with law firm.

Offering fixed fee or value billing in unbundling does not preclude the lawyer from accepting retainers from the client. In the limited-scope engagement agreement, lawyers may require that the representation not commence until the client has returned the signed agreement along with the first payment for services. This is also the ideal time to set out payment plans in a schedule that includes online bill payment or other methods of collection that are set at each of the milestones within the unbundled project. As with all billing methods used in unbundling, they should be reevaluated by the law firm on a regular basis based on client feedback, the collections process, and any changes in competition for unbundled services in the legal marketplace.

Checklist for Determining Alternative Billing in Unbundled Cases

Note: These steps are to be taken in addition to the complete client intake process:

- Decide whether to place a fixed fee on the entire unbundled project or to charge a separate fee for each stage of the project. Are there existing timetables or deadlines in place for completing the work? Find out when the work needs to be completed and how quickly the firm will have to respond.

- Ask the client what he or she expects from the limited-scope representation.

- Ask how the client expects to communicate with you, including methods of communication, how much and how often, and with which individuals in the firm.

- If clients are coming to you from full-service representation, talk to them about why they transferred and what they liked and did not like about the billing practices of their full-service firms.

- Know what the competition charges in legal fees for the unbundled services you would be providing the client. Assume the client has shopped around before coming to you.

- Find out what the client expectations are for budgeting for this legal project.

- Do they need to pay with a payment plan?

- Determine what price point would be accepted by the client and at what point your services would either seem too expensive or so low in cost as to make the client question the value of your firm's services.

- Explain how your firm determines the value of its services based on experience, reputation, resources, etc.

- Consider providing a "satisfaction guaranteed" policy.

- Offer prepaid legal services as an option.

- Be flexible based on individual client needs and consider a combination of fixed fee and value billing.

CHAPTER FIVE

Forms of Unbundling

MANY METHODS OF DELIVERING limited-scope services exist and
some of them may involve more than one form of unbundling. For example, the client who requests unbundled legal document preparation also
may request legal coaching or strategy. Or the client who requests legal
form preparation then may request a limited appearance in connection
with the case. This chapter will provide an overview of the primary forms
of unbundling. The ethics issues and best practices discussed in the previous chapters apply to each of these methods. However, certain forms of
unbundling require extra care to avoid ethics and malpractice risks,
including those methods that face criticism from some state bars and
practitioners. These will be addressed in detail. To minimize risk, the law
firm deciding how to integrate unbundled services into its practice may
want to start with only one form of unbundling or find methods of
adding these services to complement its existing practice areas.

Document Drafting and Legal Form Preparation

Document drafting and legal form preparation are common forms of
unbundling legal services for clients. The use of technology to handle
document drafting is becoming more prevalent. These technologies are
the primary methods used by companies selling legal forms to the consumer online. Chapter Seven discusses how to use document automation
and assembly tools to streamline the process of unbundling. In some
cases, the lawyer may outsource the document drafting or form preparation to another service and then add his or her legal guidance to that final

product when meeting with the client.[1] However, for many lawyers, document drafting is still a craft they would prefer to unbundle on a case-by-case basis. There may be situations where technology is not so helpful in pulling together a legal document, and it is necessary to start from an existing template. However, it should rarely be necessary to start completely from scratch.

Almost every state bar association has state-based legal form books that may be purchased in print format by the lawyer who then may transform the templates for use in his or her unbundling practice.[2] Now many online resources also provide state-based legal forms without the document assembly and automation component that may be used for free or for a minimal fee by the law firm.[3] Many larger law firms will have in-house form and document databases to select from. Lawyers without such resources may want to locate their state bar's self-help centers to see what is available to the consumer through those sites. It might be possible to reuse these forms with DIY clients who simply need assistance with drafting the document or preparing the form. Some law firm websites choose to link to these free self-help resources for prospective online clients and make use of the forms in their practice as well.

With most document drafting or form preparation for basic legal situations, the lawyer is reusing an existing template for consistency and replacing certain provisions to customize them to meet the client's needs. This form of work is going to be more common in unbundling because the lawyer usually is being retained for the limited purpose of the document drafting and is not involved in other procedures in the resolution of the legal matter. If the client's situation requires a more complex form of document drafting, then it may be likely that unbundling is not appropri-

---

[1] Find a list of vendors providing offshore or outsourced legal services compiled by Joy London, co-editor of Law Librarian News, a global electronic newsletter for law librarians and legal knowledge managers, and Ron Friedmann, president of Prism Legal Consulting, Inc. and author of Strategic Legal Technology (last updated Feb. 2008) at **http://www.prismlegal.com/index.php?option=content&task=view&id=88&Itemid=70** (last accessed Nov. 14, 2011).

[2] A few examples of form books that are not state-specific include: American Jurisprudence Legal Forms 2d, published by West (updated 2012), and American Jurisprudence Pleading and Practice Forms Annotated, published by West (updated 2012). A few examples of practice area–specific form books include: Fletcher Corporation Forms Annotated (4th ed.), published by West; Herzog Bankruptcy Forms and Practice, by Herzog's Bankruptcy Forms and Practice, by Asa S. Herzog, Joseph Samet, Sheldon Lowe & Joel B. Zweibel (updated 2011), published by West; and Uniform Commercial Code Legal Forms, 4th (updated 2011), published by West.

[3] Both LEXIS and Westlaw also have online directories of legal forms available for a cost based on subscription terms.

ate for this matter because more continuous representation beyond the creation of the document or form would be in the client's best interest.

For more complex matters, document drafting requires a significant amount of legal expertise not only in the legal issues to be included in the document but in the ways that the document will be used and any intended outcomes or consequences. While this might be easily discernible in the drafting of basic estate planning for a client, the creation of a lease agreement, or the patent application for a company's product, it may not be so clear to the lawyer when there are other factors involved that the lawyer may not be privy to, such as in the creation of a complex acquisition agreement where there are prior relationships and history that must be involved in the creation of the document. As with any form of unbundling, the lawyer must make the determination on a case-by-case basis whether the matter is appropriate for unbundling or requires full service.

Tips for Legal Document Preparation

1. If you are starting from scratch with a legal document, review examples from other lawyers who have handled similar cases. Your state bar association may have listservs for different practice areas. Send out a request for sample legal documents from others in your jurisdiction, but be careful not to rely on the first document you read and compare strategies in several before drafting your own.

2. Check the language and law references in your final version to ensure that the sample you are using is up-to-date.

3. If you are reusing a document, review it for any references to the previous client's case. This is a significant area of risk in document drafting because it has the potential to not only reveal confidential information regarding one client but also cause the current client to question the lawyer's attention and the client's ability to trust the lawyer with the client's confidential information.

4. Make sure the form you have selected from any online resource is tailored to the laws of your jurisdiction. Do not trust that anything you obtain online for free or even for a minimal fee will be updated or correctly apply to your state's laws.

5. In some matters it may be necessary to use a court-prepared legal form. Your client may be subject to default, dismissal, or other consequences for failing to use specific court forms. Make sure you

are using the form required by the court where your client will be filing the form. If you work with clients online in your jurisdiction, this may mean contacting the specific courthouse in another geographic location from your office to ascertain which legal form is necessary and obtain copies of court-prepared legal forms.

6. Start creating your own database of legal forms and documents and categorize them by practice area or legal issues so that they may be found for future reference.

7. Avoid using legalese. Some lawyers erroneously believe that using incomprehensible language increases the presumed value of their services and that clients will not balk at paying high fees for document drafting. With the proliferation of sample forms and documents online, clients are aware that clear language and good writing are just as effective if not more effective in helping to resolve their legal needs. Clients prefer the ability to read in clear language and understand the forms and documents they are signing as does the court and any other parties required to sign or read the documents.

Ghostwriting

Ghostwriting is the term used to describe when a lawyer drafts a legal document, such as a complaint or response, for a client to use in the course of a case and the attorney does not sign his or her name to the legal document or make the court aware that the document was drafted by a licensed lawyer rather than the pro se litigant.

In 2007, the ABA published Formal Opinion 07-446, which permits ghostwriting.[4] This opinion states that a lawyer may provide limited assistance to a pro se litigant by helping him or her prepare written materials without disclosing the lawyer's involvement in the preparation to the court. In a case where it would constitute fraud or be dishonest conduct on the part of the pro se litigant to hide the limited-scope assistance from the court,

---

[4]ABA Standing Comm. on Ethics and Prof'l Resp., Formal Op. 07-446, Undisclosed Legal Assistance to Pro Se Litigants (issued May 5, 2007), *available at* **http://www.abanet.org/legalservices/delivery/downloads/aba_07_446_2007.pdf** (accessed Dec. 28, 2010). The ABA Model Rule does not require that the lawyer reveal that he or she has provided assistance to the pro se litigant.

ghostwriting might constitute the lawyer's violation of other Rules of Professional Responsibility, such as Rules 1.2(d), 3.3(b), 4.1(b), or 8.4(c).[5]

Reasons an Attorney May Choose to Ghostwrite

- The client prefers to represent himself or herself in the courtroom.

- An attorney may not want to be pulled into full-service representation on a case and fears that disclosure would require increasing the scope of representation if the client is unable to proceed alone.

- The attorney may not have a good reputation or relationship with the judge assigned to the case or fear some bias based on previous experience with the assigned judge that may not benefit the pro se litigant.

- Certain groups of pro se litigants, such as prisoners, have decreased access to materials and a lack of lawyers available to assist them.

---

[5]MODEL RULE 1.2(d): "A lawyer shall not counsel a client to engage, or assist a client, in conduct that the lawyer knows is criminal or fraudulent, but a lawyer may discuss the legal consequences of any proposed course of conduct with a client and may counsel or assist a client to make a good faith effort to determine the validity, scope, meaning or application of the law," *available at* **http://www.americanbar.org/groups/professional_responsibility/publications/model_rules_ of_professional_conduct/rule_1_2_scope_of_representation_allocation_of_authority_between_ client_lawyer.html**; MODEL RULE 3.3: "(b) A lawyer who represents a client in an adjudicative proceeding and who knows that a person intends to engage, is engaging or has engaged in criminal or fraudulent conduct related to the proceeding shall take reasonable remedial measures, including, if necessary, disclosure to the tribunal," *available at* **http://www.americanbar.org/groups/ professional_responsibility/publications/model_rules_of_professional_conduct/rule_3_3_ candor_toward_the_tribunal.html**; MODEL RULE 4.1(b): "(b) fail to disclose a material fact to a third person when disclosure is necessary to avoid assisting a criminal or fraudulent act by a client, unless disclosure is prohibited by Rule 1.6," *available at* **http://www.americanbar.org/ groups/professional_responsibility/publications/model_rules_of_professional_conduct/rule_ 4_1_truthfulness_in_statements_to_others.html**; and MODEL RULE 8.4(c): "It is professional misconduct for a lawyer to: (c) engage in conduct involving dishonesty, fraud, deceit or misrepresentation," *available at* **http://www.americanbar.org/groups/professional_responsibility/ publications/model_rules_of_professional_conduct/rule_8_4_misconduct.html**.

[6]*See* Ira P. Robbins, *Ghostwriting: Filling in the Gaps of Pro Se Prisoners' Access to the Courts*, GEO. J. OF LEGAL ETHICS 23, no. 2 (Spring 2010), 271–321, *available at* **http://digitalcommons.wcl.american .edu/cgi/viewcontent.cgi?article=1069&context=facsch_lawrev&sei-redir=1&referer=http% 3A%2F%2Fwww.google.com%2Furl%3Fsa%3Dt%26rct%3Dj%26q%3Dghostwriting%252C% 2520filling%2520in%2520the%2520gaps%2520of%2520pro%2520se%2520prisoner%25E2% 2580%2599s%2520access%2520to%2520the%2520courts%26source%3Dweb%26cd%3D1% 26ved%3D0CB4QFjAA%26url%3Dhttp%253A%252F%252Fdigitalcommons.wcl.american.edu %252Fcgi%252Fviewcontent.cgi%253Farticle%253D1069%2526context%253Dfacsch_lawrev %26ei%3DiTakTse9El6jtgevoPCWBQ%26usg%3DAFQjCNGc-FXamTVfZ3J_CDTRxq8GN- TgMg#search=%22ghostwriting%2C%20filling%20gaps%20pro%20se%20prisoner%E2% 80%99s%20access%20courts%22** (last accessed Oct. 22, 2011).

Lawyers who may otherwise not have desired or wanted to invest the time and resources to provide full-service representation to these individuals may provide limited-scope in the form of ghost-writing.[6]

♦ The attorney may feel that ghostwriting will impart a level of leniency on the pro se litigant that may benefit his or her case; it is used as a strategy to gain an edge in the courtroom.

♦ The attorney may wish to avoid a potential conflict of interest.[7]

♦ The attorney may worry that representing a pro se litigant in a particularly unpopular case might have a negative impact on the attorney's reputation in the legal community, with other attorneys, the judge, or the local bar.

♦ The attorney wants to educate and empower a pro se litigant so that he or she may navigate the justice system to find a resolution to his or her legal needs.

Rule 11 of the Federal Rules of Civil Procedure provides one of the most relied-on arguments against ghostwriting. The Rule states, "[e]very pleading, written motion, and other paper must be signed by at least one attorney of record in the attorney's name—or by a party personally if the party is unrepresented." Several court cases have held that ghostwriting violates this federal rule by being misrepresentative to the court.[8] In contrast, the ABA Formal Opinion 07-446, which has supported the adoption of other states' ghostwriting rules, "reject[s] the contention that a lawyer who does not appear in the action circumvents court rules requiring the assumption of responsibility for their pleadings."[9]

---

[7] *See, e.g.*, the large number of bankruptcy cases involving ghostwriting for the purpose of avoiding potential conflict of interest: Delso v. Trs. for the Ret. Plan for the Hourly Employees of Merck & Co., No. 04-3009, 2007 WL 766349 (D.N.J. Mar. 6, 2007); *In re* Brown, 354 B.R. 535 (Bankr. N.D. Okla. 2006); Att'y Grievance Comm'n of Md. v. Lawson, 933 A.2d 842 (Md. 2007); *In re* Potter, No. 7-05-14071, 2007 WL 2363104 (Bankr. D.N.M. Aug. 13, 2007); *In re* West, 338 B.R. 906 (Bankr. N.D. Okla. 2006); *In re* Cash Media Sys., 326 B.R. 655 (Bankr. S.D. Tex. 2005); *In re* Mungo, 305 B.R. 762 (Bankr. D.S.C. 2003).

[8] *See, e.g.*, *Duran v. Carris*, 238 F.3d 1268 (10th Cir. 2001); Laremont-Lopez v. Se. Tidewater Opportunity Ctr., 968 F. Supp. 1075, 1079–80 (E.D. Va. 1997); and Clarke v. United States, 955 F. Supp. 593 (E.D. Va. 1997); *see generally* ABA/BNA LAWYERS' MANUAL ON PROFESSIONAL CONDUCT at 61:101 (2008).

[9] *See* ABA Standing Comm. on Ethics and Prof'l Resp.'s Formal Op. 07-446, Undisclosed Legal Assistance to Pro Se Litigants (May 5, 2007), *available at* **http://www.americanbar.org/content/dam/aba/migrated/legalservices/delivery/downloads/aba_07_446_2007.authcheckdam.pdf** (last accessed Nov. 14, 2011).

Accordingly, state bars have addressed ghostwriting in different ways. Many state bars have specific rules regarding the practice of ghostwriting, and an attorney must be aware of how the local court where the client will be filing the document will handle ghostwritten documents. For example, New York's version of Rule 1.2 (c) allowing for limited-scope representation includes the statement ". . . *and where necessary notice is provided to the tribunal and/or opposing counsel.*" See the Appendix for a state-by-state list of rules that apply to ghostwriting and ethics opinions discussing whether disclosure should be required and under which circumstances.

Disclosure of Authorship

States that require disclosure of lawyer authorship are concerned that both the court and opposing counsel will be misled. They also may feel that failure to require disclosure of authorship removes accountability from the practicing lawyer and, therefore, encourages the filing of a frivolous lawsuit where the lawyer who drafted the complaint is able to shirk responsibility for lack of identification.[10] Some state bars and other critics of ghostwriting suggest that not requiring lawyer authorship on pleadings results in the creation of low-quality drafted legal documents that the lawyers themselves would not want to hand in at court with their own signatures attached. If a lawyer is not able to complete the ghostwritten pleadings in a manner that he or she would do for a full-service representation, it is his or her responsibility to decline the limited-scope arrangement and refer the client to a full-service firm or other attorney who may provide high-quality limited-scope representation.

Other state bars that require lawyer authorship argue that the courts and opposing counsel in order to provide adequate justice will provide a pro se litigant with a certain amount of leeway and patience that would not be provided to an experienced licensed lawyer in the courtroom. According to an article in *The Judge's Journal*, "[a]ll federal and virtually all state courts have precedents that papers submitted by pro se litigants will face a different standard of judicial review than those submitted by lawyers."[11]

---

[10]*See, e.g.*, the following state bar ethics opinions: Ct. Inf. Eth. Op. 98-5 (Jan. 30, 1998); Ky. Bar Ass'n Eth. Op. E-343 (Jan. 1991); Colo. Bar Ass'n Eth. Op. 101 (Jan. 17, 1998) and the Addendum to this opinion added Dec. 16, 2006; Del. State Bar Ass'n Comm. on Prof'l Eth. Op. 1994-2 (May 6, 1994); and N.Y. State Bar Ass'n Comm. on Prof'l Eth. Op. 613 (Sept. 24, 1990).

[11]For more information on how judges can work with pro se litigants, *see* Rebecca A. Albrecht, John M. Greacen, Bonnie Rose Hough & Richard Zorza, *Judicial Techniques in Cases Involving Self-Represented Litigants*, in THE JUDGES' JOURNAL, Winter 2003, ABA, Vol. 42, No. 1, *available at* **http://www.zorza.net/JudicalTech.JJWi03.pdf** (last accessed on Oct. 22, 2011).

This treatment may be an attempt to balance any disparities in education and experience that exist between the party proceeding pro se against a represented party.

Critics of undisclosed ghostwriting argue that it is not fair to the party who has clear full representation to not disclose to the court that the pro se litigant also has had lawyer guidance and that any prejudice or liberal treatment of the pro se litigant should not be included in the courtroom proceedings. Other critics argue that supporting ghostwriting will encourage the unauthorized practice of law by individuals who have lost their licenses or by nonlawyers who see a market for providing legal services with the protective cloak of anonymity.

However, proponents of undisclosed ghostwriting argue that it should be evident to the court and opposing counsel that a licensed lawyer has drafted a legal pleading for the pro se litigant merely from the construction and text of the filed document. Countering both the critics and proponents of ghostwriting should be the basic principle that the legal profession always must try to balance the need for adequate access to justice for as many as possible with the need to protect the public from being misled or taken advantage of by those with a responsibility to serve the justice system.

A Suggested Best Practice

Unless your state bar has indicated a specific procedure for ghostwriting, the safest best practice would be for the lawyer to include somewhere on the legal pleading being filed with the court that the document was written by the lawyer. While many state bars do not require this step, this preserves fairness at court by providing notice to the judge and opposing counsel that the pro se litigant has received assistance with his or her case and may not require the same level of leniency or handholding as a pro se litigant who is proceeding without instruction or assistance.[12] Even though in most cases the court will be able to detect from reading the document that it was prepared by a licensed professional, the addition of the law firm's name to the document provides the court with this knowledge before the matter proceeds.

The attorney should discuss the need for disclosure of authorship with the client ahead of time. This is important so that the attorney does

---

[12] *See generally* Ira P. Robbins, *Ghostwriting: Filling in the Gaps of Pro Se Prisoners' Access to the Courts*, GEO. J. LEGAL ETHICS, Spring 2010; Rothermich, *Ethical and Procedural Implications of "Ghostwriting" for Pro Se Litigants: Toward Increased Access to Civil Justice*, 67 FORDHAM L. REV. 2687 (1999).

encounter problems later of having to protect client confidentiality while also complying with a court's potential request for notification of authorship. Remember, if necessary, the court may decide to compel the pro se litigant to provide the name of the lawyer who provided the limited assistance.

Limited Appearances

Appearances before the court are one of the significant needs of self-help individuals that are not easily overcome in the same way that they may find unbundled assistance to draft legal documents or obtain legal guidance. Pro se litigants may be intimidated by the court, the unfamiliar procedures, and the rules, and for any number of other reasons, including cultural or language barriers, they may not be able to adequately articulate their positions at hearings or trials.

Limited appearances are another area of unbundling considered by some to be a high-risk practice. When a lawyer enters an appearance on behalf of a client for the purpose of full-service representation, he or she is listed as the responsible party on the client's case who receives notices of the status and moves the process forward. To withdraw from representation, the lawyer must file a motion to withdraw and go through a hearing to obtain permission from the court. The concern with limited appearances is that they may cause confusion with the court as to who the responsible party is for the case and for which part the client is represented.

One ethics issue that arises in limited appearances is the interpretation of Model Rules 4.2 and 4.3 regarding the proper communication between parties to a case.[13] These rules cover pro se litigants or fully represented parties, but do not address how the other side should handle communica-

---

[13]MODEL RULE 4.2, Communication with Person Represented by Counsel: "In representing a client, a lawyer shall not communicate about the subject of the representation with a person the lawyer knows to be represented by another lawyer in the matter, unless the lawyer has the consent of the other lawyer or is authorized to do so by law or a court order," *available at* **http://www.americanbar.org/groups/professional_responsibility/publications/model_rules_of_professional_conduct/rule_4_2_communication_with_person_represented_by_counsel.html** (last accessed Nov. 6, 2011). MODEL RULE 4.3, Dealing with Unrepresented Person: "In dealing on behalf of a client with a person who is not represented by counsel, a lawyer shall not state or imply that the lawyer is disinterested. When the lawyer knows or reasonably should know that the unrepresented person misunderstands the lawyer's role in the matter, the lawyer shall make reasonable efforts to correct the misunderstanding. The lawyer shall not give legal advice to an unrepresented person, other than the advice to secure counsel, if the lawyer knows or reasonably

tions in the case when the party has representation for a portion of the process but is proceeding pro se otherwise. Some states, such as Colorado, Washington, Florida, and Maine, have provided guidance for their lawyers on how to communicate when there is a limited appearance in a case.[14] If more states provide this form of guidance or amendments to their rules, then it would facilitate the ability of more practitioners to unbundled limited appearances.

Critics of limited appearances cite a comment to Model Rule 1.16, which states, "[a] lawyer should not accept representation in a matter unless it can be performed competently, promptly, without improper conflict of interest *and to completion*. Ordinarily, a representation in a matter is completed when the agreed-upon assistance has been concluded. See Rules 1.2(c) and 6.5."[15] (Emphasis added.) However, Rule 1.16 leaves the interpretation of the process up to the local and state courts, stating "[a] lawyer must comply with applicable law requiring notice to or permission of a tribunal when terminating a representation."[16]

Because of the confusion that it may cause for the court and opposing counsel, some states have added guidance to their versions of Model Rule 1.2(c) as it pertains to limited appearances. Most of this guidance merely provides clarification to the lawyer about how to file the appearance, how to withdraw, and how the other parties and the courts must be notified of the limited appearance. Clear procedures for this process are lacking in most states' rules and may depend more on the lawyer's local court procedures. However, in most cases, even if the lawyer provides the court with a copy of the limited-scope engagement agreement with the client, the

---

should know that the interests of such a person are or have a reasonable possibility of being in conflict with the interests of the client," *available at* **http://www.americanbar.org/groups/ professional_responsibility/publications/model_rules_of_professional_conduct/rule_4_3_ dealing_with_unrepresented_person.html** (last accessed Nov. 6, 2011).

[14] *An Analysis of Rules that Enable Lawyers to Serve Pro Se Litigants*, ABA Standing Committee on the Delivery of Legal Services (November 2009), at 13. For a description of these states' procedures for limited appearances, *see* Alicia M. Farley, *An Important Piece of the Bundle: How Limited Appearances Can Provide an Ethically Sound Way to Increase Access to Justice for Pro Se Litigants*, 20 Geo. J. Legal Ethics 563 (Summer 2007). *See also* the Appendix for links to these states' rules related to limited appearances.

[15] Comment 1 to Rule 1.16 at **http://www.americanbar.org/groups/professional_responsibility/ publications/model_rules_of_professional_conduct/rule_1_16_declining_or_terminating_ representation/comment_on_rule_1_16_declining_or_terminating_representation.html** (last accessed Nov. 6, 2011).

[16] Rule 1.16 at **http://www.americanbar.org/groups/professional_responsibility/publications/ model_rules_of_professional_conduct/rule_1_16_declining_or_terminating_representation.html** (last accessed Nov. 6, 2011).

court may not allow withdrawal. This risk alone deters most lawyers from offering limited appearances as a form of unbundled legal services. If your law firm is considering adding limited appearances to the list of unbundled offerings, consult not only with your state bar's rules but also with the procedures at the local courthouse where you would be providing this form of limited-scope assistance for clients.

Legal Coaching and Strategy

Legal coaching and strategy is most often a method of unbundling that is coupled with another service, such as drafting legal documents, ghostwriting pleadings, negotiation, or limited appearances. However, some law firms will add coaching and strategy as a separate a la carte legal service. For a fixed fee and amount of time, the lawyer may agree to review the client's legal situation and provide suggestions for the client to resolve the legal matter. This sounds familiar to what many attorneys do as part of their regular practice: initial consultations. However, when a law firm unbundles coaching and strategy, it can become far more comprehensive than an initial law firm consultation.

For example, a law firm that chooses to provide coaching may set up a detailed plan with the client that would include the following items: an initial interview and gathering of information related to the legal matter is conducted by the lawyer and client, the lawyer researches and thinks through solutions, and, finally, the lawyer meets with the client for one or two scheduled meetings to lay out a plan of action. After this plan is created, the lawyer terminates the limited-scope representation by providing a termination letter and checklist to the client that lays out the strategy that was created. The client then must proceed on his or her own to handle the legal matter based on that coaching and strategy.

In the past, a popular form of legal coaching included legal telephone hotlines where lawyers would advertise an 800 number for clients to call for coaching by phone. The client would pay a minimal fee per minute or by the hour with a credit card to discuss his or her legal matter and hopefully receive the legal guidance necessary to proceed on his or her own. The updated form of unbundled coaching is handled online with web-conferencing tools or real-time chat technologies. The clients pay for these services online ahead of time and communicate via the Internet. Web-based forms of legal coaching and strategy also allow the law firm to create an online resource center and library where the client may have access to either free self-help information on the legal matter to add to the legal strategy and coaching the firm provides or the client library itself may be populated with state-specific legal forms or documents and guidance that the client will pay a monthly or annual fee to access.

Collaborative Law

Collaborative law is a form of unbundling where both parties and their attorneys elect to settle the case without adversarial court involvement and with the goal of settling their conflict by working together outside of the courtroom to create a solution. The process is initiated by an agreement that is signed by both parties as well as each party's lawyer. This is sometimes called a "four-way" or "participation" agreement.[17] The lawyers signing agree that if no solution is met, they will withdraw from the representation and not be involved in any further court proceedings that may ensue with regard to the matter. When a final decision successfully results from the process, it is filed as a final decree with the court. Collaborative law encourages clients to work through their disputes in a less adversarial environment and to find solutions that meet the needs of both parties.

Collaborative law has become more popular in family law practices but also may be used as a form of alternative dispute resolution in other practice areas.[18] On August 9, 2007, the ABA Standing Committee on Ethics and Professional Responsibility published Formal Ethics Opinion 07-447, "Ethical Considerations in Collaborative Law Practice."[19] This opinion states that collaborative law is an acceptable form of limited-scope representation under Model Rule 1.2(c). A handful of state bars have published ethics opinions that support collaborative law and several collaborative

---

[17]Collaborative law should not be confused with "cooperative law," which is another method of dispute resolution that removes the four-way agreement from the process and poses potentially more ethics risks. *See generally* John Lande, *Possibilities for Collaborative Law: Ethics and Practice of Lawyer Disqualification and Process Control in a New Model of Lawyering*, Ohio State L.J., Vol. 64:1315 (2003) **http://www.law.missouri.edu/lande/publications/lande%20collab%20law.pdf**, last accessed on October 23, 2011.

[18]*See generally* Forest Mosten, Collaborative Divorce Handbook: Effectively Helping Divorcing Families Without Going to Court (Jossey-Bass, 2009), and Pauline H. Tesler, Collaborative Law: Achieving Effective Resolution in Divorce Without Litigation (ABA, 2001, 2008).

[19]Opinion at **http://www.collaborativelaw.us/articles/Ethics_Opinion_ABA.pdf** (last accessed Oct. 23, 2011).

law organizations have emerged to educate lawyers and clients on the practice.[20] However, there are many critics of collaborative law as a form of legal service delivery. For example, the Colorado Bar did not agree with the ABA Opinion and found that the practice creates a "nonconsentable" or "nonwaivable" conflict.[21] Comment 1 to ABA Model Rule 1.7 states that "Concurrent conflicts of interest can arise from the lawyer's responsibilities to another client, a former client or a third person, or from the lawyer's own interests." The four-way agreement may be seen by critics as creating a responsibility to a third person that violates Rule 1.7(a)(2) by creating a conflict of interest.

However, as the ABA Ethics Opinion on Collaborative Law points out, the client may provide informed consent to the self-interest conflict, which is allowed in Rule 1.7(b)(4), as long as the lawyer seeking that consent believes he or she can provide competent and diligent representation. The conflict only exists if the lawyer believes that he or she cannot represent the client because the lawyer's responsibilities to third parties, as dictated by the four-way agreement, would materially limit his or her ability to do so.

Because collaborative law is a form of limited-scope representation, the lawyer's client has signed a limited-scope engagement agreement stating that he or she understands the limitations of the representation and has elected to choose this over full representation. If the parties in the process are unable to resolve their matter and the client must seek out other legal representation to proceed, this is in line with the nature of unbundled services—the lawyer having fulfilled his or her limited representation to follow the collaborative law process in the matter and go no further.

---

[20]*See* Ky. Bar Ass'n Op. E-425 (June 2005), Participation in the "Collaborative Law" Process, *available at* **http://www.kybar.org/documents/ethics_opinions/kba_e-425.pdf** (last accessed Oct. 23, 2011); N.J. Advisory Comm. on Prof'l Ethics, Collaborative Law, Op. 699 (Dec. 12, 2005) (not available online); N.C. State Bar Ass'n 2002 Formal Eth. Op. 1 (Apr. 19, 2002), Participation in Collaborative Resolution Process Requiring Lawyer to Agree to Limit Future Court Representation, *available at* **http://www.ncbar.com/ethics/ethics.asp?page=2&from=4/2002&to=4/2002** (last accessed Oct. 23, 2011); and Pa. Bar Ass'n Comm. on Legal Eth. & Prof'l Resp. Inf. Op. 2004-24 (May 11, 2004), *available at* **http://www.collaborativelaw.us/articles/Ethics_Opinion_Penn_ CL_2004.pdf** (last accessed Oct. 23, 2011). *See, e.g.,* Int'l Academy of Collaborative Professionals at **http://www.collaborativepractice.com/** (last accessed October 23, 2011).

[21]Colo. Bar Ass'n Ethics Op. 115 (Feb. 24, 2007), Ethical Considerations in the Collaborative and Cooperative Law Contexts, *available at* **http://www.cobar.org/index.cfm/ID/386/subID/10159/ Ethics-Opinion-115:-Ethical-Considerations-in-the-Collaborative-and-Cooperative-Law-Contexts,-02/24//** (last accessed Oct. 23, 2011).

A strong debate still surrounds collaborative law and both sides raise valid arguments that should be considered before adding this form of unbundling to a law practice.[22] Consider the following conditions of a client and his or her legal needs to determine whether this method of unbundling is appropriate for the circumstance:

Reasons Why a Lawyer Might Consider Collaborative Law

- The lawyer is skilled in mediation and dispute resolution.
- The lawyer prefers to settle rather than enter into litigation.
- The parties to the case are willing and able to discuss their situation and a solution in a reasonable manner.
- All parties are interested in a fair resolution and want to avoid appearing in court.
- Parties want to save the expense of litigation.
- In divorce matters, the parties may have children and wish to spare them a drawn-out process as dictated by the courts.
- Clients seek more privacy for resolution of their legal matter.
- It is important that both parties preserve the relationship for business or personal reasons.
- Time is of the essence and the client needs the matter resolved faster than it would take to litigate.
- The client wants to pursue the collaborative law process but clearly understands that if the method fails, he or she will be required to select other counsel for any future representation related to the matter.
- Both parties will be able to agree on the exchange of information needed to resolve the matter and the method of communicating (in-person meetings, web conferences, etc.) through the process.
- Negotiation might benefit both parties by bringing mental-health-care professionals or social workers to assist in aspects of the settlement process, including them in "participation agreements."[23]

---

[22]*See generally* Robert F. Cochran, Jr., *Legal Ethics and Collaborative Practice Ethics*, 38 HOFSTRA L. REV. 537 (Winter 2009).

[23]Regarding multidisciplinary collaborative law practices, *see, e.g.,* Boston Law Collaborative, LLC at **http://www.bostonlawcollaborative.com/blc/what-we-do/multidisciplinary-practice.html** (last accessed Oct. 23, 2011), or Collaborative Law Training Assocs., Inc. at **http://www.collabtrainers .com/index.htm** (last accessed Oct. 23, 2011).

When Collaborative Law Would Not Be Good for Your Client

- ♦ Spouses are dependent or in an abusive relationship or otherwise are unable to stand up for themselves or their interests even when urged to do so by their lawyer.

- ♦ The client and his or her children require protection that a court process could better provide.

- ♦ Based on the circumstances, the client would have a stronger case if he or she went to court.

- ♦ The lawyer is using this method of unbundling as a way to avoid going to court or providing zealous or competent full-service representation to the client.

- ♦ The lawyer is not certain that ruling out litigation would be in the best interests of the client even when the client has assured the lawyer that he or she is determined to settle the matter. If the inability to settle is a risk, then collaborative law is not appropriate.

- ♦ Forgoing the filing of a legal action with the courthouse to attempt to handle the matter using collaborative law process first will not disadvantage the client or affect the case.

- ♦ If the parties fail to reach a settlement, having to find and start over with a new lawyer would be detrimental to the client's case and his or her emotional and financial well-being. The party then may be forced to proceed as a pro se litigant for lack of funds to retain new representation.

- ♦ A matter may require ongoing and continuous representation even following the completion of the collaborative law process, such as in the case of complex child-custody and support matters, where the parties may be required to come back to the table additional times over a period of years to adjust terms of the agreement based on changed circumstances.

- ♦ The client is not comfortable disclosing all relevant information to all parties involved as would be required by the agreement.

- ♦ Participation in a collaborative law network might violate a lawyer's duties under Rule 1.5 regarding accepting or paying referral fees or under Rule 7.2(c) prohibiting a lawyer from providing anything of value for recommendations.

- ♦ The lawyer or his or her client suspects that the other party may be using the method as a way to disadvantage the client by starting the process and then threatening litigation or halting the negotiations, which under the four-way agreement would cause both parties to lose their representation and be forced to seek out other counsel and start back at square one.

Best practices for collaborative law are the same for other forms of unbundled services. However, it could be argued that the informed consent component is even more important in collaborative law because the client is signing away his or her right to litigate using his or her chosen lawyer. A lawyer providing this method of unbundling must be careful to provide adequate guidance and information to the client about the risks of signing the four-way agreement and ensure that the client understands what additional services would be provided under full representation that will not be available to him or her under the collaborative law process.[24] For example, a law firm might consider creating a self-assessment in the form of a web application or adviser that would walk the prospective clients through the collaborative law process and through their circumstances to help them understand which method of divorce would be best for them. An organization in Raleigh, North Carolina, called Separating Together,[TM] is an example of a collaborative family law group made up of attorneys and other professionals.[25] The website for this group provides educational videos and walk-throughs of the process as well as a web-based self-assessment for educational purposes.

As with other unbundling methods, the lawyer should put information about the process and the scope of representation in writing and provide a copy for the client to refer to as well as a copy for the lawyer's files to ensure that there are no later misunderstandings about the scope of representation and that the risks and benefits were thoroughly discussed. Rather than relying solely on the "participation" or the four-way agreement, the lawyer should have his or her client sign a separate limited-scope engagement agreement specifically clarifying the limited scope of the collaborative law process before sitting down with the other lawyer and parties to the case.

---

[24]*See generally* MODEL RULE 1.4(b): "A lawyer shall explain a matter to the extent reasonably necessary to permit the client to make informed decisions regarding the representation," *available at* **http://www.americanbar.org/groups/professional_responsibility/publications/model_rules_of_ professional_conduct/rule_1_4_communications.html** (last accessed Oct. 23, 2011).

[25]Separating Together website at **http://www.separatingtogether.com/index.html** (last accessed Oct. 28, 2011.

Unbundling Criminal Law Cases

A solid rule in unbundling is that if the legal case requires ongoing and continuous representation, then it needs full-service representation. Criminal law is one of those areas of legal practice in which unbundling is not recommended and may even be prohibited by state ethics rules. For example, Alaska's and New Hampshire's rules specifically state that limited appearances are possible but only in "non-criminal cases."[26] Unlike most forms of unbundling, criminal defense is one practice area where there are far more outspoken critics than supporters.

If criminal law matters are unbundled at all then it most likely should be at the very beginning of a legal matter, for example, before a plea is entered, and should be in the form of guidance or strategy without the attorney making an appearance on behalf of the client. The general belief is that in these cases it is in the best interest of the client to have defense counsel present throughout the entire matter. Some would argue that unbundling of legal services in criminal defense matters might be useful where the client has been assigned a lawyer who is either not competent, lacks experience in defense work, or who was appointed to the position and is not particularly enthusiastic about handling the case.[27] Defense counsel may be provided for the defendant who cannot afford counsel, but increasingly the individual who qualifies for this service based on income levels may not adequately reflect an individual's financial ability to add full-service representation to his or her budget. Those individuals who do not qualify must proceed pro se and without any guidance. In this instance, if the client wishes to retain the unbundled services of another lawyer for guidance or as a second opinion to the court-ordered

---

[26]*See* ALASKA R. CIV. P. 81(d), *available at* **http://www.courts.alaska.gov/civ2.htm#81** (last accessed Nov. 5, 2011); and N.H. R. CIV. P, 17(c).

[27]There was an interesting study conducted in 2004 in Nova Scotia, Canada, titled "The Unrepresented Defendant and the Unbundling of Legal Services," which was prepared for the Administration of Justice Sub-Committee, Nova Scotia Barristers' Society, by Don Clairmont of the Atlantic Institute of Criminology. This report considered a strategy for adding unbundled criminal legal services to the existing criminal court system to alleviate the phenomenon of pro se criminal litigants and increase access to justice. The report suggests that one solution might be a balance between appointed representation, unbundled guidance, and a more informed client. However, it is important to note that Canada supports judicial assistance to pro se litigants in both civil and criminal cases. *Available at* **http://sociologyandsocialanthropology.dal.ca/Files/ the_unrepresented_defendant_and_the_unbundling_of_legal_serv.pdf** (last accessed Nov. 5, 2011).

lawyer, then this might be one area of unbundling that would give defendants an affordable alternative to either relying on the free counsel that was appointed by the court or going it alone. This concept has been called "hybrid representation" in the context of criminal law matters and has been rejected by most courts, which have adhered to an "all or nothing" approach.[28]

For defendants who refuse appointed counsel, would unbundled services at their own expense be an alternative to proceeding pro se without any guidance? Private counsel might not be affordable to them and if they do not trust or get along with their court-appointed counsel, unbundled services that are provided at lower cost might provide at least minimum assistance.[29] As with other forms of unbundling, the complexity of the legal case as well as the education level of the pro se litigant are major factors in whether unbundling would be appropriate in these instances. Lawyers interested in providing limited-scope assistance in criminal law matters should first find out how their state approaches the matter and whether any form of hybrid representation is permissible at any point in the process of a criminal case.

Unbundling Alternative Dispute Resolution Legal Services

Alternative dispute resolution (ADR) is a term that encompasses a number of different methods of resolving legal disputes outside of the traditional courtroom. Sometimes it may be referred to as simply dispute resolution

---

[28] *See* McKaskle v. Wiggins, 465 U.S. 168, 178 (1984); United States v. Washington, 353 F.3d 42, 46 (D.C. Cir. 2004); *In re* Lee Max Barnett, 73 P.3d 1106, 1111 (Cal. 2003); *In re* Sondley, Sr., 990 S.W.2d 361, 362 (Tex. Ct. App. 1999); McCulloch v. Velez, 364 F. 3d 1, 8 (1st Cir. 2004); State v. Cook, 821 P.2d 731, 739 (Ariz. 1991); *see generally* Jona Goldschmidt, *Autonomy and "Gray-Area" Pro Se Defendants: Ensuring Competence to Guarantee Freedom,* 6 Nw. J. L. & Soc. Pol'y 130 (Winter 2011). However, two states appear to allow a pro se criminal defendant to obtain some form of limited-scope assistance: *See* in Mississippi: Goff v. State, 14 So. 3d 625, 642–43 (Miss. 2009); Metcalf v. State, 629 So. 2d 558, 565 (Miss. 1993); and in North Dakota: City of Fargo v. McMorrow, 367 N.W.2d 167 (N.D. 1985).

[29] "The Supreme Court . . . established special rules and principles governing access to justice for prisoners in order to maintain a fair and accessible justice system. So, too, should the Court recognize the reasonableness and necessity of establishing a judicial duty of reasonable assistance to "gray-area" pro se defendants, and permit the use of innovative forms of assistance and representation in lieu of unwanted counsel." Jona Goldschmidt, Associate Professor, Dep't of Criminal Justice, Loyola Univ. Chicago, J.D., DePaul Univ.; Ph.D., Ariz. State Univ., *in Autonomy and "Gray-Area" Pro Se Defendants: Ensuring Competence to Guarantee Freedom,* Nw J. L. & Soc. Pol'y (Winter 2011).

or appropriate dispute resolution. Regardless of the term used, the concept focuses on tools to resolve legal matters. There may be opportunities for lawyers to provide unbundled assistance in traditional forms of ADR, such as court-ordered ADR in the form of mediation or arbitration.[30] Chapter Seven provides a discussion of online dispute resolution (ODR) as a form of unbundling.

Collaboration between private practitioners and the courts is greatly needed to help decrease the burden of the large numbers of pro se litigants passing through the system without any guidance. By providing unbundled legal services to the pro se litigant, the mediator or neutral involved in the process is not placed in the difficult situation of being asked specific legal advice from the litigant that the neutral is not allowed to answer. Suggested forms of ADR unbundling might include the following:

- ◆ The lawyer could provide consultation to the self-help litigant prior to the start of the legal matter in the form of coaching, strategy, general education about the process, and what will be expected of him or her and what to expect from the other side. The lawyer could review the facts of the situation and based on his or her years of experience in litigating and settling similar cases provide the client with a reasonable settlement offer or starting point for the process.

- ◆ Without making an appearance in the case, the lawyer might be contacted at other points in the process when the litigant has questions about how the matter is proceeding. Part of the lawyer's service could include providing education that the litigant's process is not like a courtroom proceeding that the litigant has seen on television and how it differs, and providing a resolution to his or her case.

---

[30]Mediation is the process of having a neutral third party, called a mediator, work with both parties to provide a resolution to a legal matter. Mediators do not determine the outcome of the legal matter; they encourage the parties to openly discuss their needs and to come to a solution between themselves, but a total resolution to the matter is not required by the end of the process. Arbitration is the process by which both parties agree upon an arbitrator and how to present their cases to this individual. The arbitrator makes a final, binding decision about how to resolve the case based on the information presented by the parties. The resolution may be finalized in a binding or nonbinding agreement. *See generally* the "ABCs of ADR," from the Alliance for Education in Dispute Resolution, *available at* **http://www.ilr.cornell.edu/alliance/resources/Basics/ABCs.html** (last accessed Oct. 31, 2011), and the Resolution Systems Institute at **http://aboutrsi.org/** (last accessed Oct. 31, 2011).

CHAPTER SIX

Pro Bono Opportunities for Unbundling

MOST OF THE STATES have adopted ABA Model Rule 6.5, which was created in 2002. This rule excuses the lawyer from conflicts searches when the lawyer provides short-term, limited-scope legal services to a client "without expectation by either the lawyer or the client that the lawyer will provide continuing representation in the matter" under a program sponsored by the courts or a nonprofit organization.[1] The rule is intended to encourage lawyers to engage in pro bono service using a method that may be more convenient for them to volunteer their time and removes concerns that this form of volunteer unbundling would result in conflicts of interest or disqualify their law firms from representing prospective clients. The rule does not remove compliance with any of a lawyer's other obligations and it only applies to nonprofit and court-annexed legal service programs, which means that the normal conflict of interest rules would apply if a law firm or other for-profit entity attempted to create a program offering pro bono limited-scope assistance.

Some attorneys who are interested in unbundling begin learning about limited-scope representation through volunteer work with a legal service

---

[1]*See* MODEL RULE 6.5, *available at* **http://www.americanbar.org/groups/professional_responsibility/ publications/model_rules_of_professional_conduct/rule_6_5_nonprofit_court_annexed_limited_ legal_services_programs.html** (last accessed Oct. 23, 2011); the following states have adopted Model Rule 6.5: Arizona, Arkansas, Delaware, the District of Columbia, Idaho, Indiana, Iowa, Louisiana, Massachusetts, Montana, Nebraska, Nevada, New Jersey, North Carolina, Ohio, Oregon, Pennsylvania, Rhode Island, South Carolina, South Dakota, Utah, Virginia; *see also Nonprofit Limited-Services Programs*, ABA BNA LAWYERS MANUAL ON PROFESSIONAL CONDUCT, at 91:6501.

or court-based program. The Wills for Heroes Foundation is a well-known example of a nonprofit organization set up to encourage and provide assistance to lawyers who want to provide pro bono estate planning guidance and legal documents to first responders across the country.[2] Other examples of unbundling volunteer opportunities for lawyers include legal-advice hotlines, such as the North Carolina Bar Association's Justice4ALL program by which lawyers across the state volunteer to provide free legal advice over a toll-free hotline one day a year and free clinics that provide online legal advice or guidance for pro se litigants.[3] Under these circumstances, the volunteer lawyer must advise the client that the representation is limited and that the lawyer may not be in a position to conduct a thorough conflict of interest check or obtain a limited-scope engagement agreement before proceeding to provide advice. In these situations, the lawyer must advise the client that he or she should seek the guidance of another lawyer if the client requires additional assistance and explain orally the limitations of what the lawyer can provide. However, the limited contact between the volunteer lawyer and the client in these situations prevents any conflicts of interest from occurring because the lawyer tends to be in situations where he or she is providing general legal advice without the benefit of a full client intake and assessment that would occur in a traditional, full-service representation.

State bars and other legal professional associations have created awards and other incentives for law firms that devote time to pro bono assistance. Model Rule 6.1, Voluntary Pro Bono Publico Service, suggests that lawyers provide 50 hours a year of pro bono service.[4] To find a state-based or national program that provides an opportunity for pro bono unbundling, visit the ABA's National Pro Bono Volunteer Opportunities Guide online at **http://www.probono.net/aba_oppsguide/**.

Some states also have required litigant awareness programs that pro se litigants must engage in before proceeding.[5] For example, Missouri Rule of

---

[2] *See* the Wills for Heroes Foundation website at **http://www.willsforheroes.org/** (last accessed Oct. 23, 2011).

[3] *See* the NCBA Justice4ALL website at **http://4allnc.ncbar.org/** (last accessed Oct. 23, 2011); for another example, *see* the District of Columbia Employment Justice Center, providing unbundled workers rights and employment law services, at **http://www.dcejc.org/** (last accessed Oct. 23, 2011).

[4] *See* Model Rule 6.1 at **http://apps.americanbar.org/legalservices/probono/rule61.html** (last accessed Oct. 23, 2011); *see also* the ABA Standing Committee on Pro Bono and Public Service at **http://www.americanbar.org/groups/probono_public_service.html** (last accessed Oct. 23, 2011).

[5] Other states have created robust online resource centers for pro se litigants to supplement or take the place of required pro se litigant awareness programs. *See, e.g.,* Minnesota's LawMoose Legal Reference Library at **http://www.lawmoose.com/index.cfm?action=library.&topic=mn102097** or New York's LawHelp/NY website at **http://www.lawhelp.org/ny/** (last accessed Nov. 14, 2011).

Civil Procedure 88.09 requires that unrepresented parties complete a litigant awareness program and assists them with filling out court-approved forms.[6] Even if these forms were completed as an unbundled service through legal aid or a volunteer attorney, the pro se litigant must attend the program before proceeding. For states that lack such a requirement, the legal-aid service or attorney providing the unbundled pro bono work may provide guidance that explains courtroom procedures and exactly how the litigant will be expected to dress and behave before the court.

Legal Services Corporation and Court System Initiatives

Some Legal Services Corporation–funded offices and court systems offer limited-scope services for self-help individuals. LawHelp Interactive is a web-based program powered by ProBono.Net and sponsored by the Legal Services Corporation, State Justice Institute, and HotDocs.[7] LawHelp Interactive links to the different participating state legal-aid programs offering guided online assistance in completing legal forms using the A2J Author discussed in the following paragraph. The site also provides free legal-aid referrals and real-time chat services. The disclaimer for use of the services by self-help individuals provides that ". . . it is not a substitute for legal advice from qualified counsel. . . . Documents created using the website may require consultation with an attorney prior to execution or filing." Illinois Legal Aid Online has created a web application for download on Apple's iTunes Store that provides a guide to Illinois law to self-help individuals.[8] The application covers divorce, custody, criminal records, small claims, eviction, foreclosure, unemployment, name change, guardianships, and more and provides step-by-step guides and resources for further assistance.

Another example of technology used to deliver unbundled legal services to self-help individuals is the Access to Justice Author (A2J Author) sponsored by the Chicago Kent College of Law and the Center for Computer-Assisted Legal Instruction (CALI).[9] This free, open-source software tool allows individuals such as court administrators and those from legal-service programs who do not have a background in programming to create a

---

[6]*See* Mo. R. Civ. P. 88.09, *available at* **http://www.courts.mo.gov/courts/ClerkHandbooksP2Rules Only.nsf/C0C6FFA99DF4993F86256BA50057DCB8/0C6B8391A4BCA286862574790047AC31** (last accessed Oct. 26, 2011).

[7]*See* the LawHelp Interactive Website at **https://lawhelpinteractive.org/** (last accessed Oct. 24, 2011).

[8]**http://itunes.apple.com/us/app/illinois-legal-aid-app/id466092937?mt=8&ign-mpt=uo%3D4** (last accessed Nov. 14, 2011).

[9]*See* the Chicago-Kent College of Law Center for Access to Justice and Technology at **http://www .kentlaw.edu/cajt/** (last accessed on Oct. 24, 2011).

user-friendly, web-based interface that walks self-help litigants through a process that helps them fill out the legal forms to be filed at the courthouse. After an A2J "Guided Interview" for the prospective pro se individual has been created using the Author tool, it is uploaded to the National Public Automated Documents Online (NPADO) Server for Nonprofit Legal Services, which uses web-based document-assembly services powered by HotDocs, a document-assembly and automation software.[10] As the use of the software spreads to more court systems across the country, e-filing capabilities are being added as well as additional developments based on user feedback. According to the program's website, Legal Aid of Western Ohio has begun a project to coordinate online intake among all participating legal-aid programs in the state that will use the A2J Guided Interview as the online interface for the client intake process.[11] Iowa Legal Aid has already implemented such a program with a case management program used nationally by many legal-aid offices.

Case Study
Ronald Staudt

Ronald Staudt is a Professor of Law and Associate Vice President for Law, Business, and Technology at the Illinois Institute of Technology Chicago–Kent College of Law. Staudt is a fellow of the College of Law Practice Management and Director of the Center for Access to Justice & Technology (CAJT), a law school center using Internet resources to improve access to justice with special emphasis on building web tools to support legal-services advocates, pro bono volunteers, and pro se litigants. He has written numerous articles and books on technology and law, including "All the Wild Possibilities: Technology That Attacks Barriers to Access to Justice," Loyola of Los Angeles Law Review *(2009).*[12]

---

[10]*See* the A2J Author Community Website at **http://www.a2jauthor.org/drupal/?q=node/125** (last accessed Oct. 24, 2011).

[11]*See* undated presentation titled "A2J Online Intake presentation for Legal Services Corporation Technology Initiative Grants," by Debra Jennings, Managing Attorney, Legal Aid Line and Cynthia Vaughn, Statewide Technology Project Manager, OLA, *available at* **http://tig.lsc.gov/TIG/LSC_A2J_Online_Intake_Session_011310.pdf** (last accessed Oct. 24, 2011). *See* a full list of Online Intake and Online Screening Systems in Legal Services, an Informal Survey of Programs (June 2011) by Legal Assistance of Western New York, Inc., at **https://docs.google.com/document/d/1gV6pwHK3A39h8hGENJfyR_T_SlfTCYLU6CCfjp4cjvM/edit?hl=en_US&authkey=ClfZ1JkH&pli=1#** (last accessed Oct. 24, 2011).

[12]**http://llr.lls.edu/docs/42-4staudt.pdf** (last accessed Nov. 14, 2011).

The legal-aid world has been unbundling forever. Because of resource limitations, only 20 percent of the legal needs of the poor can be addressed by staffed legal-aid organizations. So legal aid has provided limited service to thousands of clients over the years. Lots of clients of legal aid get "advice only" or "advice and referral" or "advice and short services" where staff lawyers and paralegals guide people to represent themselves in simple matters. Years ago, legal-aid societies launched telephone hotlines staffed by legal-aid lawyers. These hotlines were later enhanced with web resources to manage calls on hold and to provide substantive and procedural guides for the advocate on the telephone. This combination works well with pro bono volunteers who can get good training in a narrow area and then volunteer to provide advice on the telephone, for example, as the "landlord/tenant" expert for a discrete block of time.

In the past 10 years, every state has launched a single authoritative website to provide information and guidance to low-income people seeking legal help and information. All the statewide legal-aid websites are linked to **http://www.lawhelp.org**. The websites offer great information and often links to A2J Guided Interviews and HotDocs templates that self-represented people can use to prepare their own forms for court or for simple transactions.

If a justice customer is confused by the website, often he or she can click on a chat box for "LiveHelp" and ask written questions about the forms or procedure. These chat sessions also are opportunities for pro bono volunteers to assist low-income people achieve access to justice. Many of my law students volunteer to be "LiveHelp" operators and guide self-represented people to the right spot on the Illinois Legal Aid Online. The "LiveHelp" volunteers also can push their website customers directly to the top of the right queue on the hotline in Cook County, Illinois, so that someone seeking advice about evictions will get a quick call from the landlord/tenant expert on the Cook County hotline. Full circle!

Our Apps for Justice initiative is aimed at encouraging all law schools to set up a clinical course in which law students learn to write A2J Guided Interviews and other content for legal-aid statewide websites. The delivery platforms are there in every state, but there is a great need for more content. Our model is a course called Justice & Technology Practicum where students observe self-represented litigants trying to navigate the justice system. Then students work with a legal-aid expert to prepare automated solutions to lower barriers faced by those poor litigants.

Finally, there are increasing numbers of courthouse self-help desks that can be staffed by attorney volunteers. Our Self Help Web Desk is designed to be a place in the courthouse where self-represented people can use computers to contact Illinois Legal Aid Online and other web resources. Our law students also volunteer at this web desk to help low-income people navigate the web and complete A2J Guided Interviews for fee waivers and simple complaint and answer forms. More extensive service can be provided at these web desks by licensed attorneys who can advise self-represented people and provide more nuanced documents and forms. Pro bono volunteer lawyers at these court sites are able to rely in many states on relaxed rules about conflicts of interest and need not do a full check of all the clients of their partners. They are barred only by conflicts that they know exist without such a search.

These devices, telephone hotlines, limited representation for advice only, web-assisted form creation and chat and in-person guidance to self-represented people, are types of unbundling. While some are disappointed that all the justice customers who need to rely on these techniques are not able to engage the full services of a lawyer from start to finish in their cases, most would have no help at all if it were not for these unbundled services. We can't let the perfect be the enemy of the good.

There is enormous potential through the use of the online client interfaces to provide unbundled legal assistance to pro se individuals. Through Technology Initiative Grants, the Legal Services Corporation established websites for legal-aid programs in every state in the country as well as funded a national server that distributes through that website the A2J Guided Interview using HotDocs document automation.[13] The use of the technology to streamline the intake process and guide the individual through the process of creating the necessary legal forms online also serves to lessen the burden that the courts and legal-aid offices have in handling pro se individuals. Even if resulting legal documents and guidance require that the individual seek additional assistance from a licensed attorney or additional services from the legal-aid office, the time savings

---

[13]*See* LawHelp Interactive Website at **https://lawhelpinteractive.org/** (last accessed Oct. 24, 2011); *see also* the website for iCan! EFile, which is another example of a software funded by the Legal Service Corporation that was created by the Legal Aid Society of Orange County to assist individuals who are eligible for Earned Income Tax Credit and other tax credits to file their taxes without paying fees. *Available at* **http://www.icanefile.org/index.asp?caller=** (last accessed Oct. 26, 2011).

from the use of the interface is valuable. Additionally, the software tool is free and open source, meaning that legal-aid programs and other non-profits interested in the unbundling of legal services to increase access to justice may download the A2J Author software and create their own Guided Interviews.

A potential addition to a system like this would be to connect it to private practitioners interested in volunteering their time to provide unbundled pro bono assistance. At the end of the Guided Interview, if the individual did not want to proceed pro se and did not qualify for further legal-aid assistance, he or she could be provided with a list of potential attorneys willing to continue to work with the individual on a limited-scope basis pro bono and be connected with one of the volunteer attorneys online. Based on the needs of the client, the attorney then could provide unbundled pro bono assistance online or in person, making a limited appearance or providing additional guidance or coaching from the point that the Guided Interview and final legal document left off.

"As consumer-friendly, court-based, and court-supported self-help centers expand, they are likely to draw more middle-income users who will opt to self-represent or, more likely, will purchase lawyer assistance on a discrete-task basis. Thus, the private bar's unbundled legal services innovations will prosper concurrently with court reforms that welcome prepared, self represented parties."

—Jeanne Charn, Senior Lecturer on Law, Harvard Law School, in "Legal Services for All: Is the Profession Ready?", *Loyola of Los Angeles Law Review* (Summer 2009) at 1021

In April of 2011, a proposal titled "Apps for Justice: Learning Law by Creating Software" was presented at the Futures Ed Conference sponsored by New York University and Harvard Law School.[14] The proposal would engage law students across the country within law school legal clinics to create websites that would use the A2J Guided Interviews, increasing access to justice for pro se individuals via the Internet. This proposal won a competition at the Futures Ed Conference and subsequently is in line to

---

[14]*See* Apps for Justice: Learning Law by Creating Software (March 15, 2011) at **http://dotank.nyls .edu/futureed/2011proposals/11llcs.pdf** (last accessed Oct. 24, 2011), and Futures Ed Conference at **http://www.nyls.edu/centers/harlan_scholar_centers/institute_for_information_law_and_ policy/events/future_ed** (last accessed Oct. 24, 2011).

receive funding from the Legal Services Corporation's Technology Initiative Grants. This project has enormous potential to benefit pro se litigants, court systems, and law students.

Other Forms of Pro Bono Unbundling

Some DIY clients may be more inclined to learn the general details of what a particular legal matter requires from a video of the lawyer talking to them rather than from in-person meetings, text-based discussion, or articles. Accordingly, another form of unbundling used by legal-aid offices that lawyers also may wish to provide as free legal guidance on their law firm website comes in the form of short video tutorials or podcasts. Short videos may be recorded and posted on YouTube or longer videos on a site such as Vimeo, which provides more storage space. The videos then may be embedded in the law firm's blog as well as maintained on a YouTube profile for the firm.

Some state legal-aid programs have created videos of unbundled legal advice to assist the self-help litigant navigate through the necessary courtroom procedures and to understand the process that is involved in proceeding pro se. For example, the Arkansas Legal Aid has a YouTube site with a library of videos including tutorials on divorce, debt collection, taxes, and more.[15] Statistics provided by sites such as YouTube and Vimeo may provide a law firm with information regarding how often these videos are viewed.[16] Additionally, the creation of this content and linking it with other social media applications can improve the search engine optimization of the law firm's site as well as provide a basic, free unbundled service to prospective clients and the general public. As with any unbundled guidance posted on a website, the attorney should include a general disclaimer on the YouTube or any other public hosting site either on the page or in the video notifying the viewer that the material is legal information, not legal advice, and to seek additional assistance from a licensed attorney in his or her jurisdiction.

Arguably, many legal-aid organizations have more widely embraced the trend of offering unbundled legal services to self-help individuals than private practitioners have. Expect to see forms of innovation in this delivery breaking down many of the barriers on access to justice and increasing the public's awareness of the alternative options for unbundled legal

---

[15]*See* the YouTube site for Arkansas Legal Services at **http://www.youtube.com/user/LunarDog1** (last accessed Oct. 26, 2011).

[16]YouTube at **www.youtube.com** and Vimeo at **www.vimeo.com** (last accessed Nov. 14, 2011).

services delivery. Such technology used for working with pro se litigants does not only benefit those of lower means but could potentially be used by individuals of moderate and middle-class means as well. For example, a Guided Interview could be used to handle the creation of a basic name-change legal form, a document that the individual might have paid a couple hundred dollars to a licensed attorney to handle and now may be educated and empowered to handle for himself or herself. Attorneys may choose to learn more about unbundling by volunteering their time to work with a legal-aid organization or nonprofit that provides self-help assistance through one of the methods discussed previously. Drawing from these examples, the private practitioner could develop his or her own delivery methods that provide both paying and pro bono clients with unbundled legal services.

CHAPTER SEVEN

Using Technology
to Unbundle
Legal Services

NEW DEVELOPMENTS IN INTERNET technology have made it even more efficient for a law firm to offer unbundled legal services. A law firm can employ different forms of Web-based applications that can be delivered over the Internet, depending on how much it wants to automate the unbundling process for greater efficiency in delivery. These tools may be used to generate legal work product or to provide decision-making tools to guide and assist a lawyer working with a client's case. Thanks to the cost-effectiveness of cloud-based applications, a wide variety of Web-based applications that support the unbundling of legal services, may be added to the budget of any law firm from a solo practice to a larger, multijurisdictional firm. Lawyers are creating entire web-based practices that focus completely on delivering unbundled services online. Larger law firms are having customized technology solutions designed for the needs of their firm's members to deliver services to their clients through secure firm portals. Other firms are taking baby steps into the practice of online delivery and are relying on these cloud-based applications on the side of their traditional practice management software to enhance their unbundling potential. Firms delivering unbundled legal services online are not in direct competition with online legal service companies providing only auto-generated legal forms, but instead offer an alternative to the traditional law firm model with an increasing variety of limited-scope services across practice areas.

Many of the applications used to unbundle legal services operate on software as a service (SaaS), one form of cloud computing.[1] With SaaS, the tools and law office data are hosted by a third-party service. The technology provider most likely has a relationship with a hosting company that owns the data center that houses the servers storing the firm's law office data. The benefit of this form of technology is that the cost of developing and maintaining a single software application for unbundling may be spread out over a larger number of users, making it accessible for any practitioner to afford and add to his or her law practice. Thus, a large capital investment by a solo or small law firm can be avoided and a mid-size to larger law firm can cut costs related to practice management systems.

Because of this flexibility, cloud computing will most likely continue to facilitate the delivery of unbundled legal services for years to come. New innovations in the delivery of unbundled legal services are on the horizon as more attorneys realize the potential of this technology.[2] It may be used to create an unbundled client base and to deliver services in a more efficient and cost-effective manner that gives the attorney a competitive advantage over traditional firms that are not using these methods or meeting the consumer's need for unbundled legal services.[3] In this chapter, we will look at several methods of unbundling that rely on Internet-based technology and at a few emerging models of web-technology-driven delivery.

Document Assembly and Automation

Document-assembly and automation tools have been used by law firms for many years and probably are the first legal technology developed that

---

[1] As with any form of law office technology, an attorney needs to carefully do his or her due diligence in researching the chosen technology solution and understanding the terms of the service level agreement (SLA). *See generally* Nicole Black, Cloud Computing for Lawyers, ABA/LPM Publishing, 2011; Courtney Kennaday, "Sample Questions to Ask Online Storage Vendors," S.C. Bar (2006), *available at* **http://www.scbar.org/public/files/docs/VendorQ.pdf** (accessed Jan. 8, 2010); and the proposed N.C. State Bar Ethics Op. 7 (2010) (providing sample questions for attorneys to ask of third-party software vendors before subscribing to services).

[2] *See generally* Marc Lauritsen, *Five Tips for Prospering in an Age of Legal Fee Deflation*, TechnoLawyer, June 7, 2011, *available at* **http://www.capstonepractice.com/deflation.pdf** (last accessed Nov. 3, 2011).

[3] *See generally* William Hornsby, *Improving the Delivery of Affordable Legal Services Through the Internet: A Blueprint for the Shift to a Digital Paradigm, available at* **http://www.abanet.org/legalservices/delivery/deltech.html** (updated June 10, 2009) (accessed Dec. 30, 2010); and Ronald W. Staudt, *All the Wild Possibilities: Technology that Attacks Barriers to Access to Justice*, Loy. L.A. L. Rev.,. Vol. 42: 1117 (Summer 2009), *available at* **http://llr.lls.edu/docs/42-4staudt.pdf** (accessed Dec. 30, 2010); and Richard E. Susskind, The Future of Law: Facing the Challenges of Information Technology, Oxford Univ. Pr. (1996); and Richard E. Susskind, The End of Lawyers?: Rethinking the Nature of Legal Services, Oxford Univ. Pr. (2008).

greatly facilitated the unbundling of legal services. Some of the more well-known products used by law firms include Hotdocs, Rapidocs, DealBuilder, Exari, and WhichDraft.[4] These programs often use "intuitive" forms to collect information online directly from clients that are accessible through any web-browser. The client responds to the questions provided by the program and it prompts him or her with the next appropriate questions based on the previous response. The responses then are pulled into a template document which assembles the document instantly, creating a first draft for review and edit by the attorney. The lawyer may use the same legal form or even the same provisions with another client with a similar legal fact pattern without having to reinvent the wheel each time that particular legal document is required for an unbundled project. Accordingly, this reduces the amount of time that the lawyer may produce unbundled legal documents and assists in streamlining the delivery process for the unbundled offerings.

More customized systems are emerging that focus on a specific legal process or practice area. For example, Koncision is a company that provides a document-assembly and automation tool specifically for confidentiality agreements.[5] The tool is powered by software hosted by Contract Express, a company that produces a number of web-based document assembly tools.[6] Koncision provides services that may be used to create unbundled contracts by either lawyers working for clients or by companies that may need to generate these documents on a regular basis.

Case Study
Kenneth A. Adams

Kenneth A. Adams is President and Founder of Koncision Contract Automation, an online service that provides document-assembly templates for business contracts to lawyers. Adams also gives seminars in the United States, Canada, and internationally, acts as a consultant and expert witness, and is a lecturer at the University of Pennsylvania Law School. His book, **A Manual of Style for Contract Drafting** *(ABA, 2nd Ed., 2008), is widely used throughout the legal profession.*

---

[4]Hotdocs, **http://www.hotdocs.com/**, Rapidocs, **http://www.epoq.co.uk/ep/rapidocs.cfm**, Deal-Builder, **http://www.business-integrity.com/**, Exari, **http://www.exari.com/**, and WhichDraft, **http://www.whichdraft.com/** (all last accessed Oct. 29, 2011).

[5]Koncision, **www.koncision.com** (last accessed Oct. 30, 2011).

[6]Business Integrity and ContractExpress, **http://www.business-integrity.com/products/contract expresscom.html** (last accessed Oct. 30, 2011).

1. Have you noticed an increase in the number of law firms that employ document-automation and assembly processes?

From anecdotal evidence, I know that an increasing number of firms are using document assembly to allow their lawyers to create contracts. And Wilson Sonsini and Goodwin Procter have each installed on their websites a free document-assembly system that allows visitors to create some basic documents.

2. How might the services your company offers to law firms facilitate the unbundling of legal services?

Koncision Contract Automation's first product is a document-assembly template for creating a confidentiality agreement. Using the template allows users to create a confidentiality agreement more quickly than they could with the traditional copy-and-paste process. Furthermore, Koncision allows a greater degree of customization than generally is possible if you are revising a contract used in another deal. Koncision's template uses language that is far clearer and more concise than is traditional contract language. A law firm lawyer could use the product to provide drafting services more competitively. But it might be even more efficient for the lawyer and the client to complete the template's questionnaire together, either during an in-person meeting or by using an online screen-sharing service.

3. What do you think is the importance of document-assembly and automation services or other cloud-based technologies to the attorney who is adding unbundled services to his or her offerings?

Document assembly would allow a lawyer to focus on services that add real value—determining strategy and assisting in negotiations. Coming up with contract language to reflect the deal should be a commodity task.

4. How would you advise lawyers to respond to critics of unbundling or accusations from other professionals that their unbundling work is "commoditizing" the practice of law?

I understand "commoditizing" to refer to automating repetitive and routine tasks, rather than treating them as bespoke work, with all the inefficiencies that that entails. So commoditization is a good thing.

5. What role do you think document assembly and automation will take in the legal profession in the future?

At the high end of the market, document assembly will become increasingly prevalent, but it will happen slowly, particularly at law firms. Unlike companies, laws firms are asked to draft a broad and unpredictable range of contracts, and that is not as conducive to automation as repeatedly using a limited set of templates. And there are various cultural obstacles that I discuss in the following article: **http://www.koncision.com/wp-content/uploads/2011/05/Adams-NYLJ-4.1.11-The-Directors-Cut.pdf.** As regards the lower end of the market, it is falling prey to mediocrity in the form of Rocket Lawyer, LegalZoom, and comparable vendors. That's something I discuss in the following blog post: **http://www.koncision .com/rocket-lawyer-contract-automation-fail/.**

6. When the IBM computer, Watson, played Jeopardy, some thought leaders in the legal profession suggested that our current document-assembly and automation systems might one day be coupled with other forms of artificial intelligence to provide greater "diagnosis" of legal matters for lawyers.[7] How do you see the current technologies we have evolving to use AI or game theory to assist lawyers?

Document assembly spares users having to constantly re-create the language needed to articulate deal terms. But some commentators suggest that in addition, automated-document analysis allows you to determine what language you should use in a contract. But without strong editorial control, automated analysis of precedent contracts presents an insurmountable garbage-in, garbage-out problem—contract language is not susceptible to a purely technology solution.

7. Do you have any best practices or suggestions for attorneys wishing to minimize the risk of malpractice when using a document-automation and assembly software?

The risk of malpractice as a result of using document assembly to create contracts is essentially the same as with the traditional process—it arises from including in a contract provisions that don't make sense. The safeguards against such problems are old-fashioned—knowing your stuff and checking your work. But lawyers routinely rely on analyses performed by others. In that regard, a lawyer using a document-assembly system prepared by a vendor is in the same position as a lawyer using a form prepared by a bar organization. Your first line of defense is to check the credentials of whoever prepared the contract language that you are proposing to use.

---

[7]IBM's Watson was a contestant on "Jeopardy" and makes some in the legal profession ponder the use of computers to take over portions of a lawyer's work. *See* Debra Cassens Weiss, *Watson Computer, Making 'Jeopardy' Debut, Could Do Associate Research, IBM GC Says,* A.B.A. J.,, Feb 15, 2011, *available at* **http://www.abajournal.com/news/article/watson_computer_making_jeopardy_ debut_could_do_associate_research_ibm_gc_sa** (last accessed Nov. 14, 2011).

Other products allow for comparisons of versions of documents and will filter a document based on the lawyer's preference and usage of certain terms and provisions. This results in a final document that has the optimum language and that is cleaner than a template that may have been revised multiple times by a law firm with different clients.[8]

Several other methods of document assembly and automation may be used in an unbundling practice. Forms created using document-assembly technology may be used in the client intake process for an unbundling project. A law firm could use the technology to design a questionnaire that the prospective client fills out online after registering on the law firm's website or after following a link e-mailed to the client that sends the client to the application. The questions posed to the prospective client might walk him or her through the unbundling process through a series of questions while uncovering any collateral issues that surround the scope of the requested legal services. After providing this information, a completed client intake sheet then would be generated from the responses and provided to the firm for follow-up with the prospective client. However, if the prospective client responded to questions in the application that determined without a doubt based on the firm's input into the system that the case was not appropriate for unbundling and required full-service representation or that the scope exceeded what the firm would be willing to unbundle, the system would allow the lawyer or other assistant in the firm to stop the intake of data at that point and to follow up with the client to inform him or her that it would not be possible to handle the representation. This would save both the firm and the prospective client the additional time and expense of scheduling an unnecessary meeting in person or over the phone or in a web conference to determine that the unbundling in this case was not appropriate. For the client the firm wants to proceed with, when a follow-up meeting is scheduled, most of the information needed to analyze and begin the project is available.

Document-assembly and automation systems are more frequently used to generate prepared legal forms. Some law firms purchase prepared state-

---

[8]*See, e.g.*, Kiiac, **http://www.kiiac.com/**. This company has document automation and assembly tools and creates document templates and clause libraries for legal documents. The software can analyze a group of contracts to create a "reference standard" that other contracts may be based on. The owner of Kiiac, Kingsley Martin, writes about the construction of legal contracts and related issues on his blog, Contract Analysis and Contract Standards, at **http://contractanalysis .blogspot.com/** (last accessed Nov. 14, 2011).

based forms already provided in a document-assembly program, while others use their existing law firm templates to create their own forms. In some cases, the firm relies on paralegals or other assistants to enter the data related to the client's matter based on a previous conversation with the client. However, more modern systems allow for the client to input this data and for the paralegals and assistants to add to that data and modify it before generating a legal form. The final legal form generated based on the data provided by the client and firm members then may be provided to the lawyer for review. At that point, the lawyer is able to provide the finalized document to the client as an unbundled service along with the firm's instructions and checklists for the client to take the legal form and either file it at the courthouse, have it properly executed, or do whatever is necessary to complete the legal needs with that document.

One of the main benefits of these applications is the ability to streamline the data intake process. This saves time for the law firm members as well as the client and in theory should result in lower costs for that form of unbundled service. The lawyer is able to spend less time pulling together the boilerplate and standard legal-form language and more time focusing on the client's individual legal circumstances. The value to clients, therefore, should be increased through the use of the technology because it frees the lawyer to focus more on the legal advice and guidance rather than on the administrative aspects of unbundling. Document automation and assembly also may decrease the number of errors in the creation of a legal document by relying on a systematized form of data entry that may catch and correct any human-created omissions and errors in a legal document.

Some web-based technology platforms have integrated document-assembly and automation programs. Virtual law firms with secure client portals use this form of technology on a daily basis to deliver their unbundled services online. Rather than making an appointment to meet with the firm's paralegal or junior associate for an hour or more to handle the client intake process, online clients may complete this information at their own convenience on the Internet. The data from the form then is available for the firm to use with a document-automation program that takes the data, adds it to the template of the requested legal document, and creates a completed document for review by the firm within the virtual office space. If the virtual firm does not use a document-assembly program, the data may be stored digitally by the firm for an attorney to use to draft a legal document with another document-assembly program or as a client intake information sheet for the firm to keep in the client's file. If the information that was recorded in the program changes or the firm needs to change the form or document template to reflect changes in the law or to update, these programs allow the user to alter the finished product if necessary to reflect these changes and in some cases alter the template and questions generated in the web-based form. A platform such as this might provide multiple ways for a law firm to unbundle services to appeal to a larger market of consumers seeking automated online legal services.[9]

Case Study
Richard Granat

Richard Granat is President of DirectLaw, Inc., and MyLawyer.com (http://www.directlaw.com and http://www.mylawyer.com) and owner of Granat Legal Services, P.C., Maryland Family Lawyer Virtual Law Firm (www.mdfamilylawyer.com) that delivers unbundled family law services. He is the co-chair of the eLawyering Task Force of the Law Practice Management Section of the American Bar Association and a liaison member of the Standing Committee on the Delivery of Legal Services of the ABA. He is the co-author of "Best Practice Guidelines for Legal Information Website Providers," adopted by the ABA House of Delegates in February of 2003. DirectLaw provides a virtual law firm platform that supports the delivery of unbundled legal services. MyLawyer.com is a web-based portal that offers automated legal forms directly to consumers and contains a law firm directory of virtual law firms that deliver unbundled legal services online. The portal is designed to promote the work of virtual law firms that offer online legal services.

1. How do the services your company offers to attorneys facilitate the unbundling of legal services?

The platform enables a law firm to define an "unbundled" or "limited" legal service, to assign a price to the service, and to offer it through the law firm's website directly to consumers. Consumers can purchase the service directly through the website after executing a Limited Retainer Agreement.

---

[9]For example, the DirectLaw.com Platform provides these separate unbundling steps: 1) sale of legal advice alone, 2) review of a legal document, 3) documents that are bundled with legal advice, 4) court coaching with a fee assigned by the lawyer, 5) the capability of defining other services, assigning a fee, and having the client purchase the service through an integrated shopping cart, and 6) law firms can also order documents for free as a traffic generator, and as an inducement to sell more services. At **www.directlaw.com** (last accessed Nov. 5, 2011).

2. Have you noticed an increase in the number of attorneys who provide unbundling tools, such as web advisers, web calculators, legal forms, or other resources that allow the public to obtain free, unbundled services?

The increase in offering unbundled legal services has been primarily online. As SaaS vendors have moved into the market space that supports a limited legal service approach at a price that solos and small law firms can afford, we see solos and small law firms embracing this approach as a way of expanding their markets and the reach of their firms. By offering unbundled legal services online, a law firm is able to justify the time it might take to design a specific service because it can be offered over a wider area. A good example of this is the development of automated legal documents that may not be cost-effective to develop and deliver if limited to an office situation. When these documents and legal solutions are offered over a wider area, the ROI increases to the point where the cost of development is justified.

3. What do you think is the importance of document-assembly and automation services or other cloud-based technologies to the attorney who is adding unbundled services to his or her offerings?

Web-enabled document assembly is a disruptive technology because it enables the law firm to reach clients who are not normally served by law firms because they can't afford it. By enabling the client to complete an online questionnaire that instantly creates a first draft, ready for the lawyer's review, analysis, and further revision, it is possible for the lawyer to charge a lower price, but also to maintain a profit margin. These new services are by definition cloud-based. Without the availability of cloud-based technologies, these services would not be available.

4. How would you advise attorneys to respond to critics of unbundling or accusations from other professionals that their unbundling work is "commoditizing" the practice of law?

The full legal service approach is too "full featured" for what most consumers need. The broad middle class is presently priced out of the legal market and can't afford legal fees. If the legal profession is going to remain relevant, it must explore ways of serving a large underserved population base. Perhaps aspects of the "practice of law" are being commoditized. The issue is whether the legal profession will be part of this or will law firms find themselves (primarily solos and small law firms) marginalized by developments not taking place in the industry.

5. Are you aware of any existing regulations or barriers to unbundling services that exist from the state bars or another regulatory body?

Not really. The state bars have become more responsive to this trend, although we do see several constraints in some states. For example, one state requires that a Limited Retainer Agreement be hand-signed rather than have clickwrapped-acceptance and be physically mailed to the attorney.

6. Do you have any best practices or suggestions for attorneys wishing to minimize the risk of malpractice when unbundling services (online or off)?

The Limited Retainer Agreement should be clear about the scope of services, where it begins and where it ends. Boundary setting is very important in this type of practice or client expectations are not clear and this causes confusion.

7. Thinking ahead, what role do you think unbundling will take in the legal profession in the future? What currently is driving this trend?

"Unbundling," which really means that the client participates in doing some of the work that the lawyer normally does, such as representing himself or herself at a uncontested divorce hearing, will come to dominate the way legal services are delivered by solos and small law firms in some practice areas. Not all practice areas, however. In areas such as criminal-defense practice, where freedom is at stake, full-service representation still will be the primary mode of delivery.

Internet-based software applications will become more powerful, delivered to both the desktop and to mobile devices, resulting in enabling consumers to do work that was previously performed by attorneys. In this environment, the attorney needs to be able to redefine his or her services so that he or she adds value to the total legal transaction. Billing by the hour may survive but only if pricing is related to the fixed prices that lawyers now are charging for many tasks that were previously charged for by the hour.

These developments may result in income and fee compression. But they are unavoidable. Just as the iPod resulted in the price of music being reduced, these technological developments will result in lawyer's fees, at all levels, being compressed. The way to maintain profit margins is to use information technology tools to automate legal tasks wisely.

There is no rule that says that a lawyer is entitled to $200 an hour for his or her work. Doctors have experienced income compression because of developments in the medical insurance and have less income expectations than they had 25 years ago. The same developments are occurring in the delivery of legal services. It will be possible to make a good living as a solo practitioner or member of a small law firm, but except in a special area of practice such as criminal-defense or class-action litigation, more routine transactions will become commoditized and it will not be possible to "get rich quick."

At the MyLawyer.com consumer portal, we offer smart legal forms that when purchased in a bundle are less than the cost of a song on iTunes. We do this because we have the capacity to do this, and if we don't do this, someone else will. At the same time, we provide a pathway directly to a network of virtual law firms that can offer legal advice or alternative legal forms bundled with legal advice for fixed fees. The consumer signs into his or her own MyLegalAffairs page where the consumer can access legal tools, legal information, and automated legal documents. He or she also can directly select a lawyer who is listed in the MyLawyer Directory and call on that lawyer for additional assistance when needed, from purchasing legal advice to reviewing a document to even representing the consumer/client in court.

I see this as a model for the future delivery of legal services, which will become dominant in one form or another over the next five years.

Practitioners who are unbundling online will need to integrate some form of document-assembly and automation component in their process to remain competitive with the many online legal service providers, such as LegalZoom and Rocket Lawyer, which use these technologies to provide increased online usability of their system and to generate faster results. New models of document assembly and automation are turning to cloud-computing to reach a larger market of lawyers looking for automation and assembly solutions in addition to selling their free legal forms online directly to consumers. For example, WhichDraft is a company that provides a product with free legal forms, a document-assembly application for drafting legal documents, and online collaboration tools.[10] These systems may be less robust and complex in nature than the more established document-automation and assembly solutions, but also are either free or low-cost and require little training to use. They also may require that the

---

[10]*See* Whichdraft at **http://www.whichdraft.com/** (last accessed Oct. 30, 2011).

lawyer spend additional time creating templates of forms that are unique to the firm's practice rather than supplying state-specific forms that are ready to use.

Future document-assembly and automation features may be enhanced so that the questions and forms are revised automatically or suggested changes made to the formation based on data collected from a large body of users, such as the members of a law firm or the firm's clients' responses related to the creation of specific unbundled services, and the record of consistent and frequent edits made by the lawyers using the program.

Depending on the selected technology, systems may be used to set up client libraries of legal forms, instructions, and other documents that the attorney may store online for use with multiple clients. Document-assembly and automation technology may be integrated into a virtual law office to use with these libraries or a traditional law firm may use them in-house in conjunction with the firm's other software applications. Online limited-scope agreements may be created through web-based interfaces and the client's consent for use of the document-assembly process may be collected online and recorded within the client's file.

The attorney may set up unbundled "packages" of services that a prospective client may select from the firm's website when shopping for online legal assistance. The prospective client then would click on the desired legal service and the link would send the client through an automated process on the attorney's virtual law office from registration through a conflict of interest and jurisdiction check, and provide the specific client intake forms and automated responses required of that specific unbundled package. These web-based tools are used most often by transactions-based law firms, but they also may be employed by full-service, litigation-based practices interested in adding unbundled services to the firms' offerings or just to use with in-person clients as a form of speeding up the client intake and document-assembly process as part of larger projects for the clients.

Decision-Making Tools

Products are available that can assist a lawyer in creating a proposed settlement for a legal matter based on the information available before engaging in the lengthy process of preparing to go down the road to litigation. Treeage Pro, for example, helps a lawyer assess the value of settlement before litigation by allowing the lawyer to create decision trees, influence diagrams, and useMarkov models based on the issues identified in the client's legal matter.[11] Even if the client does not choose to settle, the lawyer may provide this unbundled service as a way to inform the client strategically where to focus on the trial or in the discovery process. "Choiceboxing" is another decision-making tool that may be used by law firms to provide unbundled assistance.[12] Marc Lauritsen, president of Capstone Practice Systems, Inc. and Legal Systematics, Inc., has created a system for supporting decisions that, if implemented in a software program, could be used to assist lawyers in making decisions about strategy for their clients' legal matters. The description of the method from the pending patent explains the process in more detail.

Embodiments of the present invention use a construct referred to herein as a 'choicebox' to support choice-making within a conceptual choice-space. The choicebox allows the identification of one or more options, one or more factors, and one or more perspectives for a particular choice. Each choice is associated with one or more categories. The options, factors, and perspectives are logically mapped to imagined x, y, and z axes and can be envisioned and graphically represented as a three-dimensional assessment matrix or box. Within the context of the present invention, choiceboxing is the activity of deliberating about a choice using such matrices. Choiceboxes are built and manipulated using software that renders their data into visual and interactive form. They serve as shareable places for collaborative deliberation.[13]

This type of decision-making tool works best when fixed choices must be made without any clear-cut way of determining which of those choices is going to have the greater benefit for the client. Choiceboxing allows the choices to be analyzed in a way that includes multiple people's input and emotions surrounding a decision without limiting the decision making to a checklist of tangible outcomes.

Lawyers who make use of decision-making tools such as Choiceboxing might provide them to clients through an interactive web application on

---

[11]*See* Treeage website at **http://www.treeage.com/industrySol/legal.html** (last accessed Nov. 2, 2011).

[12]MARC LAURITSEN, THE LAWYER'S GUIDE TO WORKING SMARTER WITH KNOWLEDGE TOOLS, ABA/LPM, 2009 at chapter 14.

[13]*See* the summary of the pending patent application for this concept, Patent No. 20100057645, filed by All About Choice, Inc. at **http://www.faqs.org/patents/assignee/all-about-choice-inc/** (last accessed Nov. 14, 2011).

a law firm website so that prospective clients might use these tools to help determine their choices in a legal matter based on the personal decisions of what matters most to them before approaching the law firm for unbundled or full-service assistance. A law firm might also use a tool like this only internally with clients and only when appropriate to help the lawyers provide unbundled work with the clients to come to the best outcome for their legal matters based on a collective decision-making process and then assign the unbundled tasks and responsibilities to the client and the lawyer, respectively. Clearly, there is a lot of room for innovation and different implementations of a system like this. However, in terms of using these methods for the benefit of self-help individuals as a form of unbundling, providing decision-making tools to clients are going to be most effective with more-educated clients who know how to use the information provided by the tools and continue to represent their own interests.

Online Case and Client Management

Providing a secure client portal with case access for your unbundled clients is an excellent way to keep a digital record of the legal documents and/or guidance and instruction that you have provided to the client. If clients have their own secure home pages online, the clients may log in at any time to access the information that they need to complete the legal matters on their own.

Online case and client management may be used to streamline the process of working with unbundled clients. The attorney may also use the system as a way to set up reminders for clients or to check back in with clients at later dates to ensure that they were able to complete their processes. This form of digital communication may especially appeal to the DIY clients who would appreciate the convenience and easy accessibility of their own case files and documents.

Even after the scope of the legal matter is completed by the attorney, the termination of the limited representation may be noted in the client's online case file. The clients would still retain access to their home pages and the ability to download and review the assistance provided by the attorney during the representation. In terms of converting unbundled clients into full-service clients, providing clients with online access to their legal matters shows clients that the firm is willing to use technology to provide efficiency and help cut the cost of traditional in-person legal services.

Case Study
Jack Newton

*Jack Newton, President of Clio, **www.goclio.com**, is a frequent speaker and author on the subject of security and cloud computing. Clio is a comprehensive, cloud-based practice-management product specifically designed for solo practitioners and small law firms. Clio provides case/ matter management, time tracking, billing/reporting, client contact and document management, task scheduling, trust accounting, and perform- ance metrics for independent lawyers to benchmark their business goals. Clio includes Clio Connect, a secure portal for document sharing and collaboration with clients, and Clio Express, an offline time-capture application.*

1. How do the services your company offers to attorneys facilitate the unbundling of legal services?

Clio facilitates the delivery of unbundled legal services via its Clio Con- nect client portal. This portal allows lawyers to securely communicate and collaborate with clients in a lower-overhead, efficient manner. Lawyers can securely send and receive "Secure Messages" to clients and can easily collaborate on documents with clients via Clio Connect's inte- grated document-management system.

2. How would you recommend that attorneys follow up or monitor the progress of unbundled clients after termination of the limited- scope representation?

As with any engagement, even after a full-service representation, I would recommend attorneys periodically follow up with their clients by e-mail, phone, or even via their virtual law practice platform, to evaluate and understand the outcome of the engagements. It also is important to view this as an opportunity to measure customer satisfaction and to identify ways the attorney's unbundled services could be delivered more effectively.

3. Have you noticed an increase in the number of attorneys who provide unbundling tools, such as web advisers, web calculators, legal forms, or other resources that allow the public to obtain free unbundled services?

I have observed a large increase in the number of attorneys looking to integrate unbundling tools directly into their websites. The broad sense seems to be that clients are looking for ways of engaging more meaning- fully with attorneys online without having to go to the extent of making a phone call or sending an e-mail. An online adviser, legal form, calculator, client intake form, or other similar "active" online tools do a much better job of fully engaging prospective clients while they are visiting the attorney website, and I believe an increasing number of attorneys recognize this fact and are responding appropriately.

4. What do you think is the importance of document-assembly and automation services or other cloud-based technologies to the attorney who is adding unbundled services to his or her offerings?

Document-assembly and automation services are critical tools for any attorney who hopes to compete effectively on unbundled offerings. I feel that document assembly and automation offer such compelling benefits via improved efficiency and reduced errors that they will become essential tools for almost all attorneys, whether for the delivery of full-service or unbundled representation.

5. How would you advise attorneys to respond to critics of unbundling or accusations from other professionals that their unbundling work is "commoditizing" the practice of law?

Certain aspects of legal work should be commoditized, and for those types of work attorneys can choose to respond by offering competitive, unbundled legal work or risk losing that portion of the market to competitors such as LegalZoom, Rocket Lawyer, and LawDepot. Work that is suitable for "commoditization" will be work that is highly repeatable and mechanizable by using tools such as document automation.

6. Thinking ahead, what role do you think unbundling will take in the legal profession in the future? What is currently driving this trend?

I believe unbundling will take an increasingly large role in the legal profession. Enabling technologies for unbundling are becoming increasingly widespread and affordable for solo and small-firm attorneys, and market demand for these types of limited-scope engagements is only increasing.

Delivering Unbundled Services Online

Comprehensive consumer Web portals are emerging that assist attorneys in delivering legal services online rather than giving them the tools to create their own unique virtual law offices. For example, Rocket Lawyer provides a product that is marketed to consumers who can subscribe for different levels of access to the service's libraries of legal forms to create their own legal documents online.[14] The consumer then may request to be matched with an attorney within his or her jurisdiction for review of the document and additional assistance at a "discounted rate."[15] The attorney who pays to join this lead-generation service then may be matched with the consumer who continues the relationship where unbundled assistance is provided or it may change to full service depending on the client's needs. The information and prefilled forms that the client completes online are transferred to the attorney when the client begins working with him or her. This legal services model does not provide the same case or client management features or the functionality of a backend virtual law office for the attorney, but it does generate leads to online clients who are interested in unbundled legal services. Another drawback of these services, is that the law firm does not have its own client-facing web and client portal, and is thus dependent on the company providing the service for brand development. Other online legal services companies may be considering similar lead-generation marketing models that also will encourage the practice of using technology and the Internet to deliver legal services online.

For the lawyer delivering legal services online, attention to security and ethics is paramount. Regardless of what Internet technology the attorney chooses, he or she needs to be aware of security risks involved in using cloud-based systems to deliver legal services online.[16] Additionally, there are ethics risks that may arise from the use of a service providing a comprehensive consumer Web portal. Many of the legal service companies and other free to low-cost legal forms found online may not involve the communication of a licensed attorney with the client. However, a lawyer participating in these consumer portals is subject to disciplinary action if the consumer portal is not ethically compliant. The company has no liability, only the lawyer participating in the service. Below is a list of questions that a lawyer might consider before participating in a service that provides a web-based consumer client portal. These services, unfortunately, are not held to the same standards as is an attorney who must protect the confidentiality of the client's data.

---

[14]Rocket Lawyer, **http://www.rocketlawyer.com** (accessed Jan. 8, 2010).
[15]*Id.*
[16]*See* "Suggested Minimum Requirements for Law Firms Delivering Legal Services Online," ABA LPM eLawyering Task Force (Oct. 15, 2009), **http://meetings.abanet.org/webupload/ commupload/EP024500/relatedresources/Minimum_Requirements_for_Lawyers_2009_ 10_24.pdf** (accessed Jan. 8, 2010).

1. Who has access to the client data?

2. What is the security of the process and how does it protect the confidentiality of the client's data?

3. Can I download client data to my local computer?

4. Is a written limited scope engagement agreement executed?

5. How are lawyers added to the service? Is there a qualification for use of the service by a lawyer? Does the company check that the lawyer is licensed and in good standing with his or her bar before allowing them to respond to consumer requests for legal services?

6. What is the process the prospective client goes through in selecting the lawyer he or she works with and how does that process comply with the lawyer's state bar rules regarding the establishment of the attorney/client relationship and duty to prospective clients?

7. Is the client provided with adequate notice of the limited scope of representation and the use of the technology to deliver the services?

8. How does the client know when an assignment or project has been completed? What is the termination of representation process? Does the client retain access to his or her account following termination or does the client have another way of contacting the lawyer for follow-up after termination of representation?

9. Are any revenues split between the non-lawyer provider of the consumer portal and the law firm? If so, how does this avoid the prohibition on divisions of fees with nonlawyer entities?

There may be additional questions to consider when researching whether or not to use a service that provides a web-based consumer portal service. Features provided by the companies offering these services are being developed and updated on a regular basis and most of these companies are well aware of the regulations that lawyers must follow and their concerns about ethics risks. Given the fast pace at which these online services are being developed, the use of these services will require regular re-evaluation by the lawyer to weigh the risks and benefits of using it to deliver unbundled legal services online.

Web Calculators and Web Advisers

Some law firms may choose to start out by providing unbundled services in the form of web calculators or web advisers that directly appeal to self-help, prospective clients, but which do not directly involve interaction with the firm's lawyers. These tools are embedded in the law firm's website for the use of the prospective client. In some cases, they provide information that can educate the prospective client on his or her legal needs and guide the client to retain the law firm for unbundled or full services. In other cases, they may provide an entire unbundled service, such as a legal document or legal guidance on a matter. In most cases, the law firm uses these tools on the law firm website as part of a larger marketing strategy to improve the search-engine optimization for the firm's website by providing unique and useful content, but also in the hopes of converting those self-help individuals into paying clients. Some lawyers may even consider providing the online document-assembly and automation tools for free to the client in addition to other web calculators or web advisers.[17]

One example of this is Road Traffic Representation's "expert system."[18] This system was developed by a UK solicitor and serves as a web adviser for an individual who has been accused of a traffic offense. Individuals are able to use the online tool and, by answering questions as prompted, receive tailored legal advice that lets them know what the penalties and outcomes might be in their situations. At that point, the law firm has armed the self-help individuals with the information and then also will provide them with an attorney if they decide that based on the information from the legal diagnostic tool, they would prefer to have a lawyer represent them on their matters in court.

Expect to see more free or low-cost iPad, iPhone and other tablet and smartphone computer applications that are geared toward the self-help individual.[19] These may be developed by forward-thinking law firms that can then redirect those individuals downloading the application to the law firm's website and potentially convert a few of those leads into paying unbundled or full-service clients.

The other benefit of prospective clients using these tools is that when they finally sit down to work with the lawyers in the firm, they are armed with the basic knowledge of their legal matters. This saves time and frustration for both parties and allows the parties to jump deeper into handling the legal matter because many of the decisions already have been made by the client through that initial process.

---

[17] *See, e.g.,* legalmove.com at **http://www.legalmove.com/**. Legalmove is the online division of Fidler & Pepper Solicitors, at **http://www.fidler.co.uk/**, a conveyancing law firm in the UK. It provides conveyancing quotes online from its website and allows clients to track their cases online and receive SMS texts with alerts.

[18] *See* RoadTrafficRepresentation at **http://roadtrafficrepresentation.com/RTR/PublicForms/ Home.aspx** (last accessed on Nov. 2, 2011).

[19] *See, e.g.,* **http://lawlibe.thelawpod.com/**.

Other companies may develop web-based applications for use by law firms which the lawyer may use for unbundling legal guidance and may choose to share with the client to assist him or her in the future self-representation of the case. For example, in November 2011, a company named Picture It Settled, LLC released an application for iPhones and iPads to help litigants analyze and develop negotiation strategies.[20] The application reviews the settlement negotiations of "over thousands" of cases to help the lawyer plan a negotiation strategy. A simplier version of the software tracks the dollar moves in negotiation allowing users to calculate future offers based on the opponent's moves and the concession rates of both parties. A lawyer might use such software by assisting the client in entering the data into the application related to his or her case. The lawyer might then provide the client with legal guidance based on the returned analysis along with a strategy for negotiation for the self-help client to proceed.

Online Dispute Resolution

In Chapter Five, alternative dispute resolution (ADR) was presented as another method of unbundling legal services. Increasingly, the DIY client is encountering the use of another form of web-based ADR called online dispute resolution, or ODR. ODR is a term that encompasses any methods of dispute resolution—arbitration, negotiations, mediation, and other methods of settlement—that are handled online. Most emerging methods of ODR are conducted by web-based, independent software systems created for the purpose of dispute resolution and involve only the parties to the dispute and the computer. These highly automated systems are owned by for-profit companies that may contract the use of the software out to other companies that focus on e-commerce or other markets that experience a large number of smaller claims.[21] Many clients are familiar with purchasing items from online retailers, such as eBay or Craigslist. Whether or not they read through the terms of use before signing up for the site, clients most likely agreed to the site's ODR process in lieu of litigation. When disputes arise between the buyer and the seller online, there is the opportunity for the parties to resolve the dispute using the retailer's ODR process. The need for a lawyer is cut out of the picture unless one of the parties wishes to retain the unbundled guidance by a lawyer who may be familiar with this form of dispute and can provide strategic guidance in the process.

---

[20]Picture It Settled, LLC at **http://www.pictureitsettled.com/**, last accessed December 11, 2011.
[21]SquareTrade is the most well-known example of a company that has created an ODR system and licensed the use of this to online trading website eBay.

One of the more familiar examples of separate web-based ODR systems is Cybersettle.[22] Used by trial lawyers, Cybersettle uses a double-blind bidding process that results in a faster resolution of the legal matter.[23] According to the company's website, using this system reduces the average time to settle a case by four to six months.[24] The cost savings from using this in place of full litigation are not insignificant and may allow a law firm to work with more clients by offering to use this form of settlement and reserve full-service litigation services for cases where full service is necessary. There is little danger from attempting to use this form of service because if the case does not settle through the process, the information provided by the client and the lawyer remains confidential, and the parties still may proceed through litigation.

SmartSettle is another web-based ODR tool that uses a blind bidding process, but its products focus more on negotiation and can be combined with face-to-face meetings online or in person.[25] Clients who decide to use this tool are asked to sign a mediation agreement before proceeding and then may request to work with a neutral mediator and from there may conduct the entire process online or proceed with a combination of communication methods. Legal matters that could be addressed by such a system include separation agreements, property distributions, estate-planning conflicts between parents or parents and their children, small business disputes, disputes related to elder-care issues, and potentially more situations. The company also provides a more robust version of the software for multiparty and more complex situations. Additionally, Smart-settle provides what it calls "Dampened Pendulum Arbitration," which occurs when both parties have agreed to arbitration but no settlement could be reached by the end of the blind bidding process.[26] This final stage offered by the company pulls in a neutral third party who will favor the party whose last accepted value during the process was closest to fair.

ODR works well with legal situations where the parties must continue to have contact with each other following the resolution of the case. While litigation may leave the parties feeling adversarial from having to go

---

[22]Cybersettle, at **http://www.cybersettle.com/pub/home/about/users/attorneys.aspx** (last accessed Nov. 3, 2011).

[23]*Id.*

[24]*Id.*, based on an Accenture® study and results from its clients.

[25]SmartSettle, at **http://www.smartsettle.com/** (last accessed Nov. 3, 2011). SmartSettle is a division of iCan Systems, Inc. and was founded by Dr. Ernest Thiessen, a pioneer in the field of eNegotiations.

[26]*See* explanation of the Dampened Pendulum Arbitration at **http://www.smartsettle.com/ dampened-pendulum-arbitration/** (last accessed Nov. 3, 2011).

against each other in a process that does not encourage amicable resolution, ODR attempts to preserve the relationship of the parties. Therefore, ODR might be most appropriate in cases such as family-law disputes where children are involved, employee/employer disputes where the employee will continue to work for the employer, disputes arising between neighbors or others who must continue to live and work around each other, worker's compensation matters where the employee must return to work, or e-commerce disputes and business disputes where the company wants to avoid class-action suits and ensure that the customer does not leave with a negative impression of the company that then may affect its reputation or that of a particular product or service the company sells based on negative online customer comments and reviews. The growth of ODR will continue to increase in these particular matters because it benefits both parties in these circumstances to be on the same page without negative feelings after the resolution of the dispute.

Case Study
David Bilinksy—ODR

David Bilinsky is the Practice Management Consultant/Adviser for the Law Society of British Columbia and has studied and written about ODR. He is a fellow of the College of Law Practice Management and past editor-in-chief of ABA's **Law Practice** *Magazine. Bilinsky, an adjunct professor at Simon Fraser University, teaches a graduate-level course in the Master of Arts in Applied Legal Studies program. Bilinsky's Thoughtful Legal Management blog has won numerous awards: http://thoughtfullaw.com.*

1. How do you see more attorneys becoming involved in the process of online dispute resolution?

ODR is advancing on least four fronts. One is the macro level: United Nations Commission on International Trade Law (UNCITRAL), the Organization of American States, and other organizations are working on model laws for the resolution of business to consumer disputes that take place across borders. The aim is to increase lower-value cross-border trade by providing an effective and cost-sensitive dispute-resolution mechanism that can be relied on by vendor and purchaser alike.

The second is the micro level: Australia, for example, is using ODR for the resolution of family-law disputes. They have found that it is particularly effective for lowering the emotional temperature of such disputes, for the parties do not need to be in the same physical space at the same time, as the technology bridges the geographical distances.

The third is private law: Businesses are seeking to incorporate ODR as the dispute-resolution method to avoid litigation. Witness the use of ODR by eBay and PayPal—together they deal with more than 60 million disputes per year. Of those disputes, 90 percent are resolved *entirely* by software (without any human intervention by eBay or PayPal).

Also small-claims courts are looking at how they can incorporate ODR into their dispute-resolution process. For example, Singapore, the UK, and Ireland all have ODR as part of their small-claims resolution process.

> **2.** How do you believe ODR can impact access to justice in both individual disputes and within the larger judicial system?

It has been commented by many that the "middle class" has been left behind by the legal system. High costs, delay, and the uncertainty of going to court have led many to either not pursue their claims or abandon them entirely. It is recognized that pursuing a dispute is a Pyrrhic victory at best if the cost of so doing exceeds the eventual settlement or award.

Litigation results in settlements by what has been described as the "shadow of trial" model. The parties seek to resolve a dispute outside of court to avoid an "all-or-nothing" result. They seek to save the costs of going to trial and they seek to try to "divide the pie" in a way that maximizes their return. Furthermore, the "fair trial" principle means that the court process is by definition:

- ♦ adversarial,
- ♦ independent,
- ♦ impartial,
- ♦ very public,
- ♦ concerned with the efficient use of court resources, and
- ♦ accessible to all.

By way of contrast, ODR is founded on interest-based negotiation. It is concerned with speed, flexibility, and reduced cost. The "game theory" approach of ODR can result in parties seeking to "grow the pie" rather than just dividing it (as is typical in litigation).

Since ODR is a subset of ADR, then ODR offers all the benefits of ADR. However, because ODR is Internet-based, it also has the following benefits:

- disputants don't have to meet face-to-face, lowering the emotional temperature of the dispute;
- mediation can occur at any time, not just in the shadow of trial; and
- it lowers transactional costs of resolving the dispute, since geographic, time, and transportation aspects can be minimized.

However, ODR may not offer all the procedural fairness that is built into the trial system. The less expensive and faster resolutions have their price in the lowering of procedural fairness. Accordingly, best practices have been proposed (by the ABA, for example) that seek to delineate the ways that ODR can develop in ways that minimize the lowering of procedural fairness.

3. To what extent do you believe computer systems will become integrated into the delivery of legal services?

When I look at how technology has been applied to the litigation system, it has largely been in a support role that seeks to make existing processes faster. There has not been a great deal of innovation in the actual court system resulting from technology. We still go to court (rather than appearing via videoconference), produce evidence (perhaps in electronic form rather than paper), wait to be heard (synchronous processes), etc.

ODR, on the other hand, is very creative in that the technology is integral—one would say essential—to the dispute-resolution process. The technology is driving the innovation, whether it is using online dispute-resolution methods (such as the Meeting Room) or eBay's dispute-resolution system (that results in virtually all disputes being resolved without any intervention by anyone other than the two parties and the computer system).

In one very real sense, the future is here, given the volume of disputes that are already being resolved by such parties as eBay, PayPal, and ICANN. So disputes are being resolved (mostly) outside of the court systems in the world. What remains is for ODR to be formally integrated into the court systems, such as in small-claims courts, family courts, and the like. There are projects under way now, such as in British Columbia, that are examining ODR in terms of its possible integration into the formal court process.

4. Do you believe computer processing will ever have a place in legal decision making in our profession?

Absolutely. The adoption of computer processing will continue to advance as the abilities of computer systems continue to increase in power and scope. Ray Kurzweil has become well known for his ability to predict the future. In such an environment as Kurzweil predicts (and we have already seen by the explosive growth of the Internet and associated technologies and the impact that just this level of technology has had on the world), it is next to inconceivable that the legal profession and legal decision making will remain immune to these influences.

We have people working on artificial intelligence systems at this present time, including legal analysis. No matter how skeptical you remain regarding the ability of computers to mimic how we as humans think, there have been examples such as IBM's Deep Blue, the chess-playing computer that defeated world champion Garry Kasparov, and IBM's Watson, the "Jeopardy"-playing computer that beat Brad Rutter, the biggest all-time money winner, and Ken Jennings, the record holder for the longest champion streak, that have shown that computer processing can beat the best of us. As long as Moore's Law holds, computers will continue to grow in power. I don't know at which point the processing capability will be sufficient to mimic (and beat) the best legal analysis and decision-making humans, but I have no doubt that this day will come.

5. What do you believe the next steps might be in promoting the use of ODR in the legal profession and with the justice system?

The National Center for Technology and Dispute Resolution (**www.odr.info**) will continue to be the clearinghouse and thought center for ODR. More and more lawyers and others will take an interest in the NCTDR as well as the Internet Bar Association (**http://internetbar.org/**) and the eLawyering Task Force of the American Bar Association (**http://apps.americanbar .org/dch/committee.cfm?com=EP024500**). UNCITRAL's Working Group will continue to explore ODR for low-value, international business to consumer (B2C) trade disputes.

Corporations will look to incorporate ODR dispute-resolution clauses and methods into their business agreements and business processes. International ODR forums will continue to be held around the world. Universities will develop degree programs in ODR such as Singapore Management University's Master's in Technology and Dispute Resolution. There will be further experimentation in incorporating ODR into legal dispute resolution such as ADR.eu in Europe and the City of Vancouver, British

Columbia, Canada, for parking tickets. Not the least of which, governments and court officials will look to incorporate ODR into their systems. The Organization of American States (OAS), for example, is looking into developing a draft model law for ODR for transnational commerce as is the U.S. State Department.

6. What role do you think unbundling legal services will take in the legal profession in the future?

I think the challenge is for the legal profession to realize that the competitive environment has changed drastically. Competitors are delivering legal services in a way that consumers desire. Lawyers and law firms need to rethink the "bespoke" method of delivery of legal services and approach this issue from the perspective of a consumer and not as a provider.

This is another way of saying that innovation is going to take place. Whether it takes place within or without the legal profession as a whole is perhaps the next challenge facing all of us. I hope, for the profession and for consumers and society alike, that we have those within our ranks that will drive this innovation and bring the rest of the legal profession along with them into the future.

Case Study
The National Center for Technology and Dispute Resolution (NCTDR)—
http://odr.info

Lawyers interested in learning more about ODR both in the States and abroad should visit the website for NCTDR. Sponsored in part by the National Science Foundation, this organization "supports and sustains the development of information technology applications, institutional resources, and theoretical and applied knowledge for better understanding and managing conflict. The Center believes that networked information technology can be uniquely leveraged to expand and improve conflict management resources and expertise."[27]

Working to promote the development of ODR in the legal system, NCTDR views the Internet as an environment where technology may be used to find solutions to conflicts that are both online and off, domestic and international. The NCTDR website features a list of ODR providers and standards created by organizations concerned with ethics issues that may

---

[27] http://odr.info/about.

arise from the practice. NCTDR regularly posts ODR news updates and publication announcements on its blog and works closely with the Internet Bar Organization (IBO).[28]

Since 1998, the organization has hosted Cyberweek, a free, annual online conference focused on ODR. This conference precedes the 11th annual congress on ODR that will be held in Prague in June 2012. The focus of this congress will be on "continued preparatory work on the design and development of a global resolution system to handle cross-border, low value disputes. Principal initiatives include the preparation of Rules for cross-border ODR by UNCITRAL, the development of cross-border ODR infrastructure connecting ODR providers in different parts of the world (ODR Data Exchange), current policy development by the European Commission, Organization of American States (OAS) and others."[29] The website for the Prague ODR conference contains a resources page with the most current publications, including information on the formation of a global ODR system.[30]

Tools such as those used in ODR provide greater opportunity for the lawyer to work with online systems to provide effective unbundled legal services to DIY clients involved in online purchasing disputes or for any client whose circumstances might benefit from the use of the online system rather than in-person ADR. For example, there may be situations where one of the parties is geographically located at such a distance that it would not be cost-effective to have both parties fly out to meet together with their lawyers face-to-face. Or one of the parties may have medical reasons why he or she may not travel to meet with the other party for the process. One or both of the parties to the process may even be incarcerated and unable to leave to resolve the matter. The use of the technology breaks down these barriers to provide greater access to the ADR process. The lawyer or law firm may suggest to a self-help client that these ODR services are an option in his or her circumstance and explain how the lawyer may assist the client in going through the process. The lawyer then defines the scope of ODR services based on what the lawyer agrees that the client would benefit from with the potential to add additional legal services as needed.

---

[28]See the Internet Bar Organization at **http://internetbar.org/**.

[29]See the website for ODR 2012 Prague at **http://www.odr2012.org/**.

[30]See Del Duca, Louis, Colin Rule and Zbynek Loebl, "Facilitating Expansion of Cross-Border E-Commerce—Developing a Global Online Dispute Resolution System (Lessons Derived From Existing ODR Systems—Work of The United Nations Commission on International Trade Law) at **http://www.odr2012.org/files/pilot.pdf**.

This form of unbundling may have a great amount of potential value for the unbundling lawyer where the law firm has experience in reaching settlements in a specific practice area. For example, if the law firm has more than 30 years of experience in settling insurance claims, its lawyers will know that given the circumstances of the case, a reasonable settlement amount would be X. Accordingly, the client armed with this information would have the confidence going into the ODR system that the asking settlement amount is reasonable and fair under the circumstances. The fact that both parties may not have full-service representation may simplify the process and prevent unnecessary and lengthy negotiations by starting the process with reasonable terms given the circumstances. At some point in the future, it may be possible that computer systems will be able to learn different outcomes and settlements based on input entered from prior cases. When similar circumstances arise in a new case, the computer could parse the data to provide suggested starting points for the parties. In the meantime, the lawyer's own experience may be provided as an unbundled legal service to the ODR client using these technology tools.

These forms of technology-driven ODR focus on online arbitration and this is an area of ADR that may benefit more from the use of the web-based technology. There is less need for the lawyer to unbundle services with the systems when he or she will be providing full-service representation. However, mediation, as a form of ODR, may provide additional opportunities for the lawyer to unbundle. The law firm might consider distinguishing itself by gaining experience in online mediation, where the parties to the case and the mediator communicate with each other online as well as share testimony, evidence, and other information related to the case with the mediator. Initial attempts at online mediation may have been questioned in the past because of the lack of interpersonal communication and the reliance on text-based forms of communication, such as e-mail. However, today, online mediation should be reconsidered given the ease of web-conferencing tools that allow all parties to meet face-to-face online and to have those meetings recorded and shared for future reference.

The international business community is increasingly looking at ODR as a way to circumvent many of the barriers in cross-border law practice. Other companies are creating their own systems and rules for use of the technology that clients are agreeing to follow. These rules are not based on any jurisdiction's laws, but the laws created by the company and the users based on the circumstances on the online activity and e-commerce transactions. As these new systems of ODR evolve, lawyers interested in capitalizing on the need for experienced legal guidance within these systems will find unique opportunities for unbundling.

The use of these tools can also prevent the frivolous filing of lawsuits by encouraging the parties to move toward settlement prior to engaging in litigation. Accordingly, it is not difficult to see the value that this process would have for companies that provide third-party litigation funding. The use of a form of ODR prior to litigation might be included in the review process for that funding company to help it determine the amount and likelihood of providing the funding for the matter to be litigated.

Practice areas where ODR might be an option include:

◆ Business

◆ Insurance

◆ Small claims

◆ Commercial law

◆ Worker's rights (employers may provide some form of ODR system to resolve employment disputes)

◆ Landlord/tenant

◆ Intellectual property

◆ Family law

◆ Distribution of property

◆ Contract law

◆ Other transactions-based practices

Game-Theoretic Bargaining Systems

Game theory is the science of strategy and interdependent decision-making. It uses principles of logic and mathematics to analyze and illustrate the actions that "players" should take in order to secure the best outcomes for themselves in a wide variety of "games." The games in question range from simple card games to highly complex transactions and military conflicts.[31]

In recent years game theory has been used to conduct extensive studies of the dynamics underlying legal conflicts and legal negotiations. Thousands of articles using game theory to analyze the legal field have been published in journals dedicated to such studies.[32]

---

[31]See a general summary of game theory in the Concise Encyclopedia of Economics at **http://www .econlib.org/library/Enc/GameTheory.html**.

[32]See for example, the American Law and Economics Review, published by the American Law and Economics Association at **http://www.amlecon.org/** and the Journal of Empirical Legal Studies, published by the Society for Empirical Legal Studies at **http://www.lawschool.cornell.edu/sels/**.

Practical applications of some of this work have recently been developed and made available to lawyers and to the public at large. For example, several computerized bargaining systems that employ procedures grounded in game theory can currently be accessed and used online.[33] Such systems can be and are being used by parties and lawyers involved in litigation and legal negotiations, including lawyers providing unbundled legal services.

Case Study
Fair Outcomes–www.FairOutcomes.com

James F. Ring is a partner in the Boston law firm of Chu, Ring & Hazel, LLP. He is also a principal of Fair Outcomes, Inc., a company founded by a small group of game theorists, computer scientists, and practicing attorneys to provide parties involved in disputes or difficult negotiations with access to game-theoretic bargaining systems. He has twenty-eight years of experience as a practicing trial lawyer, primarily working on business disputes. He lectures frequently, and is the author of several published articles, on using game theory to understand, manage, and resolve legal conflict.

1. **What insights and opportunities does game theory offer to lawyers, including lawyers that are interested in providing unbundled services?**

Practicing law consists, to a very large degree, of engaging in or assisting clients with various forms of bargaining. This includes overt bargaining, such as negotiating with governmental authorities, adversaries, and potential contractual partners. It also includes a great deal what game theorists refer to as tacit bargaining, such as when one takes, or threatens to take, or refrains from taking a given action in an effort to influence or induce another party to do or concede certain things. Litigation is, in virtually all cases (and like most forms of conflict), a form of tacit bargaining.

Game theory takes a scientific approach to bargaining. It sheds light on what works and doesn't work in particular contexts. In so doing, it serves to confirm much of what most experienced lawyers intuitively understand, such as that talk is cheap and actions speak louder, and are much more credible, than words. This approach has led to the development of several systems that allow various forms of legal conflict to be managed and resolved in a highly productive and efficient way.

---

[33] *See, e.g.,* the various systems offered at **http://www.fairoutcomes.com/**.

Although the theoretical work underlying these systems is deep and offers a view of legal conflict that differs markedly from the view routinely advanced by many advocates of alternative dispute resolution, the systems themselves are very simple and easy to understand. They are particularly well-suited for use by lawyers that are interested in limiting their services to helping a client identify and pursue a reasonable outcome in a credible, effective, and non-prejudicial manner.

    2. What sorts of features do these systems have that might cause them to be of interest to lawyers providing unbundled services?

There are several game-theoretic systems that can be used online, in some cases for free and in almost all cases for less than the filing fees charged to file an action in court. A party can use these systems at any time by entering some simple data identifying the parties and the underlying case and committing, in confidence, to a bargaining outcome that that party would view as acceptable. The system won't reveal that outcome to anyone else unless that outcome is achieved. The data entry process can in most cases be completed in less than five minutes, at which point that party's work is done. The system then offers the other party an opportunity to enter similar data in complete confidence and at no cost. Depending upon how the other party responds, the matter will either be resolved on terms that are acceptable to both sides or, alternatively, a party that has used the system will be given an affidavit attesting to the system's structure and to the manner in which that party, as distinct from its adversary, had used the system.

What makes these systems so attractive is that—although these systems can be and often are used by mutual agreement—they can also be initiated and used productively by one party without having to secure the other party's cooperation or consent. A party that makes a reasonable proposal will, in all cases, either achieve what it considers to be a reasonable outcome or will be able to credibly demonstrate, without having to reveal its own proposed outcome to its adversary, that its adversary had walked away from a fair solution under conditions where the adversary had no rational incentive or excuse for doing so. This is because the structure of these systems negates any incentive or excuse for either party to posture, or to fail to propose, or to walk away from, a reasonable settlement. In stark contrast to the dynamic that exists in litigation, arbitration, mediation, traditional sealed-bid arrangements and online embodiments of traditional ADR methods (all of which provide ample incentives and excuses for posturing up until the eve of trial), self-interest obliges a party that initiates a use of one of these game-theoretic systems to commit to a reasonable outcome at the outset of the process, and self-interest obliges the other party to do so by a fixed deadline.

3. What sorts of systems does Fair Outcomes presently offer?

Fair Outcomes, Inc. currently offers five distinct systems based on three different sets of patented processes. Three of these systems can be briefly summarized as follows:

Fair Buy-Sell: This system is used by joint owners of property—such as business partners, shareholders, heirs, and married couples—to bring their joint ownership to an end in a fair and efficient manner. The initiating party enters data, and the system invites the other party to enter data, confidentially specifying a price at which the party entering that data would be willing either to sell its share to the other side or buy-out the other side's share (similar to the proposal made by the initiating party under a traditional "buy-sell" arrangement). The system compares the data entered by the two parties and announces a sale to the party that specified the higher price. However, the sale price is set at the midpoint between the two values. When used by both of the involved parties, this system always produces a full and complete resolution, and it always provides each party—whether the buyer or seller—with a resolution that is equal to or (in the vast majority of cases) more favorable to it than what it had proposed.

Fair Division (the "Adjusted Winner" system): In cases in which two parties must divide up multiple items of property or resolve multiple issues that are in dispute, either party can initiate this system and thereby invite the other party to arrive at a resolution in a fair and efficient manner. This system embodies a bidding process (involving confidential bids) that guarantees each party at least 1/2 of what that party considers to be the total value of all of the items or issues in question, and usually allows each party to receive between 2/3 and 3/4 of that value. In the vernacular of game theory, the structure of this system is honesty-inducing and strategy-proof, producing outcomes that are efficient, equitable, and envy-free. Utilizing what has been recognized as some of the most important work that has been done in game theory in recent decades, this system has been used in cases ranging from marital divorce to international border disputes. It has been shown in independent empirical studies to "eminently" and "substantially" improve upon traditional approaches to legal bargaining.

Fair Proposals: In cases in which one party is seeking money or other concessions from another, such as in a lawsuit, a party on either side of such a claim can use this system to propose a resolution that it deems fair in a manner that is credible but non-prejudicial. Unlike litigation, mediation, traditional sealed-bid systems and all other forms of ADR and ODR, the system gives the initiating party a strong incentive to make a reasonable proposal at the outset of the process, and it deprives the other party of any incentive or excuse for failing to do the same prior to a fixed deadline. It has been used in cases involving claims for breach of contract, personal injury claims, whistle-blower claims, and claims for legal malpractice. Prominent economists, strategic analysts, and dispute resolution professionals have described this system as "ingenious" and as "brilliant in its simplicity."

    4. How are lawyers that provide unbundled services making use of the game-theoretic systems offered and administered by Fair Outcomes, Inc.?

As the administrator of these various systems, Fair Outcomes, Inc. is obliged to remain strictly neutral as between the parties. This has created opportunities for lawyers to assist one side, as opposed to the other, in connection with a given use of any one of these systems. Lawyers that wish to provide limited services in a given case generally use these systems in one of two basic ways. Some lawyers offer, in exchange for a fee (either fixed, hourly, or contingent), to provide people (including other lawyers) with limited services consisting of guidance and advice on how to use these systems in a particular case, such as in a divorce or personal injury case. The second way in which lawyers providing circumscribed services often use these systems is to use them to make a credible determination about whether a case can be settled on reasonable terms prior to referring the case out to another lawyer or otherwise withdrawing from involvement in the case.

    5. How can people learn more about these systems and about this general approach to dealing with litigation and legal negotiations?

All of these systems can be accessed, examined, and tested free of charge at **www.FairOutcomes.com**. In-depth information about each system, including access to analytical papers, can be accessed via the "Learn More" pages corresponding to each particular system, along with additional information about this general approach to managing and resolving legal claims.

Touching on the cornerstone rule of "doing unto others as you would have them do unto you," game-theoretic systems oblige both parties to admit to themselves that what they might want to claim in traditional negotiations and what they would actually view as a fair resolution may not be one and the same. This makes it easier for lawyers, including lawyers providing unbundled assistance, to help a client come to grips at an early stage with what would actually constitute a fair and reasonable outcome given the facts and circumstances of the case. If a client uses the system to commit to a reasonable outcome, the case will either settle on terms that the client deems fair or, alternatively, the client will be able to justify expending resources on additional legal services or moving forward on a pro se or quasi-pro se basis.

Artificial Intelligence

For most lawyers, the term "artificial intelligence" (AI) may elicit images of robots, such as Honda's well-known Asimo robot.[34] However, many other professions use AI as a useful tool that works alongside human intelligence, resulting in increased production and more predictable and stable standards and outcomes. The financial industry uses AI to predict markets and provide guidance to financial planners and investors based on economic trends. The medical industry heavily relies on forms of AI as diagnostic tools that gather input from the patient and report the findings to a medical practitioner who then has existing data from which to provide a more detailed diagnosis and health-care strategy. AI is slowly making its way into the legal profession, but it is most likely still a long way from being relied on as it is in these other industries.[35]

Neota Logic is one example of a company that has developed an artificial intelligence engine with user-friendly and power authoring tool.[36] This technology goes one step beyond basic document assembly by using decision trees, decision tables, if/then rules, calculations, weighted factors, spreadsheets, case-based reasoning and others tools to create customized

---

[34]*See* Asimo at **http://asimo.honda.com/** (accessed Nov. 3, 2011).

[35]*See generally* "Swapping Decision Trees for River Logic" by Darryl Mountain on Slaw.ca blog (accessed Sept. 14, 2011), at **http://www.slaw.ca/2011/09/14/swapping-decision-trees-for-river-logic/**, discussing eGanges as a new legal expert system shell being developed by Dr. Pamela Gray, a legal knowledge engineer from Charles Stuart University. *See also* Neota Logic at **http://www.neotalogic.com/author** (last accessed Nov. 2, 2011) as an example of a company that develops customized legal AI systems for law firms.

[36]Neota Logic at **http://www.neotalogic.com**, last accessed November 2, 2011, as an example of a company that develops customized legal AI systems for law firms.

systems for law firms. This technology may be used to assist in the decision making process for lawyers. As the expert system continues to be used by the law firm, it learns and aggregates data to increase performance of its operations as well as to create valuable reports from its database for use by the law firm. Only a limited number of law firms employ true expert systems such as those built by Neota Logic which was founded in late 2010. Michael Mills, CEO of Neota Logic, provided this background on how these expert systems are being adopted: "[o]ur discussions with corporate general counsel, compliance directors and human resources staff confirm the prospects for expert systems developed by true experts using smart technology. As one general counsel said to us, "No more memos . . . we want answers." We are finding law firms quite interested in packaging and delivering their expertise in new ways—ways that do not cannibalize traditional legal work but instead enable creation of new services that meet clients' needs in ways that traditional services cannot."

Mills provides an example of how these new services might be offered: "An expert system on human resources law deployed inside a major employer can answer for line supervisors and HR staff many routine legal questions that at present do not benefit at all from legal guidance, because it is simply too costly and time-consuming to consult with in-house or outside counsel. The system answers the routine two-thirds of the questions, and routes the more difficult questions to the right lawyer after collecting online much of the information that the lawyer will need to reach a judgment" However, Mills states that these systems are primarily built to be used by clients rather than by lawyers. He explains that the implementation of expert systems is practical when: "(1) the practice area offers clients advice and answers more than transaction execution or dispute resolution. (Examples: employment law, tax, financial services compliance, data privacy, cross-border issues, multi-state issues, environmental regulation), (2) the clients' business operations generate a steady flow of questions in a defined topic area, (3) the topic is complex enough to warrant consulting experts, and (4) yet routine and repetitive enough that the traditional service model is not sustainable."

Mills believes AI will become a powerful tool in the legal profession but one that is "narrow" in its focus, handling only the more repetitive tasks of moderate complexity. In terms of AI's application to unbundling, Mills sees potential for expert systems to provide unbundled legal services to self-help individuals who are proceeding pro se as well as in conjunction with paid, unbundled services from a lawyer.

He states "[a]s the many legal information web sites demonstrate, consumers of personal legal services, both those who are eligible for pro bono or otherwise free services as well as those who can afford to pay something for assistance, are very often looking for answers to very frequently asked questions. At present, the profession offers consumers two online choices—textual information (articles, FAQs, blank forms, instructions, checklists, etc.) and automated forms (DirectLaw, Law Help Interactive, etc.)—with or without the services of a lawyer. With expert systems, the profession can add a third online choice: personalized answers to legal questions based on the consumer's specific facts and circumstances. (Constraints and disclaimers are necessary of course.) Because expert systems can be, in fact, very smart, they can help consumers decide whether a problem is simple enough to handle themselves based on the systems' advice or instead needs live advice from a lawyer, i.e., needs the sort of experience-driven judgment across subtle facts that only human experts can provide. If the problem is indeed not simple enough, the system will route it to a lawyer, bundled with all the information gathered from the consumer by the systems' online interview, thus improving the quality and efficiency of the unbundled service provided by the lawyer."

Why should the unbundling lawyer care about the use of AI as it develops? Those law firms that are the first to harness the power of AI in the process of producing legal work will have a clear edge in the future. At this time, the expert system shells or programs that exist may not be especially user-friendly for the lawyer or for his or her client who may not have a technical background or who would prefer a user interface that is more in line with other current web-based applications. However, these interfaces are the icing on the cake, and it is the underlying systems that hold the great potential to streamline a large part of the legal process and to provide greater predictability in legal outcomes, which may result in faster settlements and provide the lawyer with strategic information that would benefit his or her client's case. For example, imagine a system that took all of the statutes for a state and its existing body of case law related to a specific legal matter. The computer is able to analyze the fact patterns provided to it to scan for similar situations, claims, and outcomes and then provide a statistical analysis that relates the most probable outcomes under multiple variables. A law firm that employs these tools would be able to offer coaching and strategy coupled with the use of the AI system as an unbundled legal service that is based on the outcome of the report, which may or may not result in the client hiring the law firm for full-service representation.

Ethics Concerns with the Use of Technology to Unbundle

Regardless of the chosen method of delivery, attorneys using technology to deliver unbundled legal services must comply with Model Rule 1.6(a), which requires that the attorney use reasonable care to ensure that the client's information is protected.[37] There is some dispute within the legal profession as to what level of security a law firm should be required to use when it comes to the use of technology to communicate with clients. Some attorneys argue that e-mail should be the standard because most state ethics opinions specifically permit unencrypted e-mail as a safe way to communicate with clients.

Today, however, most practitioners are well aware that there are more secure methods of digital communication that include encryption. Data privacy laws exist in Nevada and Massachusetts that require encryption in the collection of personal data.[38] Considering the confidential nature of the attorney/client relationship, one might predict that in the near future this higher standard of security also will be a requirement of legal professionals.[39]

Some states have issued ethics opinions regarding third-party hosting of law office data, the use of virtual law offices, and cloud computing in practice management.[40] A law firm considering delivering unbundled

---

[37]*See* comments for ABA MODEL RULE 1.6, Confidentiality of Information, *available at* **http://www .americanbar.org/groups/professional_responsibility/publications/model_rules_of_professional _conduct/rule_1_6_confidentiality_of_information/comment_on_rule_1_6.html** (accessed Dec. 12, 2011).

[38]*See* GEN. L. OF MASS., Ch. 93A, Regulation of Business Practices for Consumers' Protection, *available at* **http://www.mass.gov/legis/laws/mgl/gl-93a-toc.htm** (accessed Dec. 30, 2010); and NEV. REV. STAT. Ch. 603A–Security of Personal Information (2009), *available at* **http://search.leg.state .nv.us/isysquery/irl5021/1/doc** (accessed Dec. 30, 2010).

[39]For example, *see* the ABA Standing Comm. on Ethics and Prof. Resp. ethics opinion, Formal Op. 11-459, Duty to Protect the Confidentiality of E-mail Communications with One's Client (Aug. 4, 2011), *available at* **http://www.americanbar.org/content/dam/aba/administrative/professional_ responsibility/aba_formal_opinion_11_459.authcheckdam.pdf** (last accessed Nov. 14, 2011). This opinion states that the lawyer should warn clients about using workplace unencrypted e-mail to communicate or any time there is a risk that a third party might access and view those confidential communications.

[40]*See, e.g.,* Pa. Ethics Op. No. 2010-060, January 2011; Cal. State Bar, FEO 2010-179 (December 2010), *available at* **http://ethics.calbar.ca.gov/LinkClick.aspx?fileticket=wmqECiHp7h4%3D& tabid=837** (last accessed Nov. 3, 2011); Fla. State Bar Op. 00-4, Fla. Ethics Op. 00-4, 2000 WL 1505453 (July 15, 2000); N.C. State Bar 2005 Formal Ethics Op. 10, Virtual Law Practice and Unbundled Legal Services, 2006 WL 980309 (Jan. 20, 2006); N.Y. State Bar Ass'n Comm. on Prof'l Ethics Op. 709 (Sept. 16, 1998), Use of Internet to Advertise and to Conduct Law Practice Focusing on Trademarks; Use of Internet E-Mail; Use of Trade Names, 1998 WL 957924 (Sept. 16, 1998); Wash. State Bar Informal Op. 1916 (issued 2000); and Pa. State Bar Formal Ethics Op. 2010-200 (issued 2010).

legal services online should refer to these opinions for guidance. This book cannot go into all the issues related to the use of cloud-based technology in law practice but urges the reader to conduct due diligence in researching any technology product and vendor and to use reasonable care before entrusting any part of the unbundling process to a technology or technology provider.[41]

Case Study
Darryl Mountain

Darryl Mountain is a Canadian lawyer based in Sydney, Australia, with an interest in disruptive innovations in law. Mountain is a member of the eLawyering Task Force of the American Bar Association, which examines and responds to the ways in which the practice of law is changing in the Internet age. He has written a number of popular journal articles on legal technology topics, including "Disrupting Conventional Law Firm Business Models Using Document Assembly," **International Journal of Law and Information Technology** *(Summer 2007) 15 (2): 170–91. He works on projects involving legal document assembly and virtual law practice.*

1. How would you advise lawyers to respond to critics of unbundling or accusations from other professionals that their unbundling work is "commoditizing" the practice of law?

"Commoditizing" the practice of law is a narrow way of looking at it. Steve Jobs was seen not as a commodity producer but rather as a creator of premium products. Very few people talk about how digital cameras and iPhones have commoditized photography. The conversation has shifted from whether the colors are right on the developed photos to how easily the photos can be shared over the Internet. Similarly, I think that unbundling will lead to a shift in the conversations that take place when people judge the provision of certain legal services.

2. What role do you think document assembly and automation will take in the legal profession in the future?

I think the best solutions will be those that combine people and software, whether the people are lawyers, paralegals, or outsourced personnel. There are limits to what document assembly and automation can achieve, at least at their current state of development. Computers are

---

[41]*In general, see* Nicole Black, Cloud Computing for Lawyers, ABA/LPM 2011, and Stephanie Kimbro, Virtual Law Practice: How to Deliver Legal Services Online, ABA/LPM 2010.

good at logical intricacy and people are good at exercising judgment and interpreting difficult fact situations. For example, a software-generated questionnaire with built-in checklists doesn't forget to ask questions such as "Do you have a marriage agreement?" On the other hand, it takes a lawyer asking open-ended questions to discover that the testator will, in fact, be moving permanently outside the jurisdiction next month.

3. When the IBM computer, Watson, played "Jeopardy," some thought leaders in the legal profession suggested that our current document-assembly and automation systems might one day be coupled with other forms of artificial intelligence to provide greater "diagnosis" of legal matters for lawyers to use with clients. How do you see the current technologies we have evolving to use AI or game theory to assist lawyers?

Artificial intelligence may allow generalist legal practitioners to disrupt specialists. One of Clayton Christensen's famous examples is how cardiologists doing angioplasty are slowly disrupting heart surgeons doing cardiac bypass surgery. It took 11 years for angioplasty to overtake bypass surgery in terms of number of procedures. The gulf between the number of angioplasties and the number of bypass surgeries performed continues to widen, and heart surgeons are becoming increasingly marginalized. In the United States as of 2004, they were back to doing the same number of coronary bypasses as they had been doing in the mid-1980s. This example may be a prototype for legal disruption of the future: Perhaps one day a tax lawyer or tax accountant will be disrupted by a less qualified expert working with a suite of online legal knowledge products.

The UK-based Road Traffic Representation site discussed earlier in this chapter allows the client to electronically brief a barrister and bypass solicitors. This is an example of having AI provide the diagnosis and moving straight to the remedy. It is the inverse of the cardiologist example in that it is technology + specialist replacing the less specialized person rather than technology + less specialized person replacing the specialist.

How to Develop a Web-based Application for the DIY Client

Most lawyers are not equipped with the programming and developer skills necessary to create web-based applications for their own websites. If your law firm does not have the in-house talent to take your ideas for a web application and run with them, then you might consider outsourcing this task to a developer who will agree to stay within your fixed budget. Elance is a website that allows you to post your proposed project and estimated budget to a tailored group of skilled programmers and developers.[42] Developers who obtain work from the site have acquired positive reviews and ratings and there are several processes in place to protect both you and the developer from fraud or theft. Another option might be to hire the services of a consulting firm, such as Neota Logic, which will use its own customized application to generate the tool that you need for your law firm based on your practice area and needs.[43]

Remember this simple tip when looking for a developer: A web developer may understand what you want him or her to create, but he or she may not be skilled in design. Without clean design and usability of the application, there will be little benefit for the self-help client. Make sure to emphasize usability and user interface with any prospective developer.

If a lawyer or firm is interested in learning how to develop its own iPad or iPhone legal application, Stanford University has published its iPad and iPhone Application Development course for free on Apple's iTunes U.[44] For an example of a lawyer who has developed his own web-based application, see the case study for the Kelly Law Firm in the Appendix. Kelly has developed a Smartphone app for use by his clients, which may be downloaded from iTunes.[45] This application allows his clients to make online payments for legal services, obtain access to case files, and task management features.

There are significant security risks to delivering any legal services—whether unbundled or full scope—to clients online. The use of mobile devices and applications poses even greater risks because of the lack of education by many lawyers and their clients regarding best practices for securing data online and protecting the confidentiality of the law office data. When considering developing a web-based legal application, make sure the developer understands these concerns and the need for encryption if the application will be inviting your clients or prospective unbundling clients to transmit any confidential information over the Internet through the use of a mobile device.

---

[42]Elance website at **www.elance.com** (last accessed Nov. 2, 2011).

[43]Neota Logic at **http://www.neotalogic.com/author** (last accessed Nov. 2, 2011).

[44]*See* the free course for download at **http://itunes.apple.com/itunes-u/ipad-iphone-application-development/id473757255** (last accessed Nov. 15, 2011).

[45]*See* the Kelly Law Firm app at **http://itunes.apple.com/us/app/kelly-law-app-internet-affiliate/id447613097?mt=8** (last accessed Nov. 12, 2011).

Conclusion

The technology and methods of delivery discussed in this chapter will never exclusively replace the need for lawyers who unbundle their services. The goal of the legal profession should be to identify the ways in which these tools may be used to the benefit of legal practices while really questioning which processes in legal product depend on lawyers alone to complete. Computers may be better at parsing through data, and collecting and filtering information with minimum error. They can be a great form of quality control. But lawyers are superior at analytical and creative thinking. After reevaluating the roles of lawyer and machine and delegating responsibilities accordingly, we can more effectively apply innovative systems and technology into our practices for more efficient, ethical, and, hopefully, more error-free unbundling of legal services. Providing prospective clients with a web-based tool to assist them in the DIY process and to provide unbundled services directly to the client serves to differentiate your law firm's services from those of a traditional law firm.

CHAPTER EIGHT

Marketing Unbundled Services

IT IS PLEASANT TO think that the majority of lawyers would be inspired to provide unbundled services with the primary goal of increasing access to justice. However, the latent and untapped market for unbundled legal services and its potential financial gain is the true driving force behind the increasing growth of unbundled offerings. Consumers are driving this trend by actively seeking out legal services from alternative delivery methods. They will continue to do so, requiring the legal profession to address this market need. Before law firms will add unbundled services, they will closely analyze the return on investment—whether they intend to cultivate a separate limited-scope client base that is online or in person or if they intend to offer unbundled services as part of a broader marketing strategy to entice prospective clients to learn more about the firm and hope to convert those limited-scope clients into full-service clients.

To derive a profit from offering unbundling legal services, a law firm must generate a larger number of prospective clients or leads who are interested in these services. Given the current and growing competition for unbundled services online, the conversion rate for these leads is going to be relatively small. Rather than focusing on a smaller number of legal projects for clients that might result in typical billable hours or a larger collection at the end of the matter, offering unbundled services often means the firm needs to focus on generating a larger number of legal matters for clients that will result in smaller returns. The marketing necessary to generate this larger number of prospective legal matters is going to differ from traditional legal marketing. Lead generation and strong brand building are two critical components for law firms to understand and develop before investing in adding unbundled legal services.

In this chapter, we will examine the changing legal marketplace from the perspectives of the consumer, legal service companies, and lawyers. Then we will look at several marketing strategies that work well with unbundling both online and offline and provide suggestions for a return-on-investment (ROI) analysis and implementation.

What Does the Marketplace for Unbundled Legal Services Look Like?

There is a renewed interest in unbundling because of changes in the over-all market for legal services. The public is actively going online to seek out legal services for convenience and affordability.[1] Because many of these individuals are unable to find a licensed attorney who can provide online legal services, these members of the public turn to online legal services companies, such as LegalZoom, to provide limited-scope legal services. However, online methods of delivering legal services are not the only option readily available to the public anymore. There are a number of alternative legal service providers in the marketplace. There are also non-lawyers who unbundle services for the self-help individual. These include civil law notaries, legal document assistants, and immigration assistants.[2]

While online methods continue to grow at a fantastic rate, a number of self-help legal books, guides, and software programs continue to appear in book and office-supply stores.[3] As discussed in Chapter Six, a number of states have online self-service centers to provide unbundled services for limited practice areas. All these factors combine to create a legal market-place for the consumers that no longer limits them to retaining a tradi-tional attorney to meet their legal needs. As Jordan Furlong, partner with

---

[1]"Limited-scope is a consumer-driven movement, as middle-class litigants are increasingly insisting on retaining control of their legal matter and looking for a coach rather than a full-service advocate. They may well type 'unbundled attorney' into their search engine." M. SUE TALIA (2005), ROADMAP FOR IMPLEMENTING A SUCCESSFUL UNBUNDLING PROGRAM, published online at **http://www.ajs.org/prose/South%20Central%20Notebook%20Contents/Tab%206/Roadmap% 20for%20Implementing.pdf** (accessed Jan. 5, 2010).

[2]*See* page 29 of the American Bar Foundation's *Access Across America: First Report of the Civil Justice Infrastructure Mapping Project* (Oct. 7, 2011), authored by Rebecca L. Sandefur and Aaron C. Smyth, *available at* **http://www.americanbarfoundation.org/uploads/cms/documents/access_across_ america_first_report_of_the_civil_justice_infrastructure_mapping_project.pdf** (last accessed Nov. 3, 2011).

[3]For example, *see* LegalZoom, Nolo (acquired in May 2011 by Internet Brands, **http://www.internet brands.com/**), LegacyWriter at **http://www.legacywriter.com/**, CompleteCase at **http://www .completecase.com/**, SmartLegalForms at **http://www.smartlegalforms.com/**.

Edge International and a senior consultant with Stem Legal, explains, "ALSPs [alternative legal service providers] are regulated by the state, which still allows the profession to govern itself but no longer permits it to govern the legal services marketplace as a whole."[4]

Most online legal services are delivered to the consumer as legal forms that are automatically generated after the customer has registered with a service and filled out the appropriate questions in an online form that then generates the requested legal document along with instructions for the next steps. The customer pays a fixed fee that is most likely far less costly than the time and money he or she would have spent going to a traditional law office to meet with an attorney in person. The number of consumers going online to search for DIY or unbundled legal solutions continues to soar.[5] The need for unbundled legal services provided by licensed attorneys becomes clear when you add this increase in the demand for online legal services to the continued overall growth of e-commerce.

But are these the clients you really want? Can you afford to be selective in this marketplace? Who are these consumers seeking legal services through alternative methods? Critics of unbundling will sometimes argue that the only consumers seeking these services are individuals of lower to moderate means or individuals who do not qualify for legal-aid services but who cannot afford to pay an attorney and are merely looking for free legal assistance. This may be the case for a portion of this market, but more significant numbers in this untapped market are made up of the middle class. *The Wall Street Journal* interviewed Laurence Tribe, former head of the U.S. Justice Department's Access to Justice Initiative, who acknowledged that "[t]he problem is growing for the middle class."[6] Multiple reports have found that the majority of Americans know that they need some form of estate planning but almost half of them do not have

---

[4]Jordan Furlong, *Metamorphosis: Five Forces Transforming the Legal Services Marketplace*, LAW PRACTICE Magazine, Jan./Feb. 2010 Issue, Vol. 36, No. 1, p. 44, *available at* **http://www.americanbar .org/publications/law_practice_home/law_practice_archive/lpm_magazine_articles_v36_is1_ pg44.html** (last accessed Oct. 2, 2011). *See* Furlong's blog for further writings on the changing legal landscape: "Law21: Dispatches from a Legal Profession on the Brink."

[5]For example, in July 2011—one month alone—an estimated 434,000 people in the U.S. searched online for legal solutions through the Legal Zoom website. *See* Quantcast audience statistics related to websites providing online legal services. The number of duplicate people searching is not quantified. **http://www.quantcast.com** (accessed Oct. 2, 2011).

[6]Nathan Koppel, *More Strapped Litigants Skip Lawyers in Court*, WALL ST. J. (July 22, 2010), *available at* **http://online.wsj.com/article/SB10001424052748704229004575371341507943822.html** (last accessed October 2, 2011).

anything in place.[7] This is evidence of the untapped market for legal services in the estate-planning practice area alone. Family-law firms also have reported an increasing number of middle-class couples holding off on divorces because of economic factors or attempting to handle no-contest divorces without legal guidance and assistance to cut costs.

These individuals are making legal purchasing decisions based on a number of factors, and these are not always cost-driven. Affordability is important to them, but equally so is being given a variety of payment options and the ability to budget for these expenses, such as through fixed fees or payment plans. Convenience is also a factor for them as more middle-class families have two working spouses and limited hours during the business workweek to handle legal services in a traditional manner.

Distrust is another factor that sends these prospective clients away from traditional, full-service law firms. This sentiment has only increased since the recession and, combined with the potential intimidation factor of meeting with an attorney if they have never had any interaction with the legal profession before, may be enough to turn prospective middle-class clients to a less intimidating and more convenient self-help option or encourage them to put off their legal needs.

With unbundling, law firms can provide both the affordability and convenience that is needed by this middle-class market while being able to cost-effectively develop an unbundled client base and generate additional revenue for the firm. The law firms that can create this balance within their existing practice-management structures are the ones that will have an advantage in the legal marketplace and greater access to this latent market for legal services.

The Effect of ABS on Unbundling in Australia, England, and Wales

American law firms have been closely watching the changes that have occurred in Australia, England, and Wales over the past five years. In the UK, the enactment of the Legal Services Act of 2007, which as of October of 2011 has gone more fully into effect, has the potential to revolutionize

---

[7] A national survey commissioned on behalf of EZLaw[TM], an online legal document creation service by LexisNexis®, reported that the majority of Americans (60%) believe that adults should have a last will and testament or other form of estate planning. However, only 44% reported currently having these in place. From the 2011 EZLaw[TM] Wills & Estate Planning survey reported online July 19, 2011, at **http://www.lexisnexis.com/community/ideas/blogs/product_corner/archive/ 2011/07/20/ezlaw-survey-finds-most-americans-recognize-the-importance-of-a-will-or- estate-planning-yet-few-have-necessary-documents-in-place.aspx** (last accessed Oct. 2, 2011).

the way consumers in that country receive legal services.[8] A significant part of that expected delivery is in the form of limited-scope representation. Part of the act allows for alternative business structures (ABSs), which means that nonlawyers will be able to invest in and assist in the operation of law firms. Australia also allows for a form of ABS called "Incorporated Legal Practices," which allows for the creation of publicly traded law firms and multidisciplinary law firms.[9] In both countries, these changes are driving competition for legal services providers and legal professionals.

As a result, the public's access to affordable, unbundled legal services has increased as more options become available to them. The Legal Services Consumer Panel's Consumer Impact 2011 Report provides an overview of the impact on the consumer to the changes since the UK Legal Services Act of 2007.[10] The ABA Commission on Ethics 20/20 has closely studied the creation of ABSs in these countries as the Commission considers how similar changes would affect the American legal profession and access to justice in our country.[11]

What Do the Law Firms Think the Marketplace Looks Like?

Even law firms are acknowledging that unbundled services will continue to grow. An Altman Weil Flash Survey conducted in April and May of 2011 polled managing partners and chairs at 805 U.S. law firms with 50 or more lawyers and received surveys from 240 firms, which included 38 per-

---

[8]*See* the Legal Services Act 2007 at the Solicitors Regulation Authority website, **http://www.sra.org.uk/lsa** (last accessed Oct. 21, 2011). *See also* the Legal Services (Scotland) Act passed on October 6, 2010, by the Scottish Parliament, which allows for ABSs and was created largely in response to expected changes from the UK Legal Services Act, at **http://www.scotland.gov.uk/Publications/2011/02/09105855/0** (last accessed Oct. 21, 2011).

[9]For additional information on this topic, *see* the Legal Profession Act 2004, *available at* **http://www.austlii.edu.au/au/legis/nsw/consol_act/lpa2004179/**, and Legal Profession Regulation 2005, *available at* **http://www.austlii.edu.au/au/legis/nsw/consol_reg/lpr2005270/**.

[10]*See* report at **http://www.legalservicesconsumerpanel.org.uk/publications/research_and_reports/documents/ConsumerPanel_ConsumerImpactReport_2011.pdf** (last accessed on Oct. 21, 2011).

[11]*See* ABA Commission on Ethics 20/20 Working Group on Alternative Business Structures Issues Paper Concerning Alternative Business Structures, issued April 5, 2011, *available at* **http://www.americanbar.org/content/dam/aba/administrative/ethics_2020/abs_issues_paper.authcheckdam.pdf** (last accessed Oct. 21, 2011). *See also* Discussion Paper on Law Practice Structures, issued Dec. 2, 2011, *available at* **http://www.americanbar.org/groups/professional_responsibility/aba_commission_on_ethics_20_20.html**.

cent of the country's largest law firms.[12] More than 80 percent of the respondents answered affirmatively that "more commoditized legal work" would be a "permanent trend going forward." Almost 70 percent responded that they thought "competition from nontraditional (including nonlawyer) services providers" would be a permanent trend in years to come. Respondents to the survey found other trends in the marketplace to be permanent, including an increase in price competition (89.6 percent), more commoditized legal work (81.3 percent), more nonhourly billing (74.9 percent), and a focus on improving the firm's efficiency in practice management (93.5 percent). The growth of all these trends supports the incorporation of unbundled legal services into the structure of the law firm.

Law firms will need to get over the stigma that limited-scope representation may have for more traditional practitioners. In interviewing attorneys for this book, some of them would become defensive when the author pointed out that they were already offering limited-scope services along with their traditional offerings. They would protest that they did not offer unbundled services, but full services all the time, interpreting "limited" or "unbundled" to mean "incompetent" or "not what the client needs." Or they wanted to reassure me that their clientele was not made up of a "certain class of client," but that they command a somehow "better," paying client base. This form of misunderstanding about unbundling and the perceived bias toward the practice as a lower form of legal service delivery is detrimental to the public interest and to law firms that hope to evolve and keep pace with the new legal marketplace.

In fact, larger, more established and perhaps traditional firms have offered unbundled legal services for years to their clients. Often this work is handled as an on-the-side amenity that may or may not be billed on the client's regular invoice. Or if the client is a corporate entity, this work may be provided to in-house counsel for the internal legal department to do. See the sidebar on the *Qualcomm* case involving unbundling of legal services by outside counsel for in-house counsel. Offering limited-scope assistance does not doom a law firm to increased collections problems and a clientele unwilling to pay. It does, however, require that the firm and its attorneys take a close internal look at the services offered and identify areas of growth for unbundling that fit in with the firm's existing marketing strategy and target client base. Based on the statistics from the Altman

---

[12]The Altman Weil Law Firms in Transition Survey 2011, Altman Weil, Inc. (May 2011). Full survey online: **www.altmanweil.com/LFiT2011** (last accessed Oct. 2, 2011).

Weil Flash Survey, many firms acknowledge these changes in the legal marketplace and are making moves in their management structure to adapt. However, these statistics were from larger law firms. It may take more time for smaller and medium-size firms to not only change their approach to services delivery but also find ways to develop cost-effective means to do so as well as get over any perceived professional stigma about unbundling.

Unbundling for In-house Counsel—The *Qualcomm* Case

Lawyers may have the opportunity to unbundle their services for in-house counsel that need to outsource part of a legal project that cannot be completed by its own available resources. For example, a lawyer who specializes in handled matters that the in-house counsel is not familiar with may be asked to conduct research, provide an opinion, or draft a legal document. A lawyer also might be asked to unbundle discovery work or help take on some of the caseload from in-house counsel on a temporary basis by unbundling the needed tasks. This form of unbundling should operate no differently than when the client is a layperson in terms of the lawyer making the determination of whether to handle the matter and obtaining an agreement for the limited scope of work. However, when lawyers are working together, it may be tempting for them to assume that because both parties are lawyers, there is a clear understanding of the services that are expected to be unbundled. Strong communication and a written record of the limited-scope representation is key in these cases.

The *Qualcomm* case is a good example of an unbundling project for in-house counsel that did not end up being handled as both parties expected.[13] *Qualcomm* was a case in which the lawyers were sanctioned for "massive discovery failure," which the judge found to be a result of the lack of communication between in-house counsel and the lawyers retained to conduct unbundled legal services to assist in the discovery process for the case. The responding lawyers in the case were not sanctioned, but the court explained the reason for the breakdown as a result of mismanaged unbundling of the project, citing "a lack of agreement amongst the participants regarding responsibility for document collection and production." The in-house counsel that relied on the unbundling of legal services from outside counsel also failed to supervise those tasks

---

[13]Qualcomm, Inc. v. Broadcom Corp., 05-CV-1968-B, S.D. Cal., 2010 WL 1336937 (S.D. Cal. Apr. 2, 2010).

that were outsourced and failed to establish a clear scope of the services that were supposed to be handled by outside counsel. The court stated: "The fundamental problem in this case was an incredible breakdown in communication. The lack of meaningful communication permeated all of the relationships (among Qualcomm employees [including between Qualcomm engineers and in-house legal staff], between Qualcomm employees and outside legal counsel, and amongst outside counsel) and contributed to all of the other failures. The court was not presented with any evidence establishing that either in-house lawyers or outside counsel met in person with the appropriate Qualcomm engineers . . . at the beginning of the case to explain the legal issues and discuss appropriate document collection. . . . Finally, no attorney took supervisory responsibility for verifying that the necessary discovery had been conducted . . . and that the resulting discovery supported the important legal arguments, claims, and defenses being presented to the court."

Would a clearly defined limited retainer agreement between the unbundling law firm and the in-house counsel have prevented this miscommunication? Regardless of the existence of an agreement, best practices for unbundling, even when the customer is more sophisticated as is in the case of providing unbundled services for in-house counsel, the use of checklists and clearly defined responsibilities and checks at each stage in the process of unbundling are critical to avoid problems such as those that arose in the *Qualcomm* case.

DIY Will Writing in the UK

The Legal Services Consumer Panel of the Legal Services Board in the United Kingdom conducted a study comparing the quality of wills written by solicitors and those written by nonlawyers.[14] The Legal Services Board is the body responsible for deregulation of the legal profession in the UK. This is significant because in the UK anyone may open shop and provide unbundled will writing to members of the public. The report notes that "banks, independent financial advisors, charities, trade unions, will-writing companies and providers of paper and online self-

---

[14]*Regulating Will Writing, Report of the Legal Services Consumer Panel of the Legal Services Board,* July 2011, *available at* **http://www.legalservicesconsumerpanel.org.uk/publications/research_and_reports/documents/ConsumerPanel_WillwritingReport_Final.pdf** (last accessed Oct. 8, 2011).

completion wills have made significant inroads into the market" and, in fact, created around one-third of the wills produced in the past year.[15] The report notes that "[u]sage of will packs or online services has also risen significantly. This is likely to reflect new online services offered by major retailers working outside of legal services regulation."[16] For example, a company named LawPack is the leading provider of DIY will kits in the UK, but also provides landlord/tenant, family law, personal injury, business, and other DIY services online.[17]

The panel's report found that the poor quality of wills being drafted for citizens indicated that standards for will writing need to be sharply improved and the sales practices for these services also need to be more strictly regulated. Consumers were found to have a low awareness or understanding of the fact that will writing was not regulated and that a solicitor was not required to review the document before the consumer purchased it.[18] As with many online legal services options in the United States, online providers in the UK of online wills are able to use technology to filter out the clients who have complex estate-planning needs and provide disclaimers that the online service is not appropriate for their needs. However, beyond this disclaimer, it is up to the consumer, who does not have a legal education, to determine whether or not he or she needs more complex legal services from a licensed professional or whether the online DIY service will suffice. The panel's report found that consumers recognize that "you get what you pay for," but recommended that regulation of these services should be kept under review and initiatives for educating the public at large should be developed.[19] Arguably, that the same educational initiative would benefit the American public.

The panel concluded that will writing should be made a reserved legal services activity to protect the consumer, meaning that any business, not just a solicitor's firm, would be able to provide this service only after satisfying a regulator's entry standards.[20] Arguments against this regulation on providing unbundled will writing are similar to those arguments that are

---

[15]*Id.* at § 1.1.

[16]*Id.* at § 3.7.

[17]LawPack, **http://www.lawpack.co.uk/** (last accessed Oct. 8, 2011).

[18]*Id.* at § 3.31. The report found that "while most solicitors offered a clear and transparent service, will-writing companies were less reliable" (report at § 5.9).

[19]*Id.* at §§ 4.44 and 4.47.

[20]*Id.* at § 1.23. The Legal Services Act has a list of "reserved" legal services, which means that only those services authorized by an approved regulator designated by the Legal Services Board may provide those services to the public.

heard in the United States regarding the restriction of LegalZoom or other online legal services companies from providing direct-to-consumer legal services: It would not be in the consumer interest and might place a chill on innovation in legal service delivery, which would limit choice and access to justice.[21] However, one in four wills written in the UK under this study were found ineffective.[22]

Why is this relevant to limited-scope representation in the United States? Our legal marketplace is expanding with the number of companies offering unlicensed, unbundled legal services directly to consumers. While at this time we have a higher level of regulation of these services than exists in the UK, questions about the deregulation of the legal profession have come to the center of attention recently and part of this debate centers around the quality and effectiveness that unregulated legal services providers would add to the market. The results of the panel report in the UK could be a telling indicator of what would occur here in the states if unbundled legal services were deregulated.

What Do the Alternative Legal Service Providers Think This Marketplace Looks Like?

With more consumers turning to the Internet to conduct many different transactions, including professional services such as banking and investing, the legal services companies see a growing opportunity in this marketplace. Alternative legal service providers are not restricted by the same rules and regulations of licensed lawyers. Their biggest obstacle is avoiding claims of unauthorized practice of law (UPL) from a state bar. However, with the ABA and many state bars unable to clearly define the "practice of law," it is difficult for claims of UPL to stick. Multiple companies have sprung up to meet the need for unbundled services in the legal marketplace and are true disruptors to the way that consumers shop for and purchase legal services. Some of these companies include LegalZoom, AVVO, TotalAttorneys, Rocket Lawyer, MyLawyer, Law Pivot, JustAnswer, LawBidding, Nolo (acquired by Internet Brands after 40 years in the legal services industry),[23] and AttorneyFee.com.

---

[21] *Id.* at § 2.12.

[22] *Id.* at § 4.12.

[23] *See* press release about Internet Brands' acquisition of Nolo, May 2, 2011, **http://static.ibsrv.net/ ibsite/pdf/2011_5_2_Internet%20Brands%20Acquires%20Nolo%20the%20Definitive%20Online %20Source%20for%20Consumer%20Legal%20Information.pdf** (last accessed Oct. 8, 2011).

Disruption of the marketplace comes with a price. LegalZoom has perhaps undergone the most trials with claims of UPL from Missouri,[24] Alabama,[25] North Carolina, and Washington.[26] The settlement in Washington bars LegalZoom from making comparisons between the costs of its online documents with the fees of a law firm unless LegalZoom first discloses that its service is not a substitute for obtaining legal assistance from a licensed attorney.[27] On August 2, 2011, a federal district judge for the Western District of Missouri published an opinion denying, in part, Defendant's Motion of Summary Judgment in the class-action suit. The court held that document preparation by nonlawyers was conduct not entitled to First Amendment protection.[28] However, later in the month a settlement was reached in the Missouri class action allowing LegalZoom to continue to provide services in that state as long as it makes certain modifications to its business, which were not disclosed to the public.[29]

In September of 2011, LegalZoom filed suit against the North Carolina State Bar, asking it to declare that the company is authorized to sell its

[24]LegalZoom was sued in the 19th Judicial Circuit Court in Cole County, Missouri, for engaging in UPL on December 18, 2009. *See* "LegalZoom Sued in Class Action for Unauthorized Law Practice " on IP Watchdog Blog, Feb. 9, 2010, at **http://ipwatchdog.com/2010/02/09/legalzoom-sued-in-class-action-for-unauthorized-law-practice/id=8816/** (last accessed Oct. 8, 2011).
[25]On June 10, 2011, the DeKalb County Bar Association filed a lawsuit asking a judge to prohibit LegalZoom from doing business in the state, claiming that the company is involved in the unauthorized practice of law. *See Alabama Bar Group Files Suit to Ban LegalZoom*, A.B.A. J., July 15, 2011, *available at* **http://www.abajournal.com/news/article/alabama_lawyer_group_files_suit_to_ban_legalzoom/** (last accessed Oct. 8, 2011).
[26]In September 2010, LegalZoom entered into a settlement with the state of Washington, *available at* **http://www.atg.wa.gov/uploadedFiles/Home/News/Press_Releases/2010/LegalZoom AOD.pdf** (last accessed Oct. 8, 2011). Under the settlement, LegalZoom may provide only an online form service for consumers to "choose and complete legal documents on their own" and found that just selling legal forms to the consumer online does not constitute the practice of law. *See* the Washington State Office of the Attorney General's press release, Washington Attorney General zooms in on LegalZoom's claims, Sept. 16, 2010, *available at* **http://www.atg.wa.gov/pressrelease.aspx?id=26466** (last accessed Oct. 8, 2011).
[27]*See* press release from the Washington State Office of the Attorney General, *available at* **http://www.atg.wa.gov/uploadedFiles/Home/News/Press_Releases/2010/LegalZoomAOD.pdf** (last accessed Oct. 8, 2011).
[28]Janson v. LegalZoom.com, Inc., USDC W.D. Mo. Central Div., case no. 2:10-CV-04018-NKL, filed August 2, 2011. An online copy may be found at **http://www.directlaw.com/courts-order-in-LegalZoom.pdf** (last accessed Oct. 8, 2011). *See also* a law review article by Professor Catherine J. Lanctot, *Does LegalZoom Have First Amendment Rights: Some Thoughts About Freedom of Speech and the Unauthorized Practice of Law*, TEMPLE POLITICAL & CIVIL RIGHTS L. REV., Villanova Law/Public Policy Research Paper No. 2011-07, June 30, 2011.
[29]*See LegalZoom Can Continue to Offer Documents in Missouri Under Proposed Settlement*, A.B.A. J., Aug. 23, 2011, *available at* **http://www.abajournal.com/news/article/legalzoom_can_continue_to_offer_documents_in_missouri_under_proposed_settle/** (last accessed Oct. 8, 2011).

online services in the state.[30] Several years prior, a series of inquiries by the state bar had brought up the issue of whether the company was engaged in unauthorized practice of law in North Carolina. In March of 2003, the bar's Authorized Practice of Law Committee had opened its first inquiry regarding LegalZoom's services and sent a letter notifying the company of its inquiry and concerns. After reviewing LegalZoom's response, the bar issued a letter stating that it found no evidence of UPL and it dismissed the claim. Then again in January of 2007, the Committee issued another letter, this time concerned about LegalZoom being named as an "incorporator of corporations" in some of its online North Carolina legal business forms. In 2008, the North Carolina Bar sent LegalZoom a cease-and-desist letter finding that its practices constituted UPL in North Carolina. LegalZoom responded to this cease-and-desist letter but never received a return response. The September 2011 lawsuit brought by LegalZoom seeks to require the North Carolina Bar to allow the company to register its prepaid legal services plan in North Carolina (which is separate from its DIY online legal document service) and to acknowledge that the company is in compliance with North Carolina state law. However, all the claims of UPL and lawsuits do not appear to have slowed the company down significantly, and the company may be in the process of preparing to go public.[31]

In part as a response to some of these legal issues as well as to adapt to the changing needs of the online consumer, LegalZoom has added a new service that provides attorney support on demand in the form of a prepaid legal services plan for a monthly fee.[32] The service includes attorney support for the creation of the legal documents as well as an annual "legal checkup" with the attorney, unlimited revisions of the document through the Legal-Zoom system, unlimited access to LegalZoom's other legal forms, and other discounts on its legal services. It is not evident how an attorney is selected or assigned to the DIY client who chooses this option, but the fact that this has been integrated into the company's unbundled options shows an effort to collaborate with licensed professionals to avoid UPL claims in additional states and to provide a higher level of legal assistance as an option.

The struggles of an online service company such as LegalZoom may continue to generate a fair amount of press in the legal profession. However, the general DIY consumer seeking legal services does not seem to be

---

[30]LegalZoom.com, Inc. v. N.C. State Bar, Wake County Super. Ct., 11-CVS-015111, Sept. 30, 2011, *available at* **http://online.wsj.com/public/resources/documents/LegalZoom.pdf** (last accessed October 8, 2011).

[31]*See* Matthew Lynley, *Source: LegalZoom in early stages of preparing to go public*, VENTURE BEAT, Feb. 28, 2011, *available at* **http://venturebeat.com/2011/02/28/legalzoom-ipo-preparations/**.

[32]*See LegalZoom Advantage Plus Option for Last Will and Testament*, at **http://www.legalzoom.com/legal-wills/wills-pricing.html#lap** (last accessed Oct. 20, 2011).

deterred. Debates continue to spring up among attorneys who feel threatened by the existence of companies such as LegalZoom and who strive to find ways to distinguish their unbundled legal services from those of the online legal services companies. No technology can fully replace the personalized analysis and attention to a client's legal needs and the relationship and trust formed—whether online or in person—between an attorney and his or her clients. The issue is whether the consumer is educated to know the difference in the quality of assistance, not just whether the legal documents are legally enforceable and accurate in a generic sense, but whether the necessary guidance and customization to individual needs will be met.

While there is certainly a need for more accessible and affordable basic legal services, the question is whether consumers are able to determine which services they need and to know that there are other alternative options that would provide more customized services that are provided by a licensed attorney. Virtual law offices are one method of obtaining this higher quality of attention, but other traditional firms integrating limited-scope representation offerings into their practice also may provide more affordable DIY legal services that rival those of online legal service companies. Unfortunately, no individual law firm or practitioner will be able to rival the million-dollar advertising budgets of companies such as LegalZoom, which would be necessary to educate the public about these other options.

Regulation of online legal services companies might push consumers to discover DIY services from licensed legal professionals in their own state, but until the legal profession more widely embraces unbundled services and online delivery methods, such regulation would significantly decrease access to certain basic legal services for many.

One solution to this dilemma may be found in collaboration between online legal services companies and legal professionals: the branded network concept.

Working with the Legal Services Companies— The Branded Network Concept

The branded network concept combines an online marketing strategy for attorneys interested in tapping into the market of DIY clients with the power of a large company's advertising budget. There are several variations of the model, but, in general, lawyers are able to register online to be part of a directory of attorneys who provide legal assistance to consumers who have completed and purchased legal forms from the company website. Consumers may directly take the legal forms and do the rest of the footwork themselves or they may select from the directory of attorneys in their jurisdiction to receive additional assistance with the forms and to purchase additional legal services. These services might be over the telephone, in person, online, or a combination of methods. The work might be limited in scope or extend the DIY services from the company to a full-scope representation with the licensed attorney.

Several of these companies have sprung up over the past couple of years, the most notable being Rocket Lawyer, which does have an online meeting space for consumers who have selected an attorney to handle additional work with them. Rocket Lawyer partnered with LexisNexis, and in August of 2011, Google Ventures invested $18.5 million in the company.[33] Google Ventures stepping into the legal services industry both with investments in Rocket Lawyer and in LawPivot, a legal crowd-sourcing website, has raised speculation about what the injection of capital into Rocket Lawyer would mean to the services it offers both directly to consumers and to attorneys. Some of this investment undoubtedly will go to increase advertising for the service targeted directly to consumers, many of whom are primarily aware of the LegalZoom model and no other alternatives. Rocket Lawyer also appears to be focusing on growing its network of licensed attorneys who may choose between a free listing or a monthly fee for additional online services and greater access to consumers looking for limited-scope representation online.

Case Study
Charley Moore

Charley Moore is the founder and Chairman of Rocket Lawyer Inc., http://www.rocketlawyer.com. As an expert in corporate partner development, Moore has advised both early-stage companies, large enterprises, and their investors on strategic partnering strategy. Rocket Lawyer corporate partners include LexisNexis, H&R Block, TransUnion, Avanquest Software, and many other leading companies. Moore has been at the forefront of Internet corporate development since beginning his career as an attorney at Venture Law Group in Menlo Park, California, in 1996. Rocket Lawyer was founded in August of 2008 to make legal services easy and affordable for everyone. With Rocket Lawyer, users create customized legal documents that can be downloaded and

[33]Google Ventures, **http://www.googleventures.com/portfolio.html** (last accessed October 8, 2011).

shared instantly. Legal plan members have access to free document reviews from local attorneys and receive discounted rates on legal services for more complicated legal needs. Lawyers can access online marketing tools and targeted client referrals.

1. How do the services your company offers to attorneys facilitate the unbundling of legal services?

Legal fees should be transparent and predictable. So, we help lawyers streamline their practices and pass the benefits on to clients. Specifically, we provide lawyers and consumers alike with unlimited access to document-assembly tools and a cloud-based collaboration platform. By better enabling everyone to work online, we make it easier for lawyers to integrate unbundled services into their practices. Rocket Lawyer provides easy-to-understand legal documents that can be shared, e-signed, and edited (by consumers and attorneys alike). Many attorneys also participate in our Rocket Lawyer On Call™ program at no cost to them. In this program, lawyers receive requests from clients for free consultations and document reviews, as well as other flat rate or hourly legal services. Lawyers get access to a steady stream of new clients that can turn into long-term or repeat clients, which is great for attorneys who are looking to break into the "unbundled" business model.

2. How would you recommend that attorneys follow up or monitor the progress of unbundled clients after termination of the limited-scope representation?

As we all know, many transactions never get "tested." For those that do, it's a very stressful time for a lawyer because documents can be sitting out there like time bombs. Did I miss something? Did a law change? And so on. Lawyers generally are stretched enough with their existing clients, let alone with the additional expectation that they follow up with former clients. Yet, there are steps they can take to ensure some follow-up.

We recommend lawyers become more active in the legal community, both online and offline, to protect the interests of their existing and former clients. Lawyers can do this quite simply by doing something they already do all the time—write and speak. When a new law arises that may affect clients who you have written agreements for, such as a change in landlord-tenant law for a lease you wrote, you could write a newsletter about it and send it to your clients. By educating your community on these evolving aspects of the law, you are both following up with your clients as well as performing great business development.

Those clients who originally sought a limited engagement earlier will be more likely to come back to you.

3. Have you noticed an increase in the number of attorneys who provide unbundling tools such as web advisors, web calculators, legal forms, or other resources that allow the public to obtain free, unbundled services?

Yes. Thousands of legal documents are generated everyday by lawyers and/or consumers using Rocket Lawyer. In fact, we see more and more lawyers using Rocket Lawyer to complete new documents or repeat a document they've already completed for a client. We believe that technology makes the practice of law more efficient, which, in turn, makes it more affordable for clients to access legal services and more profitable for lawyers to deliver legal services. This works because it connects clients who may have completed legal documents (e.g., last wills) on their own, with a lawyer who is ready to review it for them, and educate the client on the benefits of a more complete estate plan. The clients make informed decisions on their legal lives without a big commitment up front, and the lawyers get the chance to develop relationships with new clients.

4. What do you think is the importance of document-assembly and automation services or other cloud-based technologies to the attorney who is adding unbundled services to his or her offerings?

It's of paramount importance. Technology makes the practice of law more efficient and allows lawyers to do more, and faster. Before word processors, lawyers would spend hours rewriting or typing essentially the same document with customized changes for each deal and client. Once the word processor came along, we could all do this with a find-and-replace tool. While that was marginally more efficient, mistakes still could be made and the essential questions could be missed. With Rocket Lawyer's assembly tools and automation process, the lawyer does not just cut and paste a new name into a form. Rather, the lawyer responds to specific questions generated, which then creates a document that is ready to be reviewed and further customized if necessary.

The last and most important step for a nonlawyer creating a document is that he or she needs to get the document reviewed by an attorney. That is why Rocket Lawyer provides the user with instant access to the document, and allows the user to share it with an attorney for review. The client can share it with any attorney or use an attorney from Rocket Lawyer On Call.

5. How would you advise attorneys to respond to critics of unbundling or accusations from other professionals that their unbundling work is "commoditizing" the practice of law?

Unbundling is a natural evolution of the market in response to innovation. Clients are telling the legal profession that there are aspects of legal representation that they're ready to pay for and those that they're not—some lawyers will meet this need, and the clients, in the end, will decide who they want to do business with. By providing services in the way that clients want to receive them, lawyers are, in fact, evolving to meet new market opportunities.

6. Thinking ahead, what role do you think unbundling will take in the legal profession in the future?

Lacking a crystal ball, the data we have shows pretty clearly that clients want the tools to enable them to do more legal work themselves and to engage with lawyers collaboratively as needed. So, as this trend continues, it is only reasonable to expect that the end result will be more lawyers practicing unbundling to meet the growing opportunity. Unbundling services will help lawyers break away from the billable hour and develop more favorable pricing structures for themselves and clients. This will include the rise in flat rate services for discrete pieces of a matter. As a result, these unbundled services will be more predictable in the amount of effort they involve for the attorney, and the risk in offering a flat rate price will be greatly alleviated.

7. Do you have any best practices or suggestions for attorneys wishing to minimize the risk of malpractice when unbundling services?

There are several steps you can take to minimize the risk of malpractice:

- Be familiar with the rules in your jurisdiction.
- Do a background check on the provider.
- Obtain recommendations from colleagues and do not be afraid to reach out to your local bar association to get these recommendations and find out what attorneys in your area are doing.
- Join networking groups where you can consistently share best practices.
- Talk with colleagues to get the most up-to-date information. Do not be afraid to share and others will be more likely to share with you.

MyLawyer.com is another site that markets directly to the consumer to provide free legal forms and then allows the consumers to choose from a directory of attorneys in their jurisdiction with virtual law offices.[34] Consumers register to receive a "MyLegalAffairs" account and select the legal forms that they need.[35] After completing the form online, the consumer may save the document online and proceed pro se or click on the Virtual Law Firm Network to contact an attorney in his or her jurisdiction to provide additional, unbundled legal assistance, or just online legal advice. Attorneys subscribed to this service may choose from a free listing or if they are subscribers to the DirectLaw virtual law office platform, they have a more complete directory listing as well as an online platform for working with the client securely online.

Legal question-and-answer (Q&A) sites are another form of a branded network concept that focuses on providing legal advice to clients online rather than legal documents. These companies work the same way in terms of marketing their benefits directly to the consumer while also subscribing attorneys to the service to provide content for the site. Oftentimes, an attorney will join up with nonlaw-related Q&A sites to provide legal guidance, such as Quora or JustAnswers.com. The risks to the public of receiving incorrect or harmful legal assistance are greater on these sites because there may be no verification process to assure the consumer that the individual providing the questions is an actual licensed lawyer in good standing in his or her jurisdiction. Sites that cater to attorneys often have a profile for that attorney that will provide bar membership and other professional information to allow the consumer to judge the qualifications of the attorney answering the consumer's question. Sometimes there is a rating system added to the website in which the attorney is ranked by the quantity and quality of the questions answered. One of the first legal Q&A websites was LawGuru.com. Since then, several more have appeared, including LawQA, LawPivot, and Just Answer.

One concern with joining these sites may be that the attorney spends his or her time providing answers online, which the service retains in threads almost like general forums that are accessible to the public at any time. The attorney in essence is generating content for the website of another business and raising the SEO of that branded network's website with his or her answers rather than placing that valuable content on the attor-

---

[34]MyLawyer.com, **http://www.mylawyer.com/** (last accessed Oct. 8, 2011).
[35]MyLawyer.com, "How it works," **http://www.mylawyer.com/howitworks.asp** (last accessed Oct. 8, 2011).

ney's own law firm website. While the branded networks such as Rocket Lawyer and MyLawyer.com send leads directly to the attorney, who will then provide additional limited legal services through a platform that is connected with the company's brand, the Legal Q&A sites make much of the legal guidance from the attorneys visible on the website, which many consumers may deem to be enough legal assistance to go with the free legal forms they found online and may not continue through to the attorney's individual website.

Before investing a significant amount of time writing responses to questions in these forums, the attorney may want to find out the percentage of direct leads generated per answered question. Additionally, if an attorney creates a profile on these sites and then decides not to answer questions or is absent for a given amount of time, his or her profile may continue to exist on the site with a low "ranking" for the number of questions answered or a title that may reflect poorly on the attorney to any prospective clients. The ability to delete a profile from the Q&A site is another factor to research before joining any such service. Many state bars also have ethics opinions discussing how attorneys licensed in their state should behave when using these sites. Before engaging in any form of branded network concept, it is advisable to check your state bar's rules and regulations regarding online advertising and marketing.

Proponents of legal Q&A services argue that these online archives of legal information provide the public with valuable legal education and guidance for free, which increases access to justice. However, critics note that many consumers are likely to follow the advice of an attorney who is not licensed in their jurisdiction or who does not practice in that specific practice area where the consumer needs assistance and may be proceeding pro se without correct guidance. No matter how many disclaimers the attorney on a legal Q&A site may provide with his or her profile and below his or her answer regarding the advice only being related to a specific state's laws and not tailored to an individual's unique circumstances, the consumer may still choose to follow that guidance to his or her detriment. As with many of these online marketing methods, legal professionals using them must find a balance between their responsibilities to serve the public with their need to provide adequate access to justice. Ethics issues may arise from the use of legal Q&A sites, such as the inadvertent formation of the lawyer-client relationship, the risk of breach of confidentiality, and limitation of the lawyer's ability to control the direction and nature of the online communication. Minimizing these risks must be carefully weighed against the benefit of the service as a form of online marketing.

The significant benefit of a branded network is that rather than an individual attorney having to spend a sizable fortune on his or her own online marketing and advertising to reach this consumer market, the branded network has the funds available to pool resources from all members into the creation of a single, recognizable brand that can more easily saturate the market than a single firm's advertising campaign. LegalZoom has done this for their company. Rocket Lawyer and others seek to do this for their brand while potentially benefiting their members at the same time. Currently, for an attorney offering unbundled legal services online, it is necessary to invest a significant amount of money and time to build a brand and to create an online presence for that brand that will bump it up to the top of a search engine's organic search when the consumer goes online seeking DIY legal services in a particular jurisdiction.[36] The branded network concept may charge attorneys to be part of that directory, and they are then lumped in with other attorneys in their jurisdiction on that site, but such a service does provide a more clear-cut road to obtaining leads who may be more inclined to be converted into paying clients if they have already purchased or received free basic legal forms on that site from that brand.

As more attorneys open virtual law offices as a way to deliver legal services online, the competition will increase for each practice to distinguish itself and its unbundled services to the consumers in a particular jurisdiction. This will make it even more expensive and time-consuming for those practitioners to maintain the SEO for their websites and to create online brands that will effectively reach the consumers. Collaborating with branded network concepts, at least as a significant part of an unbundling marketing strategy, may become more important in the near future.

Some ethical questions surround the branded network concept, the most obvious being the duty to prospective clients regarding whether the system acquires informed consent from the prospective clients to the unbundled representation or uses some form of limited-scope agreement, as well as technology questions regarding the security of the platforms provided to the attorneys to work with the clients online. Lawyers engaging in a branded network service should pay close attention to the formation of the lawyer-client relationship in the online process of joining the net-

---

[36] An "organic" search result is a result that is produced by an online search engine when certain keywords are entered and is based on the search engine's unique algorithms that compile online data rather than based on SEO rankings that the law firm paid for, such as sponsored sites with higher and highlighted placement, AdWords, etc.

work. Lawyers also should be aware of the restrictions of Model Rule 7.2(b) regarding payment of "anything of value" to a person for recommending the lawyer's service. There is also the question of how much access the company might have to the privileged communication between the client and the attorney after the legal forms purchased by the client are transferred to the chosen attorney in the network. These issues are not that different than those that would be brought up for any cloud-based third-party service to which an attorney chose to subscribe. Close attention to the terms of the service-level agreement regarding confidentiality and access is critical. Attorneys subscribing to a branded network service, whether a free or paid version, should understand the transfer of information from the attorney and the client to the third-party provider and any hosting service where that sensitive data is being housed. For additional guidance before selecting to work with any cloud-based service provider, I recommend reading Nicole Black's book, *Cloud Computing for Lawyers,* published by the ABA LPM Section, 2011, or see the International Legal Technology Standards (ILTSO) for guidance.

The Franchised Law Firm

Another marketing model for unbundled services may be on the horizon in the form of franchised law firms. This is a concept that may be taking off soon in the United Kingdom with the announcement in the fall of 2011 of a new venture entitled "Simplify the Law," in which a company called Evident Legal is attempting to create a national network of law firms in the UK.[37] The company has already identified more than 400 firms that will fit the criteria to join their franchise. The company's website promises to "aggregate marketing spend to build the financial muscle that independent firms need to compete."[38]

Before this new entry into the legal marketplace, a company called QualitySolicitors had developed a similar branded model of selected law firms across the country.[39] In the spring of 2011, it announced a deal

---

[37]Evident Legal website, at **http://www.evident-legal.com/** (last accessed Oct. 20, 2011). *See also* "Exclusive: 'Simplify the Law' enters the fray in latest bid to build national legal network" on Legal Futures blog, Oct. 12, 2011, at **http://www.legalfutures.co.uk/legal-services-act/market-monitor/exclusive-simplify-the-law-enters-the-fray-in-latest-bid-to-build-national-network** (last accessed Oct. 20, 2011).

[38]Evident Legal website, at **http://www.evident-legal.com/** (last accessed Oct. 20, 2011).

[39]*See* QualitySolicitors, at **http://www.qualitysolicitors.com/about.html** (last accessed Oct. 20, 2011).

with the large UK bookstore chain WHSmith to place legal self-help kiosks in bookstores across the country. Employees of the company staff the kiosks and use iPads to book in-person appointments with the firm's members as well as provide basic unbundled legal services, such as estate-planning packages or other transactional legal work and fixed-fee consulting sessions, in addition to providing free legal education guides and firm advertising in the bookstores.[40] In October of 2011, QualitySolicitors announced that it had secured private equity investment for the purpose of expanding its brand across the country.[41] In December of 2011, Instant Law UK, another UK-based legal services company, announced the launch of a videoconferencing kiosk in a shopping center that provides access to a solicitor for a fixed fee.[42] The public may access the same videoconferencing service from home over the Internet. The company plans to develop a network of 120 kiosks in shopping centers in the UK by the end of 2012. Other UK franchise models include face2face solicitors, HighStreetLawyer.com, The Legal Alliance, and LawNet.[43]

A franchised marketing model along with unbundling tools and legal forms that carry the franchise's branding could focus efforts on marketing to the DIY client seeking legal services and effectively compete with the online legal services companies while allowing licensed legal professionals to profit. One difficulty in replicating this model in the states is the legal profession's reluctance to accept alternative business structures (ABSs), which are now allowed in the UK under the Legal Services Act (see the sidebar at the beginning of this chapter). For example, face2face solicitors in the UK is a national franchise for solicitors in England and Wales operated by Professional Business Structures Ltd., a company that has a record of creating businesses both in the legal and other professions.[44] The Cooperative Legal Services, a company owned by the Cooperative, a company in the UK that provides banking, travel, and food services through its stores, is planning to add legal services to its bank branches in

---

[40]*See QualitySolicitors in WHSmith tie-up*, Law Society Gazette, April 7, 2011, *available at* **http://www .lawgazette.co.uk/news/qualitysolicitors-whsmith-tie** (last accessed Oct. 20, 2011).

[41]*QualitySolicitors sets sights on UK domination with private equity injection*, The Lawyer, Oct. 20, 2011, *available at* **http://www.thelawyer.com/1009880.article** (last accessed Oct. 20, 2011).

[42]*See* "Video-conferencing kiosks hit shopping centres in new legal advice push", December 5, 2011, LegalFutures blog at **http://www.legalfutures.co.uk/legal-services-act/market-monitor/ exclusive-video-conferencing-kiosks-hit-shopping-centres-in-new-legal-advice-push** (last accessed December 12, 2011).

[43]face2face solicitors website, **http://www.face2facesolicitors.net/about-us.php**; The Legal Alliance, at **http://www.thelegalalliance.co.uk/**; HighStreetLawyer.com, at **http://www.high streetlawyer.com/**; and LawNet, at **http://www.lawnet.co.uk/** (all last accessed on Oct. 20, 2011).

[44]face2face solicitors website, **http://www.face2facesolicitors.net/about-us.php** (last accessed Oct. 20, 2011).

the near future.[45] The District of Columbia is one of the few jurisdictions in the United States that allows its members to form nonlawyer ownerships in law firms as long as the ownership control remains in the hands of a licensed attorney.[46] Without the same permission from other state bars, it would be difficult for a franchised law firm model on the scale of QualitySolicitors to take off in the United States. However, a fully lawyer-owned franchise is the model that will develop here first.

The benefit of a law firm franchise is similar to that of the branded network; it is far easier to focus online marketing on a single brand and model that already is successful and has an established reputation. Some virtual law firms are considering branching into multiple jurisdictions and creating online "branch" offices that will carry the primary virtual firm's name and logo on their websites but will contribute their marketing efforts and resources to building on that brand within their own state and directing clients to their branches' unbundled and full-service offerings. In addition to each firm's website, the clients who go online and find the main firm's website will be able to select the unbundled services from a list on the website and then select which jurisdiction or branch they will use to complete that unbundled service.

Another franchising concept is more along the traditional lines of business franchising in which a successful firm franchises its brand to other separate law firms that want to replicate the model and who pay a fee for the benefit of the brand recognition, use of the firm's unbundled legal forms, web tools, and other content for use on their own websites.[47] An example is SmartWill.com, a network of estate-planning attorneys with exclusive territories, each of which has its own website, but all are tied into a nationwide consumer-oriented portal that generates leads for the firms in each of their territories. This model would be in a better position to compete with the branded network companies for certain unbundled legal work because of the pooling of online marketing and advertising resources put into the single franchised brand. This structure also avoids many of the ethics issues, such as claims of UPL, that the online legal services companies face.

---

[45]*See* The Co-operative legal services website, at **http://www.co-operative.coop/legalservices/** (last accessed on Oct. 20, 2011).

[46]*See* Dist. of Columbia R. of Prof'l Conduct 5.4, *available at* **http://www.dcbar.org/for_lawyers/ ethics/legal_ethics/rules_of_professional_conduct/former_rules/rule_five/rule05_04.cfm** (last accessed on Oct. 21, 2011).

[47]*See, e.g.,* SmarterWill.com, powered by DirectLaw at **http://www.smarterwill.com/** (last accessed Oct. 20, 2011).

Building Your Own Brand for Unbundled Services

Regardless of whether or not an attorney chooses to engage in a branded network concept or franchised law firm model, building a brand for unbundled legal services is important for attracting prospective DIY clients and for generating revenue when adding unbundled services to a full-service practice. For attorneys unbundling legal services online and when it is the core of a client base, building a brand is even more necessary for success. What does building a brand mean? It means being able to clearly define to prospective clients what makes your unbundled services unique from those of any other attorney and from any other online legal services company offering unbundled services.

As discussed previously, a large market for unbundled legal services comes from individuals who are going online to search for these DIY options. Many of those individuals may prefer to meet with an attorney at a local law office, while others are specifically looking for the convenience and presumed affordability of an online option where they do not need an appointment at a law firm. In both cases, the law firm providing unbundled services must create a strong brand for its practice that the consumer can easily find when searching online. This means that the firm must understand the way that search engine optimization (SEO) and landing page optimization (LPO) work to generate leads to the law firm's website where the consumer may learn more about the unbundled services offered. Not only does the law firm need to be found by these consumers seeking DIY services, its needs to be found by the customers seeking the specific practice area and specific unbundled work that the law firm provides.

For this to work, the firm must create a clear focus and brand for its practice. When energy and funds are invested in promoting this carefully crafted brand, it can be used at its maximum potential to pull in prospective DIY clients. For example, in California, attorney Jeff Hughes created Legal Grind as a way to unbundle legal guidance to clients over a cup of coffee.[48] Prospective clients are able to meet with an attorney at the coffeehouse to discuss their legal issues in a fixed time period for a fixed fee. He provides an explanation of unbundled legal services on the website as well as a sample limited-scope engagement agreement. Sample prices for legal document preparation and the ability to handle the client intake

---

[48]**http://www.legalgrind.com/**. Jeff Hughes was a keynote speaker at the 2000 Unbundled law conference in Baltimore, Maryland.

and preparation work online are also shown as part of the unbundled package. Prospective clients are urged to meet with an attorney first to discuss their legal needs before ordering legal document preparation. Appealing to the coffee culture and the more relaxed atmosphere of a coffeehouse, Legal Grind has developed a unique identity that makes it easier for that practice to build and expand its reach as an online brand.

Niche or bespoke practices have a unique ability to succeed in creating a brand because they are not competing with the large numbers of options in a jurisdiction that provides basic unbundled services, such as no-contest divorces or business setups. Self-help clients with legal needs related to a unique business or personal interest will recognize the importance of retaining a lawyer who has experience in that unique area of law. Some examples of this might include equestrian law, animal-rights law, wine and hospitality law, video-game law, or dental law. For example, an attorney in Michigan, Jason A. Waechter, defines himself as the motorcycle lawyer and not only represents bikers, but is an avid biker himself.[49] He appeals to his clients on a personal level and is able to use this to build an online presence for himself.

Designing an unbundling practice that is too diverse in its offerings, such as a general practice firm, will be more difficult to market because of the way that online advertising works. See the following section for an explanation of SEO and LPO and advice from Hubspot, an online marketing service. The attorneys at the firm need to answer the question of why a prospective client should choose them over another attorney. For example, the firm's partners have had X number of years of experience as plaintiff's attorneys and this would give them an edge in representing defendants on the same issue, or an attorney owned his or her own small business before going to law school and can bring that experience to other small business clients. Other attorneys or firms will focus on the individual reputation of one of their attorneys and his or her online personality.

What Are SEO and LPO?

What is SEO? Search engine optimization is an Internet marketing strategy that involves driving and increasing traffic to a website from different search engines using techniques that are not paid for directly but are embedded in the source code of the website or blog.

---

[49]Jason A. Waechter, **http://www.themotorcyclelawyer.com/** (last accessed Oct. 10, 2011).

What is LPO? Like SEO, landing page optimization, sometimes called "lead conversion," is an Internet marketing strategy, but this technique involves the conversion of visitors to a website into paying customers. LPO focuses on conversion optimization of the website by focusing the content of the landing pages (the website page where a visitor has clicked a link in an online advertisement or a blog post and ended up landing) based on where the visitor is coming from.

Case Study
Brian Whalley

Brian Whalley is SEO Manager for HubSpot, Inc., http://www.hubspot .com/. The company offers an all-in-one marketing software platform that has helped more than 5,000 companies in 34 countries increase the number of visitors to their websites and convert more of those visitors to leads and customers, including through marketing automation software.

1. What services or support should a law firm expect from an online marketing service such as HubSpot?

A firm should closely examine exactly which services and software it is being offered. Some providers offer only services (such as an agency), some offer software and services, and some offer only software (such as HubSpot). For example, we sell marketing software and training on how to use the software, but it remains a "do-it-yourself" model for the professionals who purchase the software. As a result, our costs are much lower than hiring an agency to do the work, but you still need to dedicate your own (or your staff's) time to your marketing projects. Before you purchase any software or services, examine your options and decide what the best fit is for you. If you have money but not time, an agency may be a better fit for you—like a gym membership, software doesn't help you get your marketing in shape if you don't use it regularly!

2. Why is it important for attorneys to understand SEO and LPO as components of a marketing campaign?

Depending on the focus of your firm, different elements of SEO and LPO will be crucial for your business. One of the most important considerations is to remember that most attorneys have a very localized practice, and generally focus on only a few topics as well. When someone has a specific need for your business around a keyword, they will be typing a keyword phrase "employment lawyer in Massachusetts." What attorney would not want to rank #1 for a phrase like that, when someone is seeking counsel? That is why search engine optimization is so critical—you want to rank for the general description of what you do. Once that person has clicked through to your website and wants to learn more, LPO takes over. Landing page optimization is about making sure that people who visit your site get what they are looking for and are able to give you their information or contact you effectively. Hoping that this person will call you after he or she visits your site is not enough; let the person give you his or her name and phone number through your site, and you can reach out to him or her. This way, you have a chance to track how the person found you, and you don't need to hope that he or she is good at switching between media (from the computer to the phone) to reach out to you.

3. If a law firm is new to online marketing, would you recommend DIY SEO maintenance?

A lot of SEO is just common sense and public best practices. There are no secret tricks or tools in search engine optimization. It comes down to execution and expertise. The issue is really about time commitment. SEO can be very time-consuming, so if you are a busy professional, the do-it-yourself method may not make sense. A number of prominent organizations in the Internet marketing industry have provided great guides on "How to hire an SEO and not get scammed," which provide everything from a bullet list of what to look for to questions to ask them (and what the right answer is) so that you can evaluate services providers well.

4. What are some methods that attorneys can use to create organic SEO and why is this important?

The best overall method for doing this is to create useful content and share it freely online. The more people reference your work online, link to you, or use you as a resource of information, the better your SEO efforts will be rewarded. All those references and mentions are very valuable to your website, and search engines love to see those. Many law firms already produce this type of content internally but then do not share it widely, such as "Client Alerts" to warn retainer clients of changing laws or rules that impact their businesses. You also could produce content on the state of the type of law that you practice or common misunderstandings that people have about the law. Once you've started regularly producing this content, network with the other law blogs that are in your field or region. If you aren't aware of any, try some common searches and see if you can find some. For example, Googling for "Connecticut law blog" or "Employment law blog" could help return nearby blogs on related topics and provide great professional networking opportunities. Introduce yourself and tell them about your blog content. You don't need to even ask them for anything. In general, just letting them know you exist and being on their radar is more than enough so that they know who you are. A great example of a law blog doing this well is the employment and labor law blog of Hirsch Roberts & Weinstein in Boston.

5. In terms of SEO and as part of an online marketing effort, what is the value and/or downfall of using a Q&A site for marketing?

This is a tough call, but I think in general it is best to participate where the conversation is already happening. If there already is a collection of people in one place having a conversation on the topic, then you will do the best at building visibility there than on your own. However, it's not really clear to me that there is a lot of direct SEO value to participating on these sites, for you aren't generating links back to your website or to content on your website. There is definitely marketing value. You are proving your expertise, networking with people who have questions, building a brand online around your name, and many other positive things. But that brand and expertise exists only on their sites, not yours. I generally recommend using these sites to build your marketing presence, but if you find particularly interesting questions or topics, answer them briefly on that site and then more fully on your own website with the details and interest. This way, you can use these Q&A sites to help you come up with ideas, content, and material and get the best of both worlds.

6. How can monitoring a law firm's online presence benefit its marketing strategy? What would you recommend a law firm use to accomplish this?

The most straightforward way to go about monitoring your web presence is to pick the items that you are most interested in tracking and watch them specifically. I would pay particular attention to mentions on the web via Google Alerts of your firm's main personalities and names. Google Alerts are free and will cover most of what you will be interested in watching for, such as people who have directly mentioned you or your employees. You also can track your website traffic from different sources (such as search engines, referring websites, social media, etc.) with different marketing analytics packages like Google Analytics, HubSpot, or others, which is more about the effectiveness of your overall marketing strategy.

7. With online advertising, which is more effective: creating a niche market that is focused or showcasing a variety of different services a law firm could provide?

Would you rather buy your new Ford from a Ford dealer or a general car dealer? The Ford dealer clearly specializes in what you are looking for, will have more options and expertise, and will be better suited to help you. The same is true with Internet advertising. Pick your strengths and highlight them with evidence or examples. People, as a rule, never search for general terms. When seeking a law firm, a person has a particular need and is seeking an answer to that particular need. If you have a few specialties, try creating a few different advertisements and allotting each one a portion of your budget. This is what most expert Internet marketers do. Instead of creating a few very general pages, they create a number of very specific and strong pages and then target them specifically to their audiences and advertisements. When someone has a particular need for employment representation or criminal defense, he or she will not want to dig into a firm or lawyer who professes to have broad expertise but doesn't show right away the particular strengths in the person's subject of interest.

8. The terms "lawyer" and "attorney" are used interchangeably in the legal profession. How should lawyers decide which keywords to use for online marketing and categorization in online profiles?

You should absolutely use the word "lawyer" when writing on your website. Your clients and potential clients very rarely think of the term "attorney." It's too formal and not what they search for. If you compare the relative search volume in some of the keyword search tools available, this is an easy comparison. For example, the volume of searches in Google last month for "employment lawyer" is more than double the volume available for "employment attorney." As a result, I'd recommend against optimizing for the word "attorney." The volume and potential audience is much lower. This difference is likely to decrease over time though, as search engines get better at matching semantically identical terms such as "lawyer" and "attorney."

9. Aside from the disclaimers and other bar rules regarding website design, what should be the key features of a lawyer's website?

Stay away from flashy animations or too much focus on design and make sure that the site can serve its critical functions well: Generate leads, help people find your information, and express your expertise on the core subjects that you represent people or groups on so that they know about your skills before they actually reach out to you. Provide staff biographies for all the firm's lawyers, and include nonattorney professionals who they might encounter when in your offices. On those biographies and pages, include elements that will help them seem human and three-dimensional, such as multiple photographs, professional citations, or events they've been involved in, and so on.

10. Some consumers may have a negative opinion of lawyers; what are some ways that attorneys can appear more "approachable" and less intimidating to prospective leads through their online marketing efforts?

Be up front and professional in your tone and message. Speak the language that your potential clients do. Definitely do include things on your website or presence that will make you more approachable and human in general. For example, use multiple photographs of yourself if possible on your biography page or other important pages, not just one headshot over and over. Don't be afraid to show a sense of humor or editorial voice when appropriate. The first rule of social media is always "be human."

11. If a law firm is just getting started with online marketing, what would be an estimate for the cost of a service such as Hubspot and then the average cost of a beginning marketing campaign with performance-based lead-generation methods?

If you are looking to get started with online marketing, good marketing software typically starts around $400 to $750 a month, and then include the additional costs of other things that you might want to do. For example, it will be cheaper but more time-consuming if you choose to produce your own content. If you'd prefer to hire a contract writer or expert to produce blog posts or other content, it will require much less of your time but involve a higher upfront cost. There are corners that can be cut to reduce the cost somewhat, but I do not recommend it for people who are getting started for the first time and do not have someone on staff or the background knowledge to make the best choices on saving money. For example, you can almost always host a company blog for "free" on your own server that already is hosting your website, but setting one up and optimizing it for search engines and more is not a trivial task and very time-consuming for people who are not experienced with it. Especially in a profession where hours spent on a task have a clear dollar value, it will almost always be dramatically cheaper to buy software or hire someone with experience to make these decisions for you.

12. Why is it important to run analytics on a law firm's online activity?

Analytics are a great way to watch if changes or actions that you're taking in your marketing presence are having an impact on the performance of your website. I would recommend that people establish a 10-minute plan on how to review their analytics once a week. For example, decide that you want to look at visits from search engines, leads generated from the website, and visits to each blog post you write. If those aren't good for you for some reason, choose whatever statistics are meaningful to your business. Once you have them, monitor them once a week. If you see something you don't like or that does not make sense, you can dig deeper and investigate more, but, in general, this will stop it from taking over your free time.

Checklist for Creating a Brand for Your Unbundled Legal Services

1. Narrow down the specific unbundled services the firm may provide.

2. Define who your client base is for these services.

3. Determine where these prospective clients would be going online to find you.

4. What keywords most succinctly define your unbundled offerings?

5. What is the image the firm wants evoked when its name is used online?

6. Do you plan on having a separate marketing strategy for the unbundled services your firm provides or will you integrate it into your existing business plan?

7. What funds do you plan to allocate to online marketing methods, such as lead generation, pay-per-click advertising, website development, SEO from an outside third party, analytics services to provide detailed reporting on the success of these methods, developing web calculators or other online unbundling tools, etc.?

8. What portion of your strategy will include the use of online social media applications?

9. What existing components of the firm's brand or reputation does the firm want to keep or build on along with showcasing the unbundled offerings?

10. Will the brand be built around the firm as a whole or around one or two individual personalities in the firm? Analyze how the brand will be conveyed in the chosen web-based applications and what the "voice" will be for the firm's online presence across the Internet.

Marketing Strategies for Unbundling

As discussed previously, there is a growing online market for unbundled services. However, even a firm that does not want to advertise its unbundled services online can benefit from adding the unbundling portion of its practice to the firm's marketing strategy. After you have identified a strong brand for your firm and decided how you will showcase your unbundled services as an amenity that you provide over law firms that only provide full-service services, you need to turn to the methods that will help you get that brand and message across to potential clients.

Traditional Advertising Methods

Traditional advertising methods are quickly falling to the wayside as more firms turn to online advertising to market their services to potential clients. However, there are methods to help the more traditional firm let its potential clients know that it offers unbundled services. Consider the following non-Internet-based methods:

1. Adding a sidebar to your firm's newsletter introducing unbundled packages, such as legal coaching sessions or basic legal documents, as new product offerings from the firm in addition to the full-service offerings. Adding fixed-fee prices or estimates for those services may make them more appealing to existing clients.

2. Educating office assistants and paralegals about how the unbundled services might be sold to clients as a la carte services that compliment their full-service legal matters. For example, when the paralegal meets with the client at the end of the process of completing the incorporation setup for the client's company, the

paralegal could mention that the client might consider that he or she may need to update his or her estate planning to include this new change in assets. The paralegal then could hand the client a small flyer with a list of the unbundled estate-planning services with fixed fees and explain the simplified process for the client so he or she understands that the client could handle this on his or her own after the firm sets up the basic documents without having to make numerous trips to the law office or pay the firm's full-service billable hour rates.

3. Have a section of the law office's waiting area be devoted to unbundled offerings. Set up a table with basic legal education on those services. For example, a family-law firm that provides full-service divorces may decide to put up a table educating clients about the difference between a full-service divorce and a DIY no-contest divorce. Clients who are there for an initial consultation may benefit from learning the differences in services, and it may help to weed out the clients that would be more appropriate for unbundled services than full service, given the needs of their cases and their financial concerns about paying for full-service representation. This might save time in the initial consultation with the attorney and result in a client who is willing to pay a smaller fee for unbundled services than one who leaves because he or she cannot afford the full-service fees.

4. Adding a list of unbundled services to a traditional print advertisement in a newspaper or magazine. List these options as a la carte services with fixed fees or advertise a payment plan for these services to show that the firm can be competitive on price and that the firm recognizes that transparency is important for the consumer who is shopping around for legal services.

5. Many attorneys have success with radio advertisements or short segments on local television shows showcasing their expertise. Make your firm the expert firm for unbundled services in your local practice area. Take out a short radio advertisement that showcases your unbundled services and mention that it was created with the DIY customer in mind. Offer to provide an interview for your local television's morning or evening show that features unbundled services provided by attorneys. Whether or not you focus solely on the unbundled options from your firm, you firm's name will be associated with meeting consumer demands for more affordable and convenient legal services and help establish your reputation as a firm that unbundles in addition to offering full service.

6. Engage in pro bono opportunities to unbundle services for your local legal-aid office or consider offering some of your unbundled services "low bono," depending on the client's financial needs. Some attorneys are hesitant to do this for fear that it will draw more potential clients to a firm who are seeking free legal assistance. However, if the firm is willing to create flexible payment plans based on the client's financial situation, the cost to provide these services will be minimal and the collections process spread out over several months rather than up front. The firm also may find this unbundling work to be personally rewarding for its members and that it helps build the firm's reputation as a responsible member of the local community.

Online Advertising Methods

Every law firm needs to have an online presence. At this point, it is futile to resist attempting to compete with other firms without having some website or other online presence for your firm. Whether you want your firm to be online or not, it already is. Go to any review or rating website and you can find a profile for firms and attorneys who have not claimed their profiles formally but who are listed in directories and even have reviews from former clients sitting on their unclaimed profiles. Failing to monitor and control your firm's online presence is simply a bad business practice and might lead to malpractice claims if situations arise where former clients or existing clients are attempting to communicate with you online through methods you began using for marketing or networking purposes but failed to regularly monitor.

For example, a client in the middle of a case attempts to "check in" to your firm on Foursquare.[50] The firm may not have claimed its profile, but the client is connecting to it, letting the world know when and with whom he or she is meeting to discuss confidential matters. Opposing counsel can easily go to your firm's listing, follow the client's profile, and see everywhere else the client has "checked in." Imagine the implications of this in certain domestic dispute cases. If your firm has claimed its profiles (which may already exist on certain online sites whether the firm has initiated the process or not) and monitors its online presence, it will have greater control in minimizing the risk that clients will post inappropriate information on those online networks. The firm will be able to either delete any comments posted by the client online or set the firm's security

---

[50]See Foursquare, **www.foursquare.com**.

and privacy settings on the profile so that clients and anyone else are not able to publicly or privately communicate through those online methods. Another key component to the online monitoring of the firm's reputation online is the firm's responsibility to educate and inform clients about posting sensitive information. Online monitoring not only allows the firm to protect the client but also allows it to promptly identify and address any negative reviews or comments about the firm that are made online and to protect the firm's reputation.

Aside from being a good business practice, online advertising provides a wealth of opportunity for the firm that wants to unbundle. Because many DIY clients are going online to seek out unbundled services, the firm offering these services needs to have a strong presence online to tap into that potential market and consumer need. The 2011 ABA Legal Technology Survey Report found that 88 percent of respondents reported their firms had websites.[51] However, of the content provided on those websites, only 20 percent provide "self-help legal information/guides" and only 3 percent provide "real-time communication tools," such as real-time chat, chat rooms, or Skype or Google Chat options. Consider the potential here to market the firm's unbundled legal services using these methods that will make it stand apart from the typical law firm website.

We previously discussed the importance of landing page optimization and making sure that when visitors land on your home page, they become engaged in the content that you provide. Adding "calls to action," such as buttons that prompt the visitor to click to try a free web calculator or click to fill out a free legal form, immediately engage the visiting client by offering an unbundled legal service online. After investing the time in using this online tool, the prospective client may be encouraged to retain the law firm for either full or limited-scope services.

Lee Rosen's firm, based in Raleigh, North Carolina, and at other virtual locations across the state, is a good example of a firm that uses these online unbundling tools to convert leads into paying clients.[52] The firm only advertises its unbundled services through the website and provides unbundled family-law advice and legal forms. The firm's unbundled service provides unlimited help-desk access to one of its attorneys as well as sample legal forms for different family-law situations along with video

---

[51]ABA Legal Technology Survey Report, Web and Communications Technology Survey, page viii.

[52]*See* Rosen Law Firm at **www.rosen.com**, and see the above interview with Lee Rosen, owner of Rosen Law Firm, about the unbundled portion of his practice. Lee Rosen was the winner of the 2010 ABA Keane Award for Excellence in eLawyering for his use of technology to deliver legal services to individuals of lower and moderate means.

lessons that guide the client through the process. When more extensive legal services are required, the attorneys at the firm advise the clients that unbundling is not appropriate in this case and give them the option to switch over to full-service representation. The firm also offers a money-back guarantee that may help to convince the more skeptical DIY client that the services are less of a risk. This satisfaction guarantee is also something that most legal services companies without attorney review of the work will offer to their online clients. To stay competitive with these services, attorneys might want to think about putting themselves on the same playing field. While most of Rosen Law Firm's clients are those who cannot afford the firm's "typical $7,000 minimum fee" for family-law services, the firm is able to tap into a larger potential online market for unbundled family-law services in the state of North Carolina.

Case Study
Lee Rosen

*Based in Raleigh, North Carolina, the Rosen Law Firm, **www.rosen.com**, provides North Carolina family-law services related to divorce, child custody, child support, property division, alimony and support, domestic violence, and mediation and collaborative law. Lee Rosen is the founder of the Rosen Law Firm and is a frequent speaker about divorce law and other topics related to law-practice management. His firm's website provides different forms of unbundled legal services to self-help individuals, including a regular recorded radio show, web calculators, and educational videos, along with written articles and links to additional legal education resources related to divorce. The firm also offers unbundled prepaid legal plans and a secure client portal for communicating and working with the firm's members. Lee is also the author of the popular Stay Happily Married (**http://stayhappilymarried.com/**) and Divorce Discourse (**http://divorcediscourse.com/**) blogs.*

1. How do you determine whether a case may be unbundled or needs full-service representation?

We take all comers, and if more extensive services are required, we advise the client as we go along and give the client the option to switch over to full-service representation.

2. What percentage of your unbundled clients are you able to convert to full-service clients?

We don't seek to convert clients to full service. Our online service generates far higher margins and we'd prefer that clients use the service and do the work themselves. We end up shifting about 10 percent of our clients to full service when circumstances become more than they can comfortably handle.

3. How do you follow up or monitor the progress of your unbundled clients after termination of the limited-scope representation?

We do not track a client after the conclusion of our representation except to conduct satisfaction surveys.

4. Do you offer fixed fees, alternative billing arrangements, payment plans, or billing methods other than the traditional billable hour?

On our unbundled site, we charge $199 per month. We offer fixed fees for our full-service representation. We don't offer payment plans, billing arrangements, etc.

5. How do you feel unbundling has affected your practice?

Very high margins in our model so it impacts our bottom line very favorably. The clients generally are very satisfied and we offer a money-back guarantee if they aren't. We are working with a class of clients that can't afford our typical $7,000 minimum fee.

6. How do you respond to critics of unbundling or accusations from other professionals that your work is "commoditizing" the practice of law?

The practice of law was commoditized long before we started this service. They're right.

7. What role do you think unbundling will take in the legal profession in the future?

It will assist in the elimination of lawyers in providing legal services to most middle- and upper-middle-class customers. Nonlawyers and technologists will take that business by providing better services.

Consider some of the following online marketing strategies for an unbundled practice:

1. Offer basic unbundled legal services for free or low cost on the website to increase SEO as well as engage prospective clients who may be converted at a later date into paying full-service or additional limited-scope services clients.

2. Think outside of the box and go beyond offering basic legal forms. Hire a programmer to create a web calculator, web adviser, or other online tool that you can provide to unbundled clients.

These can be based on forms or processes that your firm already may have created, just converted into a digital format for online use.

3. Integrate a secure client portal into your website for prospective clients to register for their own account pages to communicate with your firm about their legal needs.

4. List unbundled services with fixed fees or prices on the website with buttons linking each service to a video tutorial that walks the prospective client through the unbundled process for that service or links to a button to register on your virtual law office.

5. Provide an online checklist or comparison chart that helps the prospective client make a risk/benefit analysis between full-service representation and limited-scope for the service that it needs. This serves to both engage the client on your website, provides free educational content, and instills a level of trust for the firm because of its willingness to be transparent in the differences between the two types of services offered.

6. List unbundled services in the firm's online profiles. When a lawyer directory listing or free profile on a social media application has the option of listing services, include the firm's unbundled services separately with or without fixed-fee prices. Consider adding information about unbundled offerings to the firm's Facebook Fanpage or Google+ profile for businesses (when those become available). Add the list of services to the firm's Google Places account. These services will show up when prospective clients use Google to search for the firm's business and visit the profile. Be consistent with each of these listings and keep all prices and service offerings updated. Keeping a database of each place the firm has posted a profile listing the unbundled services makes it easier to go back and ensure consistency of the firm's content across the Internet.

7. Some online services, such as AttorneyFee.com, Shpoonkle, and LawBidding, may become more popular with consumers shopping for legal services based solely on price differences.[53] Adding your firm to these sites for the purpose of listing your price on unbundled offerings allows the firm to compete for online clients by comparing prices. One risk with this method is ensuring that

---

[53]AttorneyFee at **www.attorneyfee.com**, Shpoonkle at **http://www.shpoonkle.com/**, LawBidding from **ExpertBids.com**, at **www.expertbids.com** (all last accessed on Oct. 20, 2011).

when you list the firm's offerings and price point, that it is clear these are limited-scope representation services only so that the prospective client is not mislead into believing this is the cost for full-service representation when comparing it with other firm's full-service offerings.

8. Keep an eye on how firms may start using daily deal sites to advertise unbundled legal services. There are a lot of gray and untested areas in this form of online marketing, but there may be an opportunity to unbundle services as packaged DIY deals depending on the practice area and appropriateness. South Carolina Formal Ethics Opinion 11-05[54] and North Carolina 2011 Formal Ethics Opinion 10[55] both conclude that offering legal services through "deal-of-the-day" models such as Groupon and Living Social, are acceptable under certain circumstances.

9. Online advertising is a game where the rules change every few months. When Google decides to alter its algorithm for the search engine, which it does occasionally, then it may affect the use of AdWords and other pay-per-click (PPC) services as well as the SEO strategy for a firm's website.[56] Accordingly, keeping up with this game means staying on your toes or hiring a company that provides services that do this for you. If your entire practice is going to be unbundled services, then you will need higher online lead generation than a traditional firm that will be supported by both full-service client revenue as well the online stream of revenue. Consider using the services of a company that specializes in lead generation that will send target prospective clients to your firm's website.[57] This means that the visitors to your law firm website are "warm" leads—they have confirmed ahead of time that they are ready to purchase the legal services you have to offer by having first visited an "optimized landing page," a site with a form asking them to request their need for online legal services based in a specific practice area and jurisdiction. At the time of this writing,

---

[54]*See* S.C. Bar Ethics Adv. Op. 11-05, June 2011, *available at* **http://www.scbar.org/Member Resources/EthicsAdvisoryOpinions/OpinionView/ArticleId/1012/Ethics-Advisory-Opinion-11-05.aspx** (last accessed Oct. 20, 2011). *See* Groupon, at **www.groupon.com**, or Living Social, at **www.livingsocial.com** (last accessed Oct. 20, 2011).

[55]**http://www.ncbar.com/ethics/ethics.asp?page=1&from=10/2011&to=12/2011**.

[56]*See, e.g.*, Google AdWords, at **http://www.google.com/ads/adwords2/** (last accessed Oct. 20, 2011).

[57]*See, e.g.*, Total Attorneys' High Performance Marketing, **http://www.totalattorneys.com/services/high-performance-marketing/** (last accessed Oct. 20, 2011).

there are not any lead generation services for lawyers that focus on leads who are specifically seeking unbundled services or online DIY options. Most companies, such as Total Attorney's High Performance Marketing service for attorneys, will target a specific practice area, such as divorce matters or bankruptcy, but will not determine if the client is actively seeking limited-scope services. However, this more tailored customization of the leads to a law firm website may be on the horizon as these companies recognize the need for targeted lead direction to unbundling law firms.

Case Study
Kevin Chern

Kevin Chern is the President of Total Attorneys, www.totalattorneys .com. From 1997 to 2005, Chern served as managing partner of the country's largest consumer bankruptcy law firm. The firm, which began with only two attorneys, ultimately employed more than 180 people in 19 states and served approximately 450 new clients each week. As an attorney, Kevin has personally represented thousands of bankruptcy petitioners, which has helped to develop his insight into the administrative, marketing, and other support needs of busy attorneys. Total Attorneys is a cloud-based service provider dedicated to assisting small and solo law firm practice management, growth, and development. The company's services include lead generation services for law firms, a web-based practice-management system, LawQA, and a virtual receptionist service. The company's High Performance Marketing offers high-quality leads from consumers actively looking online for an attorney. HPM offers bankruptcy, DUI, personal injury, criminal defense, divorce, Social Security, and tax law leads. Attorneys can select only the law areas and ZIP codes they want to ensure high close rates and only pay for the leads received. This makes it easier to calculate and maximize the ROI.

1. Why is it important for attorneys to understand SEO and LPO as components of a marketing campaign?

Thousands of consumers are searching online every day to find an attorney. These searches are shifting from the yellow book and other offline sources, so it's important to have an online presence. But just having a website isn't likely to provide much benefit: there's a lot of competition out there making an effort to get in front of the same audience. Knowing what terms prospective clients are searching and how to get your pages to show up in those searches is the bridge to connecting with them.

Even that isn't enough, though. Whether a prospective client lands on the firm's website through an organic search or by clicking on a paid advertisement, the content on that page can be either the first step toward a new client relationship or the last thing the prospect sees about that firm before clicking back to look for other options. That means it's critical to have landing page content that's accessible, connects with the client, instills confidence and makes it easy and inviting for that prospect to take the next step.

As important is that their online presence is optimized to display a good first impression and drive new business. By using online marketing services like HPM and LawQA, attorneys can easily access the online market. This allows them to leave the marketing to the experts and do what they do best, practice law. Attorneys can capture the online market by using these services because they have national reach, so they're able to optimize all incoming traffic. With LawQA, an attorney's profile, with contact information, will be published on LawQA.com and on targeted websites in the attorney's area. With HPM, attorneys can leverage nationally recognized consumer sites, like TotalBankruptcy.com and have online prospects sent directly to them.

> **2.** With online advertising, which is more effective: creating a niche market that is focused or showcasing a variety of different services a law firm could provide?

Creating a niche market with online advertising can allow an attorney to monetize more of the traffic they receive, but it can cause them to lose out of valuable traffic from prospects searching more broadly. By leveraging a national service like HPM, attorneys can take advantage of a broader audience, but only receive volume that's targeted to their niche market.

That depends to a great degree on how specific the niche is. Often, when attorneys use the word "niche," they mean something like "divorce" or "criminal defense." Those aren't really niches, just law areas. Clearly, it makes more sense to target specific law areas. If you're focused on bankruptcy law, it's a waste of resources and of your receptionist's time to create a presence that draws in clients looking for wills and assistance incorporating non-profits and such. A true niche is much narrower: representation of floral businesses or contested interstate custody issues or some other slice of a particular law area. In determining whether to pursue the more general category (family law, for example) or the specific (interstate custody disputes), it's important to consider both your business and your prospective client base. First, do you want to limit your practice to that specific area of expertise, or is it just one thing you do well within the larger law area in which you practice? How much demand is there for your niche area, and how lucrative is it compared with your more general practice? And finally, how do your clients think about and talk about the services you render? It may be that clients don't differentiate between "custody" and "interstate custody disputes" and so will be looking for attorneys using broader terms. One simple but effective way to find out is to pay attention to the language prospects and new clients use when they make inquiries and during your initial meeting.

That said, it's important to note that you're not limited to one approach. If you're uncertain about how specific to get, put a section or blog relating to your more specific niche on your more general law firm website, optimizing different pages for general and specific terms. You can advertise on general and specific terms, too, and then track which pages, search terms and advertisements bring in the most lucrative business for your firm. The answer may be different for different firms, depending on location, competition, particular niche area and a variety of other factors. This is one of the key benefits of a large national marketing effort like HPM: we target hundreds or thousands of general and specific terms within each law area.

3. How should a law firm go about researching a pay-per-click advertising campaign—to know where to go and what to do without losing money experimenting to find the right keywords?

The main PPC advertising sites publish best practices and have tools to help drive targeted traffic, and that's always the best place to start. Your continued business is dependent on your success, so the reputable advertising sites want your campaigns to be effective. However, the idea that any business will create a successful PPC campaign without losing time and money experimenting is unrealistic. A firm needs to decide in advance how much time and money it's willing to invest in the learning curve and then budget that out. To be competitive on PPC sites, it can be expensive and may require significant resource. By leveraging a marketing service like HPM that has national coverage across numerous law areas, attorneys can take advantage of PPC traffic without the risk of losing money or wasting time.

In nearly ten years of placing PPC advertising for law firms, we have refined our process, but part of what we learned was that every time we undertake a new law area or a new niche, we'll have to experiment again and make a significant financial investment in optimizing our campaigns. We've also learned that these campaigns require constant monitoring and tweaking; your most effective and cost-effective terms today may rise in cost or drop off in conversions at any time. For our clients, that means that we're absorbing that cost and up-front time investment, but a business that wants to develop and maintain a successful PPC campaign must be prepared to make that time and financial investment.

4. If a law firm is just getting started with online marketing, what would be an estimate for the cost of a using a service, such as HPM?

Total Attorneys price ranges from $52 to $107 based on lead type. Volume varies based on zip code and product.

5. How important is it to run analytics on a law firm's online marketing activity? How can this be accomplished and what kind of time investment does it take to monitor and adjust based on analytics?

It is important for an attorney to understand the ROI on any campaign, as well as overall return on the firm's marketing investment. That means gathering and analyzing data at several points throughout the process, whether the campaign is online or through more traditional media like the yellow pages. That process typically begins with gathering data about the source of new prospects. This may include low-tech methods like asking new callers how they heard about your firm and more technical solutions such as web analytics that show the traffic source and path through your firm's website. But it's important for attorneys to recognize that that's only the beginning of the process. Getting a lot of phone calls or completed forms from a given marketing effort might feel good, but it doesn't necessarily translate to increased revenue. A law firm that wants to make the most of its marketing campaigns and maximize ROI will need to track everything from clicks and visits to inquiries to appointments scheduled to retained clients and payment actually received for every client.

6. Other guidance on online marketing?

It is important for an attorney to understand their ROI. If using the yellow pages or other sources with fixed fees and limited tracking capabilities, using site analytics can be helpful. With a service like HPM, attorneys are only charged when a potential client is delivered, so understanding ROI can be calculated and straightforward.

7. Please provide any other tips or information that you believe might benefit a law firm or attorney in learning about online marketing.

When a lead is received, follow up immediately. Many potential clients, especially those in high-emotion consumer areas like bankruptcy and divorce, have a strong sense of urgency when they reach out to an attorney. If they don't reach a live person or get an immediate call back, most will move down the list and place another call. Being the first to talk to a potential client will increase overall close rates. And don't just place a call and then move on yourself; leverage all contact information. If a call is not answered, always leave a message and follow up with an email. Create a follow-up strategy that defines how many times, at what intervals, and how often and in what manner you'll follow up with a lead, taking into account any legal or ethical restrictions in your state. This will help you stay on task and better measure your success. Keep track of those contacts and which are successful; over time, this will help you fine-tune your follow-up strategy. It can take multiple touches to close a lead, so persistence is necessary.

Conclusion

This chapter examined different approaches to marketing unbundled legal services from traditional to online methods. It should be clear from the overview of the legal marketplace that any law firm considering unbundling its services needs to stay keenly aware of developments and the direction in which the trends in online marketing are heading. Just as a firm becomes comfortable with its existing marketing strategy, a newer Internet-based model will crop up and change the game again. Some attorneys will play it safe and wait until their states pass formal ethics opinions approving each specific online marketing model. However, while waiting for the model to be approved, a newer version may be taking its place. Instead, attorneys should be able to look at the existing state rules and ethics opinions and determine what reasonable care should be in using these different marketing options.

The core purpose of the Model Rules that relate to lawyer advertising, protecting client confidentiality, duty to prospective clients, unauthorized practice of law, and other regulations that might come into play in an unbundling marketing strategy, apply the same way to traditional marketing as they will to online marketing methods for unbundled services. Many states in their recent ethics opinions on cloud computing or third-party hosting of law office data have taken the position of reminding their members of the reasonable care standard, to not mislead clients in advertising methods, and to be transparent to the consumer in the lawyer's actions online.[58] These opinions then point to other resources outside the formal rules to guide lawyers on the specifics of what constitutes reasonable care and due diligence. Relying on these sources outside of the legal industry and keeping up-to-date on technology and security developments as they affect these newer online marketing models is crucially important for lawyers.

A stable marketing strategy in a business plan for an unbundled law practice would include both traditional and transitional marketing strategies. While keeping a close eye on these marketing developments as they affect the commoditization of legal services, the unbundling law firm must continue to develop its own strong brand online and find ways to create a niche practice that justifies the value of its full-representation services. While maintaining this brand building, the firm must be careful to diversify its prospective revenue stream by also focusing more marketing efforts on cultivating a new base of DIY clients seeking unbundled services, both alone and with the assistance of these larger branded network concepts as they develop into the legal marketplace.

---

[58]*See, e.g.*, S.C. State Bar Formal Ethics Op. 11-05 (Summer 2011) regarding lawyers' use of "daily deal" services to offer discounts online to prospective clients; Cal. State Bar Ethics Op. 2010-179 (December 2010); Ala. State Bar Ethics Op. 2010-02, "Retention, Storage, Ownership, Production and Destruction of Client Files"; Ariz. State Bar Comm. on Rules of Prof'l Conduct, Op. 09-04 (Dec. 9, 2009); Pa. Bar Ass'n Comm. on Legal Ethics and Prof'l Responsibility, FEO 2010-200, "Ethical Obligations on Maintaining a Virtual Office for the Practice of Law in Pennsylvania"; N.Y. State Bar Ass'n, Op. 842, Sept. 10, 2010, regarding online storage providers storing confidential client information; State Bar of Cal. Standing Comm. on Prof'l Responsibility and Conduct, Formal Op. Interim No. 08-0002, regarding third-party storage of confidential client information.

CHAPTER NINE

Conclusion

WITH ALL THIS CHANGE in the legal marketplace and the growing frustration with the public over high legal fees and lack of access, the question has been raised by those outside of the legal profession: Is it time to deregulate the practice of law to increase access to justice?[1] Without getting into all the arguments for or against deregulation, the simple answer is "No." Part of this push-back from other professionals outside of the legal industry is a response to what they and the public see as the unwillingness of the legal profession to acknowledge that there is a disconnect between what the public needs and what the lawyers are willing to provide.

There are more innovative ways to provide access to justice that are in the best interest of the public than deregulating the legal profession. This book has pointed out the many potential ways of unbundling legal services that lawyers may use to serve the public and that will address the concerns of critics of the legal profession. Taking into account some of the disruptors of our existing legal marketplace, unbundled delivery moves away from the more traditional method of legal services delivery to more closely meet the current needs of a majority of the public and responds to the demands for accountability by those outside our profession.

---

[1]Clifford Winston & Robert W. Crandell, *Time to Deregulate the Practice of Law*, WALL ST. J., Aug. 22, 2011; and Clifford Winston, *Are Law Schools and Bar Exams Necessary?*, N.Y. TIMES, Oct. 24, 2011, *available at* **http://www.nytimes.com/2011/10/25/opinion/are-law-schools-and-bar-exams-necessary.html?_r=1&ref=regulationandderegulationofindustry** (last accessed Oct. 26, 2011).

As discussed previously, there are benefits for the professional as well as the public in unbundling legal services. Unbundling may be seen primarily as a service to be handled pro bono or "low" bono or seen as a service primarily to aid pro se litigants navigate the justice system. However, unbundling should be looked at in a much broader sense—as the middle ground between no legal representation and full-service representation. To quote the ABA Section of Litigation: "[l]imited scope legal assistance is not a substitute for adequate funding for indigent legal services programs."[2] But until the day our society can afford the resources to provide full-service representation to all, the reality is that the legal profession must find ways to provide as much assistance as possible. By following best practices for unbundling and paying attention to the different state rules and regulations regarding limited-scope assistance, unbundled services may easily be added to most law firms depending on their practice areas and the needs of their client bases.

The legal profession has established a sense of entitlement to be able to charge high fees and expect clients to pay high costs for legal services without complaint. In any profession, once a high rate is fixed and the business and its members have become dependent on that expected source of revenue, it becomes extremely difficult to change even as the business develops a larger client base. But changes in technology and consumer behavior have irrevocably changed the method of legal services production and delivery. Unbundling permits the lawyer to adapt to changes by slowly making his or her processes more cost-effective and efficient through the use of technology. Lawyers can unbundle services and then over time as they build the quantity of work with the faster process, they will be able to maintain their standard of living while providing the now-expected lower fees for their services. Unbundling may allow the lawyer to transition from inefficient traditional models of legal services delivery to newer and more cost-effective versions without having to take a big dip in revenue.

The most successful law firms will find ways to add unbundled services to their full-service representation offerings and others will create entire practices that provide only unbundled assistance. Innovative firms will be able to quickly adapt to the changing legal marketplace and learn to col-

---

[2] ABA Section of Litig., Handbook on Limited Scope Legal Assistance: A Report of the Modest Means Task Force (2003), at **http://www.ftp.abanet.org/litigation/taskforces/modest/report.pdf** (last accessed Oct. 23, 2011).

laborate as well as compete with branded networks and other companies that have the financial and brand power to directly appeal to the empowered consumer seeking DIY legal services.

Responsible adoption of unbundling by lawyers will help push the profession into the next generation of professional legal services delivery— opening up new business and practice potential for lawyers and law firms and increasing access to justice for the public they serve.

Appendix

Case Studies of Firms That Unbundle

Internet Law

Kelly Law Firm—**http://www.aaronkellylaw.com**

The Kelly Law Firm, L.L.C., is a Scottsdale-based law firm founded by Aaron M. Kelly. The firm focuses on business and Internet law, and has a client roster that includes professionals from all sides of the online community—affiliate networks, affiliate marketers, direct marketers, advertisers, online auction sites, search engine optimization (SEO) companies, web-hosting companies, and venture capitalists. Kelly also serves as general counsel to ad networks and Internet-based companies. Kelly has developed a Smartphone app for use by his clients that may be downloaded from iTunes: **http://itunes.apple.com/us/app/kelly-law-app-internet-affiliate/id447613097?mt=8**.

1. What services does your firm unbundle?

   We unbundle a variety of services, but usually they're the ones that have a low probability of developing complications. For example, trademark or copyright registrations for our clients are fairly straightforward matters, as are website terms of service agreements or privacy policies. The general rule is that if it's not something open-ended, such as research, and it doesn't involve going against an adverse party, it can probably be unbundled.

2. What is the client intake process for unbundled clients? How do you determine whether a case may be unbundled or needs full-service representation?

We use the same intake process for unbundled clients as we do for full-service clients. However, we are currently developing a service called Law La Carte (**www.lawlacarte.com**), which will be targeted at unbundled clients and permit us to intake clients using a list of standardized questions based on the services they choose. This will reduce the amount of time we need to spend conducting interviews. With the implementation of our new mobile app, we will also be able to reach out to clients who want unbundled services.

3. What percentage of your unbundled clients are you able to convert to full-service clients?

I'm unsure of the percentage, but whether they convert to full-service clients really depends on whether they get into situations where they need full service for something. Usually, my clients are repeat customers, but only if they need it. If the client comes to me for a trademark registration and needs to sue over infringement of that trademark six months later, he or she will likely use me rather than retaining the services of an unfamiliar attorney. The same applies with developing terms of service and privacy policies—most of them will have me draft those agreements, and then if they need contracts, they come back to me.

4. How do you follow up or monitor the progress of your unbundled clients after termination of the limited-scope representation?

I run a very online-oriented firm. Many if not most of my clients are on my Google Talk, Skype, or Facebook list, or more than one, so I can chat with them once in a while to see how they are doing. I also occasionally send out e-mails to past clients to make sure that they haven't run into any new legal issues. Because we provide this open line of communication, we stay in contact with all our clients regularly.

5. How are office assistants or paralegals used with your firm's process with unbundled work?

I use office assistants and paralegals to schedule meetings with clients and conduct preliminary interviews. For straightforward matters such as copyright or trademark registrations, a paralegal will have a list of standard questions to ask my clients that I know I will need the answers to in order to proceed. For example, my paralegal might instruct the client about the way to take a specimen photograph that I need for conducting a trademark registration. This speeds up the collection of information that I need to do.

6. Are unbundled services delivered online through a client extranet, client portal, or other online methods of delivery, such as e-mail or other collaboration software?

I use a variety of methods. Originally I mostly used e-mail, but now I use e-mail with the option of letting the client use Base-camp, which is an online tool that allows me to coordinate my legal team with my client and let the client upload relevant documents and messages. They also can monitor the progress of their cases through this tool. I have developed a Smartphone app (**http://itunes.apple.com/us/app/kelly-law-app-internet-affiliate/ id447613097?mt=8**) that clients can use to interface their phones with Basecamp. It's a huge hit with my clients, as most of them come from a tech-savvy group and like the idea of participating in their case management online.

7. Do you handle any pro or "low" bono unbundled work?

I volunteer for both the state bar and the Arizona volunteer lawyer program.

8. Do you offer fixed fees, alternative billing arrangements, payment plans, or billing methods other than the traditional billable hour?

We do lots of fixed-fee arrangements as long as the scope of the representation has clear limits on it. For example, I may represent someone in a straightforward breach of contract or copyright infringement lawsuit for a few thousand dollars, with a clear condition in the retainer that my services do not cover appeals. For the most part, my billing practices are flat/fixed fee. This gives my clients the peace of mind that every time they talk to me they aren't going to get billed.

9. How do you advertise or market your unbundled services to prospective clients?

For the most part, we advertise our firm in general to clients and offer them unbundled services during the intake process if unbundling would be appropriate.

10. How do you feel unbundling has affected your practice? Your clients?

Certainly unbundling has been the biggest game changer for me, as it is beneficial to both us and our clients. It enables us to attract clients who want to know exactly how much our representation is going to cost them. Our clients enjoy the fact that they don't have to worry about how many billable hours their projects are going to take.

Corporate Law
Rimon—**http://www.rimonlaw.com**

Rimon is a full-service corporate law firm with attorneys in the United States and Israel. The firm uses technology to collaborate with firm members and to cut costs for its clients. Rimon "employs an optimal combination of both virtual and dedicated office space, together with secure cloud technology." The firm delivers unbundled services in addition to its full-service offerings. As an example of some of its unbundled services, the firm's start-up package may be reviewed at /practice/Start-ups-Start-up-Financing.

1. What services does your firm unbundle?
   + Drafting contracts and agreements
   + Entity formation
   + Providing legal guidance and opinions
   + Financing
   + Patent and trademark filings
   + Form contracts

2. What is the client intake process for unbundled clients? How do you determine whether a case may be unbundled or needs full-service representation?

Our partners determine if something can be offered as an unbundled representation or needs full-service representation. For repeat situations such as opinions or basic contracts, we prefer unbundled. For a more complex, ongoing situation that requires negotiations or has other unknown or third-party variables, we generally do full-service representation.

3. What percentage of your unbundled clients are you able to convert to full-service clients?

Approximately 20 percent, because most of them need only one thing and have limited legal requirements.

4. How are office assistants or paralegals used with your firm's process with unbundled work?

They help automate the process to limit lawyers' time required on such work. We then try to just use the lawyers for top-level review and strategy consultations.

5. Do you offer fixed fees, alternative billing arrangements, payment plans, or billing methods other than the traditional billable hour?

Yes, we prefer flat fees. We also consider equity stakes in companies we represent or contingency fees.

6. How do you advertise or market your unbundled services to prospective clients?

We have a start-up package that lists and describes such services. We also tell our referral sources about them—who, in turn, tell future clients.

7. How do you feel unbundling has affected your practice? Your clients?

It has been highly profitable and efficient for our practice. Our clients love it because it is predictable and more affordable. On the negative side, however, it takes away from the close relationship with the client.

8. How do you respond to critics of unbundling or accusations from other professionals that your work is "commoditizing" the practice of law because it is not always handled face-to-face with the clients or is limited in scope?

Most corporate practice—from large corporate mergers to basic incorporations—is no longer done face-to-face. Unbundling simply allows for more efficient firms to be more profitable, while hourly billing makes lawyers miserable and forces clients to pay for wasted time.

9. Any other thoughts you might wish to share about the future of unbundling in the legal profession?

I think it is the right thing to do ethically and the future of legal practice. I think ultimately transactional lawyers will get paid to advise on strategy rather than for generating form documents. Unbundling is helping to pave the path for this, and those who don't do it will simply be left behind.

Intellectual Property Law
Firebrand Legal—**http://www.firebrandlegal.com**

Robert Valdillez and Michael McMullan are attorneys and co-founders of Firebrand Legal Services, a law firm in the North Carolina Research Triangle. The firm focuses on trademark, copyright, business formation, and contract creation legal services. The founders of the firm unbundle legal services as well as deliver full-representation services through the use of technology integrated into a traditional law firm structure.

1. What services does your firm unbundle?

At our firm, we make a number of unbundled services available, mostly centered around providing document review or creating contracts for clients to use on their own. We've also performed legal research and provided basic legal advice.

2. What is the client intake process for unbundled clients? How do you determine whether a case may be unbundled or needs full-service representation?

Our client intake process is the same for all clients. We determine if a client should use unbundled or full services on a case-by-case basis during the initial client interview.

3. What percentage of your unbundled clients are you able to convert to full-service clients?

I think that roughly 20 percent of our unbundled clients have become interested in other services.

4. Are unbundled services delivered online through a client extranet, client portal, or other online methods of delivery, such as e-mail or other collaboration software?

We've found that it's easiest for everyone involved if we use the Total Attorney Virtual Law Office, and thankfully a number of our clients have immediately seen the benefits as well.

5. Do you offer fixed fees, alternative billing arrangements, payment plans, or billing methods other than the traditional billable hour?

Almost every service we provide takes the form of a fixed fee, usually personalized to that client's needs and abilities. We're also hard at work on a set of packaged services and annual plans.

6. How do you feel unbundling has affected your practice? Your clients?

It provides a lower-cost alternative that streamlines the process on our end and clients like the lower rates involved in unbundled services.

7. How do you respond to critics of unbundling or accusations from other professionals that your work is "commoditizing" the practice of law?

I feel that by providing specific unbundled services to clients that are only in need of those particular services, and who otherwise might not seek legal assistance at all, we're working closer to the traditional idea of a lawyer as a public citizen than those who are more concerned that the profession be seen as a venerable institution.

Estate Planning

Texas Wills and Trusts Online—**http://www.texaswillsandtrustslaw.com/**

Rania Combs is the owner of Texas Wills and Trusts Online. Combs unbundles estate planning and some probate matters online. She provides only unbundled legal services through the use of her virtual law office and does not provide full-service, in-person representation. She uses document-automation and assembly tools as well as technology to communicate with and deliver legal services to her clients. Combs lives in Chapel Hill, North Carolina, but she is licensed to practice law in Texas and delivers unbundled Texas law matters to clients online.

1. What is the client intake process for unbundled clients? How do you determine whether a case may be unbundled or needs full-service representation?

The first thing I do when someone registers as a client on my virtual law office is call them to introduce myself and answer any questions they have. From that initial conversation, I am able to gauge what their needs are. Because of the web-based nature of my firm, I cannot handle any matters that will require me to make court appearances. So, for example, if someone contacts me with a contested probate matter, I refer the person to a lawyer who can meet with the client in person and make court appearances on his or her behalf.

2. How do you follow up or monitor the progress of your unbundled clients after termination of the limited-scope representation?

I typically follow up with a monthly newsletter that I send to all my clients. Before closing my clients' files, I always note their birthdays on my firm's calendar. That gives me a good opportunity to make personal contact with them at least once a year either with a card or a phone call.

3. Are unbundled services delivered online through a client extranet, client portal, or other online methods of delivery, such as e-mail or other collaboration software?

I use the Virtual Law Office Technology platform through Total Attorney for most communications with clients. Occasionally clients will correspond with me via e-mail, but I encourage them to send messages regarding their legal matter through their client account.

4. Do you use document automation or assembly or any other specific technology in your unbundling?

I use a document-assembly system as a starting point, and then customize those documents to address my clients' unique circumstances.

5. Does your law firm website provide any unbundling tools, such as web advisers, calculators, legal forms, or other resources that allow the public to obtain free, unbundled services?

Prospective clients can find answers to many of their estate-planning questions on my blog. A visitor to my website also is given an opportunity to get an e-book I wrote that gives step-by-step directions on how to appoint a legal guardian for his or her children at no cost.

6. Do you handle any pro or "low" bono unbundled work?

Yes.

7. Do you offer fixed fees, alternative billing arrangements, payment plans, or billing methods other than the traditional billable hour?

I offer fixed fees and payment plans if necessary to make my services more affordable for my clients.

8. How do you respond to critics of unbundling or accusations from other professionals that your work is "commoditizing" the practice of law?

Many people turn to document-preparation services, sometimes to their detriment, because they believe that contacting a lawyer will be cost-prohibitive. By unbundling and practicing virtually throughout Texas, I have made my services available to people who may have otherwise tried to handle their legal needs on their own or would not have had access to the legal services they require.

Family Law
Connecticut Legal Coaching, L.L.C.—**http://www.ctlegalcoaching.com**

Susan Wakefield is an attorney and owner of Connecticut Legal Coaching, L.L.C., and has been a divorce attorney and mediator for more than 23 years. Her practice provides legal coaching to individuals who are self-represented or who are contemplating self-representation in their divorce actions. She also provides unbundled services to divorcing individuals and unbundling divorce mediation services as an alternative to her full-service delivery to reduce costs and maximize clients' control over the outcome of their legal matters.

1. What service does your firm unbundle?

- An initial comprehensive consultation during which we discuss self-representation and its advantages and disadvantages to determine whether self-representation is appropriate given the client's facts and circumstances.

- Discussing the steps involved in a divorce, post-divorce, or custody matter and which divorce process is best for the case.

- Assistance in commencing a divorce or family action, such as preparing court forms and the process of serving papers.

- Guidance on court procedures and court etiquette.

- Preparation of the financial affidavit, child-support guideline worksheets, motions, and all other court papers, including ghostwriting, to ensure the paperwork is accurate.

- Educating individuals and couples on the factors considered by the court in calculating alimony and child support and explaining the meaning of equitable distribution in the division of assets.

- Preparing individuals and couples for their court conferences, hearings, and trials.

- Discussing the terms and provisions of a parenting plan and the final divorce/settlement agreement.
- Drafting and reviewing parenting plans and divorce and settlement agreements.

Assistance with drafting the motions needed to modify or enforce a divorce judgment such as motions for modification of alimony and child support and motions for contempt and preparing an individual to represent himself or herself in court for these various motions.

2. What is the client intake process for unbundled clients? How do you determine whether a case may be unbundled or needs full-service representation?

The client intake process for unbundled clients is an initial consultation. I take this time to evaluate the facts, circumstances, and history of the marriage and determine whether I believe the client has the skill set and the abilities to represent himself or herself. If I do not believe the case is suitable for unbundling, we discuss other options, including mediation or collaborative or full representation. At Connecticut Legal Coaching, we prepared a checklist that we require clients to complete who are contemplating self-representation or are considering unbundled legal services as another way to determine if unbundling is the appropriate process for them.

3. What percentage of your unbundled clients are you able to convert to full-service clients?

Although several unbundled clients have converted to full representation, it is neither my objective nor my goal to convert them. Most unbundled clients are seeking this form of limited representation because they cannot afford the retainer fee and the cost of full representation, and they are struggling financially. As we often say, unbundling is not a choice for most, it is a necessity. However, because of the complexity of the matter or an adversarial spouse, approximately 15 percent of my unbundled clients have converted to full representation because their cases became too difficult for them to manage on their own. Therefore, together, as a team, we decided that, to protect their interests and ensure a good outcome to their case, full representation was the appropriate next step.

In 2009, I designed a special service that I call "Legal Coaching" that offers individuals the opportunity to partner with me, a family-law expert for more than 20 years, for limited assistance at any stage of their case. To make this alternative legal service affordable, I reduced my rates by approximately one-third of the cost that I charge for full representation. I also have what I call "Legal Coaching Packages" that consist of half-hour, three-hour, and five-hour packages at even further discounted rates in an effort to support individuals and couples who need additional help or ongoing support throughout their divorce and family-law processes. Many unbundled clients seek just an initial consultation or limited services; however, I am finding that individuals quickly see the benefit of having a legal coach in their corner throughout their processes, and given the "a la carte" pay-as-you-go structure we created, most individuals can afford my unbundled legal-coaching services.

4. How do you follow up or monitor the progress of your unbundled clients after termination of the limited-scope representation?

At Connecticut Legal Coaching, we take great pride in the excellent relationships we establish with our unbundled clients. Clients contact us to discuss the progression of their cases, and we routinely check the Connecticut Judicial Branch website to follow the status of their cases. Clients also know we are available to them anytime for continued advice and support, and often we are the lifeline they need to move through their processes successfully and with confidence, so they will return for additional unbundled services.

5. How are office assistants or paralegals used with your firm's process with unbundled work?

My office manager handles all the initial inquiries from unbundled clients, answers questions regarding our legal coaching service, and schedules the first initial meeting between myself and these individuals. Throughout the process, she maintains a strong level of communication with these clients, and they seem to be very pleased with the overall service they receive.

6. Are unbundled services delivered online through a client extranet, client portal, or other online methods of delivery, such as e-mail or other collaboration software?

Yes, unbundled services are quite often delivered via e-mail exchange between myself and the client. This format is extremely efficient and allows for a fast response and turnaround time that includes evenings, weekends, and off-hours.

7. Do you handle any pro or "low" bono unbundled work?

Yes, from time to time I will take a pro bono case from either Connecticut Legal Services or Statewide Legal Services. They are the two largest organizations in Connecticut funded by the state offering free legal services to qualifying individuals. Since creating Connecticut Legal Coaching, I am working with increasing numbers of unbundled clients providing both pro and "low" bono unbundled work on a case-by-case basis. Given our "a la carte, pay-as-you-go" structure, reduced legal coaching packages, and my freedom to offer pro bono services in the appropriate case, I feel I can offer more individuals and couples access to affordable, quality legal services.

8. Do you offer fixed fees, alternative billing arrangements, payment plans, or billing methods other than the traditional billable hour?

Yes, I have specifically reduced fees by approximately one-third. I have designed special legal coaching packages at further reduced rates for unbundled clients, and I have worked out payment plans with clients in the past. The "traditional billable hour" does not exist among this new breed of clients because I have redesigned the scope of my practice to accommodate their financial needs.

9. How do you advertise or market your unbundled services to prospective clients?

The advertising and marketing is handled in a variety of ways that includes SEO, website, radio advertising, networking, social media, blogging, word of mouth, referrals, and, most important, recommendations from satisfied and happy unbundled clients.

10. How do you feel unbundling has affected your practice? Your clients?

I created Connecticut Legal Coaching to address the growing trend toward self-representation especially in the area of divorce and family law. Because of unbundling and this growing trend, I have completely redesigned my practice in an effort to support and accommodate the self-represented at all levels. These individuals are scared; they feel alone and they are intimidated by the system. Knowing that I can help to remove fear and uncertainty and empower them to proceed through their cases with knowledge and confidence is one of the most rewarding parts of my career thus far. Clients, therapists, financial planners, and laypersons think unbundled legal services are the best solution for a client seeking assistance but unable to afford the traditional retainer fee required with full representation. In addition, many post-divorce clients seeking help with a modification or enforcement of a divorce agreement express that they wish unbundling was available at the time of their initial divorce proceedings.

11. Have you encountered any regulations or barriers to unbundling your services, either from the state bar or other regulatory body?

The state of Connecticut is in the process of changing the Connecticut Practice Book to allow for limited appearances, a form of unbundled legal services that would offer attorneys the ability to appear for individuals for parts of their cases such as a motion, a conference, or perhaps just trial of the action, as an alternative to the full appearance that requires an attorney to remain in the case until the attorney withdraws or is terminated by the client. The approval of limited appearances has been challenged by the Connecticut Bar for many years, as lawyers feel threatened that such changes will undermine the importance and value of the attorney and legal services. I disagree, as do many among the Connecticut Bar, and given the change among the public who now demand alternative practices and more affordable options, unbundled legal services in Connecticut will soon be approved and, I believe, will be incorporated into many law practices among their other services offered, such as divorce mediation, collaborative law, etc. As for clients, attorneys, and judges, I have received only positive reinforcement for the services offered by Connecticut Legal Coaching. I call it the win/win/win—win for the client, win for opposing counsel who now has a more educated adversary, and win for the courts and judges who have prepared and informed litigants appearing before them.

Litigation Services
Skiba Law Group, P.L.C.—**www.skibalaw.com**

John N. Skiba is the principal of the Skiba Law Group, an Arizona-based law office providing legal services in the areas of bankruptcy, consumer law, and limited-scope/unbundled civil litigation. What originally began in 2005 as a "brick-and-mortar" law office has evolved into more of a mobile law office that involves traveling to various satellite offices to meet with clients as well as the incorporation of technology to meet clients via the Internet and provide legal services online. Skiba also is an avid blogger on consumer bankruptcy issues as well as unbundled legal services.

1. What services does your firm unbundle?

   I offer unbundled or limited-scope services mostly in the area of litigation. I assist clients with drafting pleadings, reviewing documents, advising on court procedures, and legal coaching, and provide general opinions on the strategies of their cases.

   While the bulk of my law practice is in the area of bankruptcy, I do not offer unbundled bankruptcy services. Most of my clients have been sued in one of the justice courts here in Arizona on debts of less than $10,000. Many of them have been sued by parties that have purchased the debts from the original creditors and often there are mistakes, or simply the wrong parties have been sued. The client doesn't have the money (or it doesn't make sense) to spend on an attorney. The unbundled services I offer help the client understand the legal process and prepare documents, such as an answer, written discovery, or even a response to a motion for summary judgment.

   I have seen some plaintiff-creditors assume that they are going to be litigating against self-represented defendants and incorporate that into their strategies. The unbundled services I offer help the client who can't afford an attorney but needs some assistance in handling his or her case.

2. What is the client intake process for unbundled clients? How do you determine whether a case may be unbundled or needs full-service representation?

   Nearly all my unbundled clients come to me through my website. I use a platform devised by DirectLaw that allows clients to review the unbundled services I offer on my website, register with my firm, provide me with information I need to complete the task, and even pay online. When I meet with clients to discuss limited-scope representation, I always lay out for them what full representation would involve as well as the unbundled service. Cost is the overwhelming reason clients choose to go with the unbundled service.

3. What percentage of your unbundled clients are you able to convert to full-service clients?

   I don't specifically approach my unbundled clients with the goal of turning them into full-service clients. That being said, I do let them know that after I complete the tasks they have hired me to do, if they need additional help down the road, to contact me and I can help them with other aspects of their cases. I also have had unbundled clients use my services in litigation matters and later come back for different matters for which they need full representation. I would estimate that approximately 65 percent of my unbundled clients either ask for additional assistance or hire me for different legal matters.

4. How do you follow up or monitor the progress of your unbundled clients after termination of the limited-scope representation?

I will contact the client to see how things are going and if he or she needs any additional services. In order to be clear with the client that the scope of my service is complete, I send a file-closing letter that lets the client know that the services I was hired for now are complete, and if he or she needs any additional assistance to please let me know.

5. Are unbundled services delivered online through a client extranet, client portal, or other online methods of delivery, such as e-mail or other collaboration software?

As mentioned before, nearly all my clients come to me through my website where I have a client portal they can log into to begin the process. I typically do meet face-to-face with most clients to review the documents that I have prepared for them and give them other general advice on the procedures and strategies of their cases.

6. Do you use document automation or assembly or any other specific technology in your unbundling?

I do have some basic documents that can be assembled through the automation process provided by DirectLaw, such as letters, bills of sale, and promissory notes.

7. Do you handle any pro or "low" bono unbundled work?

I do offer reduced-fee and pro bono work on a case-by-case basis.

8. Do you offer fixed fees, alternative billing arrangements, payment plans, or billing methods other than the traditional billable hour?

All my unbundled services are done on a flat-fee basis and payment is required at the beginning of representation.

9. How do you advertise or market your unbundled services to prospective clients?

All my advertising is done online. I blog at least four times per week on various topics related to my bankruptcy practice as well as my unbundled services. When I began offering these services, I ran a brief pay-per-click campaign through Google and Facebook to jump-start the practice area and now rely mostly on blogging. I distribute my blogs through the various social media sites.

There are not a lot of law firms out there offering these types of services. And because of this, I have found that it is not very difficult to begin showing up on the first page of the search engine results on Google with some consistent blogging.

10. How do you feel unbundling has affected your practice? Your clients?

I have received a lot of positive feedback from clients. My background is in bankruptcy and litigation. When I was more heavily involved in litigation work, I found that I was in conflict on many occasions with my clients over billings. Litigation is outrageously expensive to the typical family. They have a legal problem they need help with, but the cost simply makes it not possible to get the representation they need. The options are go at it alone, which usually ends very badly, do nothing, or hire an attorney and spend every cent they have.

Unbundling has allowed me to provide legal services to more clients, and I have found the clients to be genuinely appreciative of my services rather than despising the large monthly bills of full representation. It has improved my overall satisfaction with representing litigation clients.

11. How do you respond to critics of unbundling or accusations from other professionals that your work is "commoditizing" the practice of law?

The reaction by most attorneys that I interact with is mostly positive, with a good number just not understanding what the attraction is in offering this type of service. As I have blogged on providing unbundled services, I have been contacted by attorneys throughout the country looking to begin offering these types of services.

I have had one negative experience with an attorney who posted a negative comment on my blog, expressing some extreme concern as to this type of practice. I followed up with this attorney and frankly was shocked at the tone of disapproval. I was told that I was "harming the integrity of the system" and that this practice area was nothing but a "slash-and-burn-grab-the-money-and-run practice," and finally that I should quit trying to "reinvent the wheel." I did not personally know this attorney, so I was somewhat taken aback with the vitriol with which the attorney attacked both me and the practice area.

My response was that I was merely responding to what I saw as a need in the community. Furthermore, the services I offer typically are low-flat-fee services that are not huge revenue producers. In responding to critics, I believe that it is important to bring it back to why these services are necessary—many people cannot afford an attorney and thus have limited access to the courts. Unbundled services help both the client and the court by assisting and educating people as they move through the legal process.

As technology continues to improve and change, we are seeing legal services being delivered and sold more as a commodity and often by nonlawyers (i.e., LegalZoom, et al.). I believe providing unbundled services as an option for clients allows attorneys to not only utilize the latest technology but also compete with the other online legal services providers, with the added benefit of a lawyer being involved in the process.

12. Thinking ahead, what role do you think unbundling will take in the legal profession in the future?

Unbundling in the litigation area simply provides access to the courts to a large segment of the population that cannot afford to hire an attorney. For many, it will not be a good option; and in complex litigation, it probably is not going to be a good option. But in other areas it is greatly needed, and all my unbundled services clients have commented to me on how grateful they were that I offered these types of services.

As the one negative experience I had (mentioned previously) demonstrates, attitudes and minds will have to be changed for the legal community to fully embrace it. Lawyers seem to be a little more hesitant than most to embrace change, but the way legal services are being provided is changing, and, as we see with the many online providers, if attorneys don't step in and fill the need, other more business-minded non-attorneys will.

Entertainment Law
Law Offices of Gordon P. Firemark—**http://firemark.com/**

Gordon P. Firemark started his career working behind the scenes in theater, film, and television productions. Now, as an entertainment lawyer, he works behind the scenes in theater, film, television, and online media, putting together the deals that bring creative talent, money, and business interests together to make a compelling entertainment product. His clients include producers, directors, writers, actors, and the companies that employ them. Firemark blogs about entertainment law at firemark.com and is the producer and host of Entertainment Law Update (**http://www.entertainmentlawupdate.com/**), a podcast roundup of legal news and case law affecting the entertainment and media industries. Firemark's practice is strictly transactional, which allows him to unbundle a number of legal services.

1. What services does your firm unbundle?

   ♦ Copyright registration

   ♦ Trademark registration (application)

   ♦ Simple partnership agreements

   ♦ Corporate and limited-liability company (LLC) formations

   ♦ Music licenses for film/television

   ♦ Review and comment on talent/manager agreements

   ♦ DMCA takedown notices and/or counter-notices

2. What is the client intake process for unbundled clients? How do you determine whether a case may be unbundled or needs full-service representation?

   The primary difference in the intake process has to do with "face time." For most clients, I prefer to schedule an office meeting, in which I take down lots of information about the matter, the deal(s), etc. For unbundled clients, I try to handle more over the phone and via e-mail. In the initial call, I try to determine whether the client's need is for one of the items I offer as an unbundled service. If so, I quote the price, gather necessary information, and send out a limited-scope representation/fee agreement and invoice using my online billing service. After payment is received, I perform the service and deliver the work product. Generally, unbundling works for me when the matter is something where all the relevant information, documents, and collateral material can be gathered together right away. And the service can be performed the same day.

3. What percentage of your unbundled clients are you able to convert to full-service clients?

   More common is a full-service client who takes advantage of an unbundled service. This is similar to ordering off the a la carte menu for a particular transaction. It's often more profitable this way, especially for tasks that may take me only 10 minutes.

4. How do you follow up or monitor the progress of your unbundled clients after termination of the limited-scope representation?

   I typically schedule a follow-up call around 30 days following my last contact. I just say that I'm "circling back" to make sure that all is in order and to see how things are going.

5. How are office assistants or paralegals used with your firm's process with unbundled work?

   I fly solo and don't have staff. Most of my document forms are somewhat automated, so it's easy and fast for me to handle things. I do sometimes use a Virtual Assistant to do some basic document assembly, but I always review every line of each document myself.

6. Are unbundled services delivered online through a client extranet, client portal, or other online methods of delivery, such as e-mail or other collaboration software?

   I don't have a client-facing system for intake, document assembly, etc., but I do use my online billing system (Clio), which has a file-sharing function to provide documents to clients. More often than not, though, clients prefer e-mail, Dropbox, etc., even when I warn them about confidentiality and security concerns.

7. Do you offer fixed fees, alternative billing arrangements, payment plans, or billing methods other than the traditional billable hour?

   Almost all my work these days uses an "alternative" structure. Some clients agree to pay me a percentage of their gross earnings in exchange for my availability to advise, counsel, and negotiate on their behalf. For most other matters, I try to quote a "price" rather than a rate. This kind of fixed-fee structure makes a lot of sense when you can accurately predict the amount of work involved and the *value* of the service to both client and attorney. It's important to take care in setting the price to explain that changes or added complexity will require a revised price structure.

8. How do you feel unbundling has affected your practice? Your clients?

   Sometimes it does feel like it contributes to the "race to the bottom," but the race is under way already. It *has* helped to fill in the cash-flow valleys during slow times, and I'm building relationships with clients who would otherwise not be able to afford an attorney.

9. How do you respond to critics of unbundling or accusations from other professionals that your work is "commoditizing" the practice of law?

   That process is already happening, with or without me. We all need to adapt to changing business models. Those who don't will get left behind. How many buggy-whip manufacturers would still be in business if they didn't innovate and adapt?

10. Thinking ahead, what role do you think unbundling will take in the legal profession in the future?

    Unbundling will continue to grow. There will always be a need for traditional service models, but unbundling makes professional legal services accessible to a broader population, and that's good for society. This isn't really new for professional service providers. Medicine has had to cope with this kind of thing for decades now. Most health insurance companies require the doctors to list a code for each little service offered in a doctor's office or hospital bedside. I don't think most of us think of medical treatment as a "commodity."

Other Practices That Unbundle

Axiom Legal

http://www.axiomlegal.com/unbundle.html

Axiom is an example of a larger law firm using unbundling and alternative fee arrangements to provide unique services to clients with more complex legal matters. You can read its case-study example on unbundling litigation at **http://www.axiomlegal.com/casestudies/cs_litigation_unbundling .html**.

Finkelstein & Partners LLP
http://web.lawampm.com/

This New York–based law firm focuses its practice on personal injury law, but also provides unbundled legal services on the side of its main practice for individuals and businesses.

Granat Legal Services, P.C.
www.mdfamilylaw.com

Attorney Richard Granat founded his law firm in Maryland in 2003. It was the first virtual law firm in the state and one of the first in the United States. The firm offers "niche" unbundled legal services to "pro se" parties in family law matters. The primary services are legal advice, document review, and legal forms bundled with legal advice for a fixed fee. Contested matters are referred out to a network of attorneys who provide full-service representation. All client communications and client work is handled online. Granat moved to Palm Beach Gardens, Florida in 2004, and continues to operate his law firm for Maryland residents at a distance.

Harrington, Brewster & Clein, LLP
**http://www.harringtonbrewsterclein.com/Practice-Areas-Overview/
LimitedRepresentation.shtml**

This Denver, Colorado, firm provides unbundled family-law legal services out of its brick-and-mortar law office. The firm invites prospective clients to contact them about the possibility of unbundling legal assistance and cites sample limited-scope services on its website, including "talking with witnesses or experts, attending mediation, and drafting documents such as pleadings, child support worksheets, and financial affidavits. The lawyer can also negotiate issues with the other party or lawyer as well as advise the client when needed."

McGrath and Spielberger, PLLC.
http://mcgrathspielberger.com/

Jason McGrath and James M. Spielberger provide unbundled legal services online through a virtual law office platform that incorporates document-assembly and automation features in addition to operating a traditional, full-service law practice. The firm has physical law-office locations in North Carolina, South Carolina, and Florida, and delivers unbundled legal services in North Carolina, South Carolina, Georgia, Florida, and Ohio online and through the use of a counsel attorney. The firm provides the following services unbundled: general legal advice, court advice, mediation advice, deposition advice, document preparation, document analysis, document editing, legal research, and legal analysis and opinions.

Forrest "Woody" Mosten, "Father of Unbundling," Mediator and Collaborative Attorney
http://www.mostenmediation.com/

Forrest "Woody" Mosten wrote the book *Unbundling Legal Services: A Guide to Delivering Legal Services a la Carte* for ABA Publishing in 2000 and is also the author of the *Collaborative Divorce Handbook: Effectively Helping Divorcing Families Without Going to Court,* published by Jossey-Bass in 2009. He has been a mediator since 1979 and is an Advanced Practitioner Member of the Association for Conflict Resolution. He also received the Lifetime Achievement Award for Innovations in Legal Access from the ABA Section of Delivery of Legal Services. Mosten is a Certified Family Law Specialist and member of the California State Bar. His private practice focuses on divorce, premarital agreements, complex property issues, support, and parenting issues following divorce.

Rice Law, PLLC
www.ricefamilylaw.com

Rice Law is a full-service family-law firm in North Carolina that provides unbundled family-law services online. The firm identified and works with a niche market of legal services for individuals stationed in the military overseas who need secure access to unbundled legal services.

Partners-in-Law©
http://www.partners-in-law.com

Partners-in-Law© is a subsidiary division of Barbara S. Shea, PC, based in Connecticut. Barbara Shea has developed several unique brands to promote her concept of delivering unbundled legal services as a form of "integrative law." The firm provides unbundled legal services that include elder law, dispute resolution, divorce consultations, and domestic violence and has created several unbundling programs, including Court Coach,® Roadmap for Heirs,© The Wheel of Unbundled Services,© and Yearly Legal Check-Up.

M. Sue Talia, Private Family Law Judge
http://www.privatefamilylawjudge.com/about-mst.htm

M. Sue Talia is a private family-law judge who has presented a number of speeches and published papers on unbundled legal services. She is a Certified Family Law Specialist and member of the State Bar of California. Talia is a member of the Limited Representation Committee of the California

Commission on Access to Justice. She chaired and presented a CLE web program for the Practicing Law Institute (PLI) titled "Expanding Your Practice Using Limited Scope Representation," recorded on April 1, 2009. View it for free at **http://www.pli.edu/Content.aspx?dsNav=Rpp:1,N:4294964525-167&=&ID=54234.**

Checklist for the Unbundling Practitioner

- ☐ Research your state bar's rules and regulations regarding unbundled legal services. The following keywords may be useful in researching these rules: unbundled, unbundling, discrete task representation, limited-scope, limited representation, or assisting the pro se litigant.
- ☐ What services do we provide that can be unbundled?
- ☐ Where do we want to draw the line when issues become too complex to unbundle? For example, the firm might provide unbundled divorces, but draw the line when complex child-custody disputes are involved.
- ☐ What is our target client base for unbundled services? What types of clients would we attract with these services, and will it be cost-effective for the firm to work with them? Would these services be something that our existing clients would find useful?
- ☐ Determine billing options and pricing for unbundled services.
  - ♦ Do we want to offer alternative fee arrangements for our unbundled services?
  - ♦ Set fixed prices or determine value billing for specific unbundled tasks.
  - ♦ Will the firm require a retainer with unbundled services? Will it be a smaller amount than the firm's requested retainer for traditional full-service clients?
  - ♦ Decide whether to publicize sample or actual prices for services on the firm's website.
  - ♦ Decide how to respond to existing full-service clients about questions including the differences in pricing for your unbundled services.
  - ♦ Consider providing clients with the ability to pay their legal fees by credit card. Locate a third-party credit card–processing company for online and/or in-office credit-card services. Make sure the services are consistent with any state bar trust accounting and IOLTA rules and regulations.

☐ What percentage of our unbundling work will be pro bono or "low" bono services? Do we want to pursue a relationship with our local legal-aid service to receive referrals for unbundling cases?

☐ What is the start-up cost to integrate a technology to assist us in streamlining the unbundling process? Do we want to operate a virtual law office, focus on document-assembly programs, online case and client management, or a combination of methods to generate these services? Can these technologies be used in our firm for existing in-person client matters as well as new unbundled cases or do we want to keep these processes separate?

☐ How will we integrate unbundling legal services into our firm's existing marketing strategy? Do we want to market our unbundled services separately to new prospective clients or provide unbundled services for existing clients only?

☐ Do we want to appoint a firm member who will be responsible for following up with unbundled clients to ensure that they have followed instructions and completed their legal matters?

☐ Create the firm's process for unbundling for each service the firm intends to offer:

   ♦ Draft the standard limited-scope agreement that may be modified on a case-by-case basis.

   ♦ Set up educational comparison charts for prospective unbundling clients that compare the tasks associated with full-service representation to unbundled tasks.

   ♦ Create checklists and instructions for the unbundled client to complete his or her legal matter following the firm's completion of its services.

   ♦ Set up the document-assembly and automation tools for gathering client data and generating it into legal documents. If you are operating a virtual law office, draft the automated messages and legal advice that will walk the prospective online client through the process.

   ♦ Draft the termination or completion letter to provide to the client after the firm has completed its scope of the representation to ensure that there are no continuing expectations.

   ♦ Draft a standard letter declining to represent an individual requesting unbundled services if the firm determines that full-service representation is necessary or for any other reason declines to work with the individual.

Additional Questions for the Unbundled Client Intake Process

These questions may be added to the client intake process to help the lawyer determine whether the client is a good candidate for unbundling. They may also help the client understand the nature of limited-scope representation and how it differs from full-service assistance.

1. Have you worked with a lawyer on any issues surrounding this matter before?

2. What is the time frame or deadline for completing this project? Will you be able to work within the time frame proposed by the law firm?

3. Have you personally researched the law and legal issues involved in this matter?

4. How much is financially at stake here? How much is emotionally at stake here?

5. What do you see as a positive outcome for this case?

6. What would you be willing to settle for if that exact outcome is not achievable?

7. What aspects of this process are you willing and able to handle yourself?

8. Have you ever been involved in a lawsuit or had any experience with the legal system?

9. What resources are available to you in terms of time to devote to this matter, such as time away from work, arranging for child care, etc.?

10. What resources are available to you in terms of assistance from family members, paralegals, nonlawyer professionals, etc.?

11. What tasks do you know that you want the lawyer to provide?

12. How do you expect us to collaborate to create a strategy for your case?

13. How do you expect to communicate with the law firm? Are you comfortable using technology to communicate, such as web conferences, secure real-time chat, or encrypted e-mail?

14. How much are you able to budget for unbundled legal services?

This checklist may be modified based on the unbundled services that are being provided to the client. This may help both parties understand their responsibilities and the scope of the lawyer's work on the project. There may be some instances where the responsibility will be shared by both lawyer and client, such as attending a hearing.

This checklist might be provided to the client in the initial client intake process, along with the limited-scope engagement agreement, or uploaded to an online case-management file where the client may access it throughout the progress of the case. It also might be converted into a web-based format where the client would be able to click through the process on a mobile device connected to a calendaring system so that any deadlines for the client's responsibilities are set up as reminders that would help the client complete the legal matter on his or her own after the lawyer's assistance has ended.

Tasks	My Responsibility	My Lawyer Will Handle This
Preparing court forms		
Locating and organizing all necessary documents or items, including obtaining access to accounts and records, safety deposit boxes, items in storage, financial information and accounting, whether in paper or digital format, etc.		
Drafting legal documents		
Responding to motions and pleadings		
Drafting orders		
Filing documents at the courthouse		
Attending hearings		
Organizing documents for discovery and preparing requests for discovery, including interrogatories		
Conducting depositions		
Handling the subpoena for records		
Obtaining affidavits		
Having documents and papers served on the necessary parties to the case		
Conducting legal research		
Writing a report or opinion		
Coaching and strategy		

Tasks	My Responsibility	My Lawyer Will Handle This
Guidance on courtroom procedures and instruction on the legal process involved in the case		
Attending trial		
Handling negotiation and settlement		
Filing for an appeal		
Education on the basic underlying laws related to the case		
Coaching and strategy		
Other		

Sample Limited Scope Engagement Agreements

Links to several other sample limited-scope engagement agreements may be found in the list of state bar resources that follows.

> **1.** The following was provided with permission from Gordon Firemark. See the case study on Firemark Law Offices on page 170. Formatting has been changed.

Simplified Flat-Fee Retainer Agreement (Limited Scope)
Client(s) Date:

Legal Services:
We agree to perform only the following legal services for Client(s): _____

_____

and to be available to advise, counsel, and represent you during the next _____ days. This is a limited-scope representation and other services are not included. We cannot and do not guarantee particular results.

Fee
The fee is due at the time you sign this agreement, and you agree to pay the fee regardless of the outcome of your case.

The fee is <u>$ </u>, and is paid in exchange for our availability to represent you as detailed above. This fee will not be held in a trust account. The fee is nonrefundable, and is paid in exchange for our availability to advise and represent you during the next ___ days, and to cover the cost of opening your file.

Costs

You are responsible for all costs and expenses we incur in your representation. You agree to pay such costs in advance upon our request.

Notices

You agree to update your contact information whenever it changes during this representation.

Please note that this is a paperless office, and we do not keep paper files or original documents for clients. If we receive an original document, we will scan it for our file and send it to you or otherwise deal with it as appropriate under the circumstances.

We increasingly rely upon electronic communications such as e-mail, cellular phones, and other similar tools and media in our day-to-day business activities. Electronic communications are often not as secure as more traditional lines of communication, such as land-line telephones, U.S. Mail, and couriers. In the course of our representation of you, and unless we hear differently from you, we shall assume that you understand that some risk exists that electronic communications may be intercepted by or inadvertently misdirected to an unauthorized third party. We further assume that you accept that risk in general and, moreover, that you will let us know if you desire to have any particular communication (or class of communication) sent via a more secure means.

AGREED AND ACCEPTED:

LAW OFFICES OF GORDON P. FIREMARK

AGREED AND ACCEPTED:

Client Signature Telephone Number

Street Address City State Zip E-mail Address

2. The following are the Terms of Use for a virtual law office with a section devoted to the "nature of unbundled legal services." This was provided with permission from Rania Combs. Once

unbundling clients have clicked to accept these terms, she then provides them with a limited-scope engagement agreement that clearly defines more specifically the scope of the services to be handled and the billing structure. See the case study for Combs's unbundling law practice on page 159.

The Terms and Conditions of use ("Agreement") are provided by Rania Combs, attorney at law, an online Texas practice managed by attorney Rania Combs, a licensed solo practitioner. The Agreement will govern your use of this website, including all content provided on the website and through access to all online services provided by Rania Combs. The Agreement to provide legal services to you covers the time period from which you accept this Agreement, and we have received your payment through our funds-transfer service to the time we have provided you with the requested and purchased legal service.

You agree that it remains your responsibility to proceed as a pro se litigant by filing all legal documents and complying with Texas state and local procedures. By providing you with limited legal services, Rania Combs has not agreed to attend a hearing or trial on your behalf or provide any legal service extending beyond those services which you have purchased and we have agreed to provide. We provide only limited legal assistance and document preparation and review. After performing the services purchased by you, we have no further obligation to you.

Limitation of Services
While authorities in some jurisdiction may deem this website and this law practice to be an advertisement for legal services in their jurisdiction, our website should not be construed as a solicitation for legal services related to any other state's law. This website and this legal practice offer services related to Texas law only.

Unlike a geographically located law practice, Rania Combs will not provide physical legal representation or commence litigation on your behalf. The purpose of this law practice is to provide limited legal advice and general counseling on Texas legal matters with prompt service provided in a cost-effective manner.

If we determine during our communication with you that your specific legal matter requires the engagement of a full-service law firm, such as in the event that your situation may require the commencement of a formal lawsuit, then we will promptly refer you to a full-service firm in your area or refer you to the Texas Bar Association's Lawyer Referral Service.

Nature of Unbundled Legal Services

This law firm is not a prepaid legal service. Rather, it is an online legal practice where you are charged a one-time fee for limited legal services related to Texas law. Rania Combs provides unbundled legal services. This means that the legal services provided by us extend only to those services that you have requested and purchased and we have provided. After you have purchased a service and we have agreed to provide it and have completed the work, you cannot expect us to perform in any additional capacity.

For example, if we assist you in creating Estate Administration documents, it is not our responsibility to ensure that the forms are properly filed, to attend a hearing or trial on your behalf, or to provide any other legal services related to that matter beyond the original purchased and provided limited legal services. Likewise, after you have paid for the requested services and we have performed them, we will not expect any further payment from you other than payment for the original requested legal services performed by us.

As with any legal service, we cannot guarantee any legal outcome. By purchasing our services, you agree that it remains your responsibility to properly and timely file any legal documents and to comply with Texas state and local legal procedures.

The State Bar of Texas investigates and prosecutes misconduct committed by attorneys. Although not every complaint or dispute with a lawyer involves professional misconduct, the State Bar Office of the General Counsel will provide you with information about how to file a complaint. For more information, please call 1-800-932-1900.

Confidentiality—Security—Retaining of Records

Rania Combs provides limited legal services pertaining to Texas law only. The attorney responsible for this site is licensed to practice law only in the state of Texas. In compliance with the professional rules and restrictions of the Texas State Bar and the Texas Bar Association, and for reasons of personal integrity, this practice is bound by stringent professional standards of confidentiality. Any information received by us from our clients is held in the strictest confidence and will not be released to anyone outside this practice unless agreed to by you, or as required under applicable law.

An attorney-client relationship with this practice is established only after a specific question has been posed to an attorney at this practice through a prospective client's log-in page and that question has been confirmed as received through a reply communication from an attorney in this practice. Prospective clients should be aware that our duties of confidentiality and the attorney-client privilege may not arise until an attorney has expressly communicated the ability to respond to that prospective client. Once you have provided us with your personal information, we will first run a cross-check for any possible conflict of interest before accepting representation of your matter. We may decline to provide our service to you if a conflict of interest is discovered.

All our records are securely retained in electronic files, along with secure backups, for the period of years required under Texas law.

Articles and Other General Public Information Provided on this Website

The information contained in this website is provided for informational purposes only and should not be construed as legal advice. You should not act or refrain from acting on the basis of any content included in this site without seeking appropriate legal or other professional advice on the particular facts and circumstances at issue from an attorney licensed in your state.

Copyright

Rania Combs claims copyright protection on all the content provided in this website. The consent from this website may not be reproduced, copied, and/or redistributed in any form without the express permission of Rania Combs. Furthermore, the content from this website cannot be modified, nor can it be used for commercial purposes. Each document posted at this website shall contain the following copyright notice: © 2009 Rania Combs. All rights reserved.

Client Funds

No fee will be charged or obligation incurred by registering on this website. In most situations, a client's funds will not be transferred to Rania Combs until the legal services requested are ready to be accessed and received by the client on his or her personal log-in page.

Some requested services may require the upfront payment of a retainer fee before Rania Combs will begin work. After the client's payment of the agreed-upon price is confirmed through a Cardholder Information Security Program—(CISP) compliant credit-card processor, the client will have complete access to the legal advice, documents, research, or other services provided by the attorney.

If further communication with the attorney is required, the client may post a separate question regarding the received legal services or request a price quote for additional legal work. Rania Combs will not pay any court costs associated with your case that may be required as part of a lawsuit, filing fees, or service of process fees.

Technology—Security

Primary communications are done through this website over Secure HTTP, which provides you with the highest industry standard protection available on the web. All payments are processed by Cardholder Information Security Program—(CISP) compliant credit-card processors, and no credit card or payment account numbers are stored on our servers. The maintainer of this site has more than seven years of experience developing secure web-based applications, from tax filing to background-checking software, and uses secure programming techniques and best practices along with continual code auditing to ensure that this site is as secure as possible.

Links and E-mail Addresses

Links posted on this website to other websites are provided only as a convenience to our clients. We assume no responsibility for the content, security, or reliability of any websites to which we have posted links.

Spamming, the unsolicited broadcasts of e-mail addresses or links in this website, is prohibited and unauthorized.

Web Tracking—Cookies, Information Collection, and Privacy Policy

1. General Site
To view the articles and public documents on this site, you do not need to reveal any personal information. This site will present your browser with the option of accepting JavaScript and cookies in order to lay out the web page correctly and to store customized settings for your next visit. These features may be disabled by your browser; however, this will limit the look and functionality of the website. All page requests are logged in order to properly maintain the service and security of this website.

2. Virtual Law Office
In order to use the virtual law office, you must first register a user name and provide personal information about yourself. This information will be used during your transactions with Rania Combs to provide limited legal services in compliance with Texas law. Your information may be provided to a third party in order to provide the service you requested and/or as is

required by law. All other use of your personal information will be limited to your attorney-client relationship with Rania Combs. This site uses cookies to store a session ID. Therefore, in order to register on the website, cookies must be enabled so that we can provide you with a secure transaction.

Registration
To retain our services, you must register on our website. There will be no fee charged for registration. By registering you will receive access to a personal information page where you may request our services in a secure manner. By registering on our website, you are representing that you are at least 18 years of age and able to enter into a binding contact with Rania Combs. Furthermore, by registering you are representing that the information you provide to us is correct, accurate, and updated.

Reviewing and Updating Your Personal Content
Rania Combs requests that you keep your personal contact information current. After you have registered on our website, you may enter your personal information page at any time to review and update your personal information.

Contact Information
Because we are a virtual law practice, we would prefer that you provide your information to us using the technology provided for you on your personal client log-in page.

Limitation of Liability—No Warranties
Rania Combs assumes no liability for any errors or omissions in the content of this website. We will not be responsible under any legal theory for damages, including direct, indirect, incidental, consequential, or special, arising as a result of your use of this website. As stated above, this website pertains to the practice of Texas law only. Therefore, the content of this website is not applicable in any state other than Texas. The parties expressly agree that no oral or other representation has been made as to additional warranties or services.

The general information provided on this website is provided without warranty of any kind, express or implied. Rania Combs reserves the right to change, modify, add, and delete the content on this website.

Jurisdiction
The terms of this agreement will be governed by the laws of the State of Texas. The state and federal courts located in Harris County, Texas, will

have exclusive jurisdiction over any case or controversy arising from or relating to this agreement, Rania Combs's website, or any services provided by Rania Combs. Each person who registers on this website consents irrevocably to personal jurisdiction in such courts with the respect to any matters and waives any defense of forum non conveniens. Furthermore, each person who registers on this website is deemed to have knowingly and voluntarily waived any right to a trial by jury in any case or controversy related to this agreement, Rania Combs's website, or any services provided by her.

Assignment

The rights and obligations created for you under this agreement may not be assigned to any other party.

Force Majeure

Rania Combs will not be deemed to be in breach of this agreement for any delay or failure in performance caused by reasons out of its reasonable control, including acts of God or a public enemy; natural calamities; failure of a third party to perform; changes in the laws or regulations; actions of any civil, military, or regulatory authority; power outage or other disruptions of communication methods; or any other cause which would be out of the reasonable control of Rania Combs.

Severance

In the event that one or more of the provisions of this agreement shall be found unenforceable, illegal, or invalid, it shall not affect any other provisions of this agreement, and this agreement shall be construed as if the provision found to be unenforceable, illegal, or invalid had never been contained in the agreement, or the unenforceable, illegal, or invalid provision shall be construed, amended, and/or reformed to be made enforceable, legal, and valid.

IRS Circular 230 Disclosure

In compliance with the requirements of the IRS pertaining to the publication of Circular 230, we inform you that any advice contained on this website or in any communication originating from this website or this law practice which is related to U.S. federal tax advice is not intended or created to be used, and cannot be used, for the purpose of 1) either avoiding penalties under the Internal Revenue Code or promoting, marketing, or 2) recommending to another party any transaction or matter that is contained on this website or in any communication originating from this law practice.

Complete Understanding

This agreement supersedes any prior or contemporaneous communications, representations, or agreements between Rania Combs and the client and constitutes the complete and final agreement between the parties relating to this agreement, Rania Combs's website, or any services provided by Rania Combs.

Disclaimer

The information contained in this website is provided for informational purposes only and should not be construed as legal advice on any subject matter. No recipients of content from this site, clients or otherwise, should act or refrain from acting on the basis of any content included in the site without seeking the appropriate legal or other professional advice on the particular facts and circumstances at issue from an attorney licensed in the recipient's state. The content of this website contains general information and may not reflect current legal developments, verdicts, or settlements. Rania Combs expressly disclaims all liability in respect to actions taken or not taken based on any or all the contents of this website. Rania Combs is licensed to practice law in Texas.

Any information sent to Rania Combs by Internet e-mail or through the website is not secure and is done so on a non-confidential basis. Transmission of information from this website does not create an attorney-client relationship between you and Rania Combs Law, nor is it intended to do so. The transmission of the website, in part or in whole, and/or any communication with us via Internet e-mail through this site does not constitute or create an attorney-client relationship between us and any recipients.

Some links within the website may lead to other websites, including those operated and maintained by third parties. The Firm includes these links solely as a convenience to you, and the presence of such a link does not imply a responsibility for the linked site or an endorsement of the linked site, its operator, or its contents.

This website and its contents are provided "AS IS" without warranty of any kind, either expressed or implied, including, but not limited to, the implied warranties of merchantability, fitness for a particular purpose, or non-infringement.

Furthermore, the Firm does not wish to represent anyone desiring representation based upon viewing this website in a state where this website fails to comply with all laws and ethical rules of that state.

Reproduction, distribution, republication, and/or retransmission of material contained within the firm website are prohibited unless the prior written permission of Rania Combs has been obtained.

3. Limited Scope Engagement Agreement for Rosen Law Firm accessible at **http://www.rosen.com/diy/**. This agreement is used in conjunction with its Online Divorce Coach System, which coaches DIY clients through the process. The steps for unbundling involved in this are listed at **http://www.rosen.com/diy/**. A case study for the Rosen Law Firm is on page 140.

LIMITED-SCOPE REPRESENTATION CLIENT AGREEMENT

THIS AGREEMENT, hereinafter referred to as the "Agreement," a contract for employment for limited legal services, is made and entered into by and between Rosen Law Firm, hereinafter referred to as "the Firm," and [Client] hereinafter referred to as "the Client."

By entering into this Agreement and checking the "I Agree" box, Client employs the Firm to provide Client unlimited electronic access to an attorney with regard to Client's domestic issues or dispute. Client shall also have access to the forms, videos, articles, and other materials made available to the Client at the discretion of the Firm. The Firm is unbundling its services and offering this limited-scope representation as an alternative to its full-service legal representation.

Representation. Representation shall consist solely of unlimited electronic communication between the Client and the Firm to respond to questions regarding Client's domestic issues or dispute. Representation shall not include drafting agreements, review of settlement documents, communication with opposing counsel, telephone calls, in-person conferences, or other services. The electronic communications between the Client and the Firm are privileged and confidential communications. Representation shall terminate upon cancellation of the contract in writing by either the Client or the Firm or failure to pay fees as set forth below. A separate agreement will be negotiated between the Client and Firm in the event the Client requests further representation in addition to electronic communication, such as negotiation, verbal communication, in-person conferences, drafting settlement or other documents, litigation, or an appeal. The Client acknowledges that the Firm will not provide services to the

Client beyond the above-described electronic communications until such time as a separate agreement is executed.

The Firm shall provide limited representation to the Client in accordance with the laws of North Carolina related to the Client's domestic issues or dispute. However, due to the limited scope of representation, the Client agrees and understands that the electronic communications are based upon the limited factual information made available and are not intended as a conclusive response to the Client's questions regarding the domestic issues or dispute. The only manner in which to obtain comprehensive legal representation is to retain an attorney to provide a full range of legal services related to Client's situation. The responsive information provided by the Firm is designed to answer specific questions posed by the Client based solely on the information the Client provides.

In consideration of the limited representation to be furnished by the Firm as set forth above, Client shall pay the Firm pursuant to the following fee arrangements:

Fees. The Client shall pay the Firm a flat fee of One Hundred Ninety-Nine Dollars ($199.00) per month due on that date and subsequently due on the monthly anniversary of that date. Any payment that has come due and been paid by Client pursuant to this Agreement is a prepaid payment for the Client's continued use of the Firm's services as set forth above. This monthly payment is a flat fee for services, which is earned immediately, whether or not the Client utilizes the representation, and will be deposited into the Firm's operating account upon receipt.

Cancellation and Refund Policy. Client agrees to provide written notice of cancellation of the Agreement at least 2 business days prior to the monthly due date for payment of services. Any other cancellation or termination will be effective on the following month's due date, and monthly fee payments will not be prorated. The fee is not subject to refund unless it can be clearly demonstrated that the fee is excessive under the circumstances.

Personnel. The Client acknowledges that he or she is employing the Firm instead of any particular individual within the firm.

Termination of Services. The Client may terminate the representation at any time.

The Firm, upon written notice to the client, may terminate the representation of the Client and withdraw representation as set forth above if:

1.1. The Firm discovers any conflict of interest;

1.2. The Client fails to pay immediately when due any amounts required to be paid under this Agreement;

1.3. The Firm discovers that the Client has made any misrepresentation in connection with the representation, or the Firm discovers any material variance between the facts as related to the Firm by the Client and the facts as they actually exist;

1.4. The Client acts in such a manner that, in the discretion of the Firm, the Firm deems it necessary to terminate the representation;

1.5. The Firm and the Client have a disagreement over what legal matters the Firm is supposed to be handling for the Client.

Miscellaneous Terms

1.1. The Client may request a copy of the electronic file in digital format. By accepting this agreement, Client specifically agrees and consents that, without notice to the Client, the Firm may dispose of the electronic communications between the Firm and the Client after six (6) months have passed from the last fee paid by the Client.

1.2. Each provision of this agreement is severable. The invalidity or unenforceability of any provision, paragraph, subparagraph, sentence, clause, phrase, or term of this agreement shall not affect or impair the validity or enforceability of any other provision, paragraph, subparagraph, sentence, clause, phrase, or term of this agreement.

1.3. By checking the "I Agree" box below, Client indicates an understanding that the Firm has not made an agreement with Client or promises to Client about the outcome or result of Client's legal matters. Also, Client agrees to notify the Firm immediately in writing if Client feels or believes any matter is not receiving proper attention or is otherwise not being properly handled or Client suspects any misunderstanding about what the Firm is to do for Client.

1.4. By checking the "I Agree" box below, Client agrees that this Agreement has been thoroughly reviewed by him or her before being signed, and that Client has had ample opportunity to review this Agreement.

Additional Resources

Online ABA Guides on Unbundling

ABA's Unbundling Resource Center at **http://www.abanet.org/legal services/delivery/delunbundrules.html**

ABA Standing Committee on the Delivery of Legal Services white paper, "An Analysis of Rules That Enable Lawyers to Serve Pro Se Litigants," at **http://www.abanet.org/legalservices/delivery/downloads/prose_white_ paper.pdf**

ABA's Section of Litigation published its *Handbook on Limited Scope Assistance*, a Report of the Modest Means Task Force (2003), at **http://www.abanet.org/litigation/taskforces/modest/report.pdf**

Sampling of State-by-State Adoption and Modification of ABA Model Rule 1.2(c) and Ethics Opinions

For a regularly updated list of rules, visit the ABA Standing Committee on the Delivery of Legal Services Pro Se/Unbundling Resource Center at **http://www.americanbar.org/groups/delivery_legal_services/resources/ pro_se_unbundling_resource_center/court_rules.html**

Alabama

Alabama State Bar Association Ethics Opinion 2010-01 at **http://www.ala bar.org/ogc/fopDisplay.cfm?oneId=424**, last accessed October 22, 2011.

Alaska

Alaska Rule of Professional Conduct 1.2(c) at **http://www.courts.alaska .gov/prof.htm#1.2**, last accessed October 22, 2011.

Alaska Bar Association Ethics Opinion 93-1 (1993) at **https://www.alaska bar.org/servlet/content/indexes_aeot__93_1.html**, last accessed October 22, 2011.

Arizona

Arizona Ethics Rule 1.2 at **http://www.azbar.org/ethics/rulesof professionalconduct**, last accessed October 22, 2011.

Arizona State Bar Association Opinion 06-03 (2006) at **http://www.myaz bar.org/Ethics/opinionview.cfm?id=687**, last accessed October 22, 2011.

Arizona State Bar Association Op 05-06 (2005) at **http://www.myazbar.org/ Ethics/opinionview.cfm?id=525**, last accessed October 22, 2011.

Arizona State Bar Association Opinion 91-03 (1991) at **http://www.myaz bar.org/ethics/opinionview.cfm?id=618**, last accessed October 22, 2011.

Arkansas
Arkansas Rule of Professional Conduct 1.2(c) at **https://courts.arkansas .gov/rules/current_ark_prof_conduct/client_lawyer_relationship/ profcond1_2.cfm**, last accessed October 22, 2011.

California
California Civil Rule 3.35 at **http://www.courtinfo.ca.gov/cms/rules/ index.cfm?title=three&linkid=rule3_35**, last accessed October 22, 2011.

Los Angeles County Bar Association Prof. Resp. and Ethics Comm. Ethics Opinion 483 (1995) at **http://www.lacba.org/showpage.cfm?pageid=449**, last accessed October 22, 2011.

Los Angeles County Bar Association Prof. Resp. and Ethics Comm. Ethics Opinion 502 (1999) at **http://www.lacba.org/showpage.cfm?pageid=431**, last accessed October 22, 2011.

Colorado
Colorado Rule of Professional Conduct 1.2 at **http://www.cobar.org/index .cfm/ID/20472/subID/22373/CETH/**, last accessed October 22, 2011.

Colorado Bar Association Ethics Opinion 101 (1998) at **http://www.co bar.org/index.cfm/ID/386/subID/1822/CETH/Ethics-Opinion-101:- Unbundled-Legal-Services,-01/17/98;-Addendum-Issued-2006**, last accessed November 24, 2011.

Connecticut
Connecticut Rules of Professional Conduct 1.2(c) and 6.5 at **http://www .jud.ct.gov/pb.htm**

Connecticut Informal Opinion 90-18 (1990) not accessible online.

Delaware
Delaware Rules of Professional Conduct 1.2(c) and 6.5 at **http://courts .delaware.gov/Rules/DLRPCFebruary2010.pdf**

Delaware State Bar Association Opinion—2006-1 at **http://www.dsba.org/ pdfs/2006-1.pdf**

Delaware State Bar Association Comm. on Prof. Ethics Opinion 1994-2, not available online.

District of Columbia
District of Columbia Rules of Professional Conduct 1.2(c) and 6.5 at **http://www.dcbar.org/new_rules/rules.cfm**

D.C. Bar Opinion 330 (2005) at **http://www.dcbar.org/for_lawyers/ethics/ legal_ethics/opinions/opinion330.cfm**

Florida
Florida Rule of Professional Conduct 4-1.2(c) at **http://www.floridabar .org/divexe/rrtfb.nsf/FV/AE46B451CFA28E2885257170006BA282**

Florida State Bar Association Opinion 79-7 (Reconsideration 2000) at **http://www.floridabar.org/tfb/tfbetopin.nsf/SearchView/ETHICS,+ OPINION+79-7+Reconsideration?opendocument**

Hawaii
Hawaii Revised Code of Judicial Conduct Rule 2.2, Comment 4 at **http://www.courts.state.hi.us/docs/court_rules/rules/rcjc.htm**

Idaho
Idaho Rules of Professional Conduct 1.2(c) and 6.5 at **http://www .floridabar.org/tfb/tfbetopin.nsf/SearchView/ETHICS,+OPINION+79-7+ Reconsideration?opendocument**

Illinois
Illinois Rule of Professional Conduct 1.2 (c) at **http://www.state.il.us/ court/SupremeCourt/Rules/Art_VIII/ArtVIII_NEW.htm#1.2**

Illinois State Bar Association Prof'l Conduct Comm. Opinion 94-01 (accessible online only by Illinois Bar members).

Illinois State Bar Association Prof'l Conduct Comm. Opinion 04-03 (accessible online only by Illinois Bar members).

Illinois State Bar Association Prof'l Conduct Comm. Opinion 849 (accessible online only by Illinois Bar members).

Illinois State Bar Association Prof'l Conduct Comm. Opinion 85-6 (accessible online only by Illinois Bar members).

Indiana
Indiana Rule of Professional Conduct 1.2(c) at **http://www.in.gov/judiciary/ rules/prof_conduct/#_Toc279154321**, last accessed November 14, 2011.

Iowa

Iowa Rules of Professional Conduct Rule 32:1.2(c) at **http://www.legis .state.ia.us/DOCS/ACO/CR/LINC/02-02-2011.chapter.32.pdf**, last accessed November 14, 2011.

Iowa State Bar Association Opinion 94-35 (1995) at **http://www.iabar .net/ethics.nsf/e61beed77a215f6686256497004ce492/24c7fb05f296dffc 8625649c004cbc4c?OpenDocument**, last accessed November 14, 2011.

Iowa State Bar Association Opinion 96-31 (1997) at **http://www.iabar .net/ethics.nsf/e61beed77a215f6686256497004ce492/afc5d662305ed 915862564f400134181?OpenDocument**, last accessed November 14, 2011.

Kansas

Kansas Rule of Professional Conduct 1.2(c) at **http://www.kscourts.org/ rules/Rule-Info.asp?r1=Rules+Relating+to+discipline+of+attorneys& r2=53**, last accessed November 14, 2011.

Report on Limited Representation Pilot Projects by Art Thompson, April 2011, at **http://www.americanbar.org/content/dam/aba/uncategorized/ 20110509_ls_del_kansas_unbundling_pilot_projects.authcheckdam.pdf**, last accessed October 24, 2011.

Kansas Ethics Opinion No. 09-01 at **http://www.ksbar.org/pdf/ethics_ 09-01.pdf**, last accessed November 14, 2011.

Kansas Ethics Opinion 92-06 (1992).

Kentucky

Kentucky Rule of Professional Conduct 1.2(c) at **http://www.kybar.org/ documents/scr/scr3/scr_3.130_%281.2%29.pdf**, last accessed November 14, 2011.

Kentucky Bar Association Opinion E-343 (1991) at **http://www.kybar.org/ documents/ethics_opinions/kba_e-343.pdf**, last accessed November 14, 2011.

Louisiana

Louisiana Rules of Professional Conduct 1.2(c) and 6.5 at **http://www.ladb .org/Publications/ropc.pdf**, last accessed November 14, 2011.

Maine

Maine Rule of Professional Conduct 1.2(c) with a limited representation agreement attached at **http://www.maine.gov/tools/whatsnew/index .php?topic=mebar_overseers_bar_rules&id=87817&v=article**, last accessed November 12, 2011.

Maine State Bar Ethics Opinion No. 89 (1988) at **http://www.maine.gov/ tools/whatsnew/index.php?topic=mebar_overseers_ethics_opinions& id=91478&v=article**, last accessed November 12, 2011.

Maryland
Maryland Rules of Professional Conduct 1.2(c) and 6.5 at **http://www.lexis nexis.com/hottopics/mdcode/**, last accessed November 12, 2011.

Massachusetts
Supreme Judicial Court Order In Re: Limited Assistance Representation (May 2009) at **http://www.mass.gov/courts/sjc/docs/Rules/Limited_ Assistance_Representation_order1_04-09.pdf**, last accessed November 12, 2011.

Massachusetts Bar Association Committee on Professional Ethics, Opinion 98-1 (1998) at **http://www.massbar.org/publications/ethics-opinions/ 1990-1999/1998/opinion-no-98-1/**, last accessed November 12, 2011.

Michigan
State Bar of Michigan Opinion RI-348 (2010) at **http://www.michbar.org/ opinions/ethics/numbered_opinions/ri-348.htm**, last accessed November 12, 2011.

State Bar of Michigan Opinion RI-347 (2010) at **http://www.michbar.org/ opinions/ethics/numbered_opinions/ri-347.htm**, last accessed November 12, 2011.

State Bar of Michigan Opinion RI-301 (1997) at **http://www.michbar.org/ opinions/ethics/numbered_opinions/ri-301.htm**, last accessed November 12, 2011.

Minnesota
Minnesota Rules of Professional Conduct 1.2(c) and 6.5 at **http://lprb.mn courts.gov/rules/Documents/MN%20Rules%20of%20Professional%20 Conduct.pdf**, last accessed November 12, 2011.

Mississippi
Mississippi Rule of Professional Conduct 1.2: "A lawyer may limit the objectives or scope of the representation if the limitation is reasonable under the circumstances and the client gives informed consent." Supreme Court of Mississippi Corrected Order, No. 89-R-99018-SCT (January 28, 2011) at **http://courts.ms.gov/rules/msrulesofcourt/rules_ of_professional_conduct.pdf**, last accessed November 12, 2011.

Mississippi State Bar Opinion 176 (1990) at **http://www.msbar.org/ ethic_opinions.php?id=438**, last accessed November 12, 2011.

Advisory Committee of the Supreme Court of Missouri Formal Opinion 124 (2008) at **http://www.mobar.org/ethics/formalopinions/frontpage.htm**, last accessed November 12, 2011.

Missouri

Missouri Rule of Professional Conduct 1.2, Order from the Supreme Court of the State of Missouri with the newest version of the Rule (March 15, 2011) at **http://www.courts.mo.gov/courts/ClerkHandbooksP2Rules Only.nsf/c0c6ffa99df4993f86256ba50057dcb8/8195dff3462d90ba86256 ca6005211c1?OpenDocument**, last accessed November 12, 2011.

Missouri Bar Association Advisory Opinion 940161.

Missouri Bar Association Advisory Opinion 940049.

Montana

Montana Rule of Professional Conduct 1.2(c) at **http://supremecourtdocket .mt.gov/view/AF%2009-0688%20Rule%20Change%20—%20Order?id= %7bDF5F0047-A741-4BE0-A672-04051EF478E1%7d**, last accessed November 12, 2011.

Montana State Bar Association Advisory Opinion 900409 (1990) at **http:// www.montanabar.org/displaycommon.cfm?an=1&subarticlenbr=103**, last accessed November 12, 2011.

Nebraska

Nebraska Rules of Professional Conduct Rule 501.2 at **http://www.supreme court.ne.gov/rules/pdf/Ch3Art5.pdf**, last accessed November 12, 2011.

Nebraska State Bar Association Ethics Opinion 94-2 at **http://www.supreme court.ne.gov/professional-ethics/lawyers/ethics-pdfs/1990s/94-2.pdf**, last accessed November 12, 2011.

Nevada

Nevada Rules of Professional Conduct 1.2(c) and 6.5 at **http://www.leg .state.nv.us/courtrules/RPC.html**, last accessed November 12, 2011.

State Bar of Nevada Formal Ethics Opinion No. 34 at **http://64.77.93.72/ sites/default/files/opinion_34.pdf**, last accessed November 12, 2011.

New Hampshire

New Hampshire Rule of Professional Conduct 1.2 at **http://www.courts .state.nh.us/rules/pcon/pcon-1_2.htm**, last accessed November 12, 2011.

New Jersey

New Jersey Rule of Professional Conduct 1.2 (c) at **http://www.judiciary .state.nj.us/rules/apprpc.htm#x1dot2**, last accessed November 12, 2011.

New Jersey Supreme Court Advisory Committee on Professional Ethics Opinion 713 (2008) at **http://www.judiciary.state.nj.us/notices/ethics/ ACPE713.pdf**, last accessed November 12, 2011.

New Mexico

New Mexico Rules of Professional Conduct Rule 16-102(c) at **http://www .conwaygreene.com/nmsu/lpext.dll?f=templates&fn=main-h.htm&2.0**, last accessed November 12, 2011.

New Mexico Ethics Advisory Opinion 1987-12 (1987) at **www.nmbar.org/ legalresearch/eao/1987/1987-12.doc**, last accessed November 12, 2011.

New Mexico Advisory Opinion 1987-6 (1987) at **http://www.nmbar.org/ legalresearch/ethicsadvisoryopinions.html**, last accessed November 12, 2011.

New York

New York Rules of Professional Conduct 1.2(c) and 6.5 at **http://www .nysba.org/Content/NavigationMenu/ForAttorneys/Professional StandardsforAttorneys/NYRulesofProfessionalConduct4109.pdf**, last accessed November 12, 2011.

Association of the Bar of the City of New York Formal Opinion 2009-2 (2009) at **http://www.abcny.org/ethics/ethics-opinions-local/2009- opinions/788-ethical-duties-concerning-self-represented-persons**, last accessed November 12, 2011.

New York County Law Association Committee on Professional Ethics Opinion 742 (2010) at **http://www.nycla.org/siteFiles/Publications/ Publications1348_0.pdf**, last accessed November 12, 2011.

New York State Bar Association Opinion 613 (1990) at **http://www.nys ba.org/AM/Template.cfm?Section=Ethics_Opinions&template=/CM/ ContentDisplay.cfm&ContentID=49272**, last accessed November 12, 2011.

North Carolina

North Carolina Rules of Professional Conduct 1.2(c) and 6.5 at **http://www .ncbar.com/rules/rules.asp?page=5**, last accessed November 12, 2011.

North Carolina State Bar Formal Opinion 3 (2008) at **http://www.ncbar .com/ethics/ethics.asp?page=1&keywords=114**, last accessed November 12, 2011.

North Carolina State Bar Formal Opinion10 (2005) at **http://www.ncbar .com/ethics/ethics.asp?page=3&from=1/2006&to=6/2006**, last accessed November 12, 2011.

North Carolina State Bar Rule of Professional Conduct 114 (1991) at **http:// www.ncbar.com/ethics/ethics.asp?page=19&from=1/1991&to=12/1991**, last accessed November 12, 2011.

North Carolina State Bar Opinion 6 (2002) at **http://www.ncbar.com/ ethics/ethics.asp?page=323&keywords=6**, last accessed November 12, 2011.

North Carolina Lawyer's Mutual Risk Management Handout on Unbundling at **http://www.lawyersmutualnc.com/_public/documents/ resources/Unbundling_Legal_Services.pdf**, last accessed November 12, 2011.

North Dakota
North Dakota Rule of Civil Procedure 11(e) at **http://www.ndcourts.gov/ court/rules/CIVIL/rule11.htm**, last accessed November 12, 2011.

Ohio
Ohio Rules of Professional Conduct 1.2(c) and 6.5 at **http://www.supreme court.ohio.gov/LegalResources/Rules/ProfConduct/profConductRules .pdf**, last accessed November 12, 2011.

Oklahoma
Oklahoma Rule of Professional Conduct 1.2(c) at **http://www.oscn.net/ applications/oscn/DeliverDocument.asp?CiteID=448831**, last accessed November 12, 2011.

Oregon
Oregon Rules of Professional Conduct 1.2(b) and 6.5 at **http://www.osbar .org/_docs/rulesregs/orpc.pdf**, last accessed November 12, 2011.

Oregon State Bar Association Formal Opinion No. 2011-183 at **http://www .osbar.org/_docs/ethics/2011-183.pdf**, last accessed November 12, 2011.

Pennsylvania
Pennsylvania Rules of Professional Conduct 1.2(c) and 6.5 at **http://www .padisciplinaryboard.org/documents/RulesOfProfessionalConduct.pdf**, last accessed November 12, 2011.

Rhode Island
Rhode Island Rules of Professional Conduct 1.2(c) and 6.5 at **http://www .courts.ri.gov/AttorneyResources/ethicsadvisorypanel/PDF/Ethics Article5.pdf#openinnewwindow**, last accessed November 12, 2011.

South Carolina
South Carolina Rule of Professional Conduct 1.2(c) at **http://www.judicial .state.sc.us/courtReg/displayRule.cfm?ruleID=407.0&subRuleID=RULE %201%2E2&ruleType=APP**, last accessed November 12, 2011.

South Carolina Bar Ethics Advisory Opinion 05-18 at **http://www.scbar .org/MemberResources/EthicsAdvisoryOpinions/OpinionView/ArticleId/ 723/Ethics-Advisory-Opinion-05-18.aspx**, last accessed November 12, 2011.

South Carolina Bar Ethics Advisory Opinion 90-18 at **http://www.scbar .org/MemberResources/EthicsAdvisoryOpinions/OpinionView/ArticleId/ 354/Ethics-Advisory-Opinion-90-18.aspx**, last accessed November 12, 2011.

South Dakota
South Dakota Rule of Professional Conduct 1.2(c) at **http://www.sdbar.org/ Rules/Rules/rule_1_2.htm**, last accessed November 12, 2011.

Tennessee
Tennessee Rules of Professional Conduct 1.2(c) and 6.5 at **http://www.tba .org/ethics/2011_TRPC.pdf**, last accessed November 12, 2011.

Board of Prof. Resp. of the Sup. Ct. of Tenn. Opinion 2007-F-153 at **http://www.tbpr.org/Attorneys/EthicsOpinions/Pdfs/2007-F-153.pdf**, last accessed November 12, 2011.

Board of Prof. Resp. of the Sup. Ct. of Tenn. Opinion 2005-F-151 at **http://www.tbpr.org/Attorneys/EthicsOpinions/Pdfs/2005-F-151.pdf**, last accessed November 12, 2011.

Board of Prof. Resp. of the Sup. Ct. of Tenn. Opinion 93-F-130 (1993) at **http://www.tsc.state.tn.us/OPINIONS/Ethics/BdofProResp/_PDF_Files/ 92-99/93-F-130.pdf**, last accessed November 12, 2011.

As of November 18, 2011, the Supreme Court of Tennessee is considering proposed amendments to Rules 5.02 and 11.01 of the Tennessee Rules of Civil Procedure which would provide additional guidance on service of papers and pleadings, notice to the court, and withdrawal of counsel for lawyers providing limited scope representation. The Order and proposed amendments may be accessed at **http://www.tsc.state.tn.us/sites/ default/files/sc_order_soliciting_comments_on_tn_rules_of_civil_ procedure_12-5-11.pdf**, last accessed December 12, 2011.

Utah
Utah Rule of Professional Conduct 1.2 (c) at **http://www.utcourts.gov/ resources/rules/ucja/ch13/1_2.htm**, last accessed November 12, 2011.

Utah State Bar Ethics Advisory Opinion Committee Opinion 96-12 (1997) at **http://www.utahbar.org/rules_ops_pols/ethics_opinions/op_96_12 .html**, last accessed November 12, 2011.

Utah State Bar Ethics Advisory Opinion Committee Opinion 08-01 (2008).

Utah State Bar Ethics Advisory Opinion Committee Opinion 02-10 (2002).

Vermont
Vermont Rules of Professional Conduct 1.2(c) and 6.5 at **http://www .vermontjudiciary.org/LC/Shared%20Documents/VermontRulesof ProfessionalConduct_withamendmentsthroughJune2011.pdf**, last accessed November 12, 2011.

Standing Committee on Legal Ethics, Virginia State Bar Association Ethics Opinion 1127 (1988).

Standing Committee on Legal Ethics, Virginia State Bar Association Ethics Opinion 1761 (2002).

Standing Committee on Legal Ethics, Virginia State Bar Association Ethics Opinion 1592 (1994).

Washington
Washington Rule of Professional Conduct 1.2(c) at **http://www.courts.wa .gov/court_rules/?fa=court_rules.display&group=ga&set=RPC&ruleid= garpc1.02**, last accessed November 12, 2011.

Washington State Bar Association Informal Ethics Opinion 1763 (1997) at **http://mcle.mywsba.org/IO/print.aspx?ID=827**, last accessed November 12, 2011.

Washington State Bar Association Informal Ethics Opinion 2169 (2008) at **http://mcle.mywsba.org/IO/print.aspx?ID=1630**, last accessed November 12, 2011.

Wisconsin
Wisconsin Rule of Professional Conduct 1.2(c) at **http://www.wicourts .gov/sc/scrule/DisplayDocument.html?content=html&seqNo=45322**, last accessed November 12, 2011.

State Bar of Wisconsin Formal Opinion E-09-03 at **http://www.wisbar.org/ AM/Template.cfm?Section=News&Template=/CM/HTMLDisplay.cfm& ContentID=84115**, last accessed November 12, 2011.

State Bar of Wisconsin Formal Opinion E-97-1 at **http://www.wisbar.org/ AM/TemplateRedirect.cfm?template=/CM/ContentDisplay.cfm&Content ID=45048**, last accessed November 12, 2011.

Wyoming
Wyoming Rule of Professional Conduct 1.2(c) at **http://courts.state.wy.us/ CourtRules_Entities.aspx?RulesPage=AttorneysConduct.xml**, last accessed November 12, 2011.

State-by-State Ghostwriting and Limited Appearance Rules

If the state has a requirement for the duty of disclosure to the courts in ghostwriting, this is indicated next to the referenced rule or opinion.

For a full list of updated rules, including those related to withdrawing from a limited-scope matter, see the ABA Standing Committee on the Delivery of Legal Services Pro Se/Unbundling Resource Center at **http:// www.americanbar.org/groups/delivery_legal_services/resources/pro_ se_unbundling_resource_center/court_rules.html**.

States That Require Disclosure

Alaska
Alaska Bar Association Ethics Comm. Opinion 93-1 (1993) Duty to disclose, at **https://www.alaskabar.org/servlet/content/indexes_aeot__93_1.html**, last accessed November 12, 2011.

Alaska Rule of Civil Procedure 81 **http://www.courts.alaska.gov/civ2.htm #81**, last accessed November 12, 2011.

Arizona

Arizona Ethics Opinion 06-03 (July 2006) No disclosure at **http://www .myazbar.org/ethics/opinionview.cfm?id=687**, last accessed November 12, 2011.

State Bar of Arizona Committee on the Rules of Professional Conduct Opinion 05-06 (2005) No disclosure at **http://www.myazbar.org/ethics/ opinionview.cfm?id=525**, last accessed November 12, 2011.

Arizona Rule of Family Law Procedure 9(B) at **http://www.supreme.state .az.us/rules/ramd_pdf/R-05-0008.pdf**, last accessed November 12, 2011.

Arizona Rule of Civil Procedure 5.2 at **http://government.westlaw.com/ linkedslice/default.asp?SP=AZR-1000**, last accessed November 12, 2011.

California

Los Angeles County Bar Association Ethics Opinion 502 (Nov. 4, 1999) No disclosure at **http://www.lacba.org/showpage.cfm?pageid=431**, last accessed November 12, 2011.

Los Angeles County Bar Association Ethics Opinion 483 (Mar. 20, 1995) at **http://www.lacba.org/showpage.cfm?pageid=449**, last accessed November 12, 2011.

California Family and Juvenile Rule 5.70 at **http://www.courtinfo.ca.gov/ cms/rules/index.cfm?title=five**, last accessed November 12, 2011.

California Civil Rule 3.37 at **http://www.courtinfo.ca.gov/cms/rules/ index.cfm?title=three**, last accessed November 12, 2011.

Colorado

Colorado Rules of Civil Procedure, CRCP 121 Local Rules—Statewide Practice Standards Section 1-1: Entry of Appearance and Withdrawal, Section 5, Notice of Limited Representation: Entry of Appearance and Withdrawal at **http://www.courts.state.co.us/userfiles/file/Court_ Probation/Supreme_Court/Rule_Changes/2011/2011_13_redlined.pdf**, last accessed October 24, 2011. In the summer of 2011, the Colorado Supreme Court proposed an amendment to CRCP 121, § 1-1 that would allow for automatic withdrawal for attorneys providing limited-scope representation to clients. The proposed amendment can be found at **http://www.courts.state.co.us/Courts/Supreme_Court/Rule_Changes .cfm**, last accessed November 15, 2011.

Colorado Rule of County Court 311(b) at **http://www.michie.com/colorado/ lpext.dll?f=templates&fn=main-h.htm&cp**, last accessed November 12, 2011.

Colorado Rule of County Court 11(b) at **http://www.michie.com/colorado/ lpext.dll?f=templates&fn=main-h.htm&cp**, last accessed November 12, 2011.

Connecticut
Connecticut Bar Association Committee on Professional Ethics Opinion 98-5 (1998) Duty to disclose, not accessible online.

Delaware
Delaware State Bar Association Committee on Professional Ethics Opinion 1994-2 (1994) Duty to disclose at **http://www.dsba.org/pdfs/1994-2.pdf**, last accessed November 12, 2011.

Delaware Family Court Rules of Civil Procedure Rule 5(b)(2)(A) and Rule 5(b)(2)(B) at **http://courts.delaware.gov/Rules/?FCcivill_jan06.pdf**, last accessed November 12, 2011.

Florida
Florida State Bar Association Committee on Professional Ethics Opinion 79-7 (2000) Duty to disclose at **http://www.floridabar.org/tfb/tfbetopin .nsf/SearchView/ETHICS,+OPINION+79-7+Reconsideration?open document**, last accessed November 12, 2011.

Florida Family Law Rules of Procedure 12.040(a), 12.040(b)–(c), 12.040(d), 12.040(e), and 12.750 at **http://www.floridabar.org/TFB/TFBResources .nsf/Attachments/416879C4A88CBF0485256B29004BFAF8/$FILE/311% 20Family%20Law.pdf**, last accessed on November 12, 2011.

Comment to Florida Rule of Professional Conduct 1.2, not accessible online.

Illinois
Illinois State Bar Association Opinion 849 (Dec, 9, 1983) No disclosure, not accessible online.

"Expanding Access to Justice: Limited Scope Representation is Here" by J. Timothy Eaton and David Holtermann (April 2010) at **http://www.isba .org/sites/default/files/committees/limitedscopelegalrepresentation/ feature_eaton.pdf**, last accessed November 12, 2011.

Indiana
Indiana Rule of Trial Procedure 3.1 at **http://www.in.gov/judiciary/orders/ rule-amendments/2011/order-amend-2011-pcr.pdf**, last accessed November 12, 2011.

Iowa

Iowa Supreme Court Bd. of Professional Ethics and Conduct Opinion 96-31 (1997) at **http://www.iabar.net/ethics.nsf/e61beed77a215f 6686256497004ce492/afc5d662305ed915862564f400134181?Open Document**, last accessed November 12, 2011.

Iowa Rules of Civil Procedure 1.404(3), 1.423(1), 1.423(2), 1.423(3), 1.442(2) at **http://www.legis.state.ia.us/DOCS/ACO/CR/LINC/09-23-2010.chapter.1.pdf**, last accessed November 12, 2011.

Kansas

Kansas has published a Limited Notice of Appearance form at **http://www .kscourts.org/Programs/Self-Help/Limited-Representation/Limited-Notice-of-Appearance.pdf**, last accessed November 15, 2011.

Kentucky

Kentucky Bar Association Opinion E-343 (1991) Duty to disclose at **http://www.kybar.org/documents/ethics_opinions/kba_e-343.pdf**, last accessed November 15, 2011.

Maine

Maine State Bar Ethica Opinion 89 (Aug. 31, 1988) No disclosure, not accessible online.

Maine Rule of Professional Conduct 1.2(c) allows for limited appearances at **http://www.maine.gov/tools/whatsnew/index.php?topic=mebar_ overseers_bar_rules&id=87817&v=article**, last accessed November 15, 2011.

Maine Rules of Civil Procedure 5(b), 11(b), and 89(a) at **http://www.courts .state.me.us/rules_adminorders/rules/MRCivPONLY7-10.pdf**, last accessed November 15, 2011. Rule 89(a) states that attorneys providing limited appearances do not have to go through standard withdrawal procedures.

Massachusetts

Massachusetts Bar Association Committee on Professional Ethics Opinion 98-1 (1998) Duty to disclose Supreme Judicial Court Order In Re: Limited Assistance Representation at **http://www.mass.gov/courts/sjc/docs/ Rules/Limited_Assistance_Representation_order1_04-09.pdf**, last accessed November 15, 2011.

Michigan
State Bar of Michigan Opinion RI-347 (2010) No disclosure required, at **http://www.michbar.org/opinions/ethics/numbered_opinions/ri-347.htm**, last accessed November 15, 2011.

Mississippi
Mississippi Rule of Professional Conduct 1.2(c) permits limited appearances without the lawyer having to appear on record with the court.

Missouri
Missouri Rule of Civil Procedure 55.03 No disclosure required, requires attorney in limited appearance to file a "Termination of Limited Appearance" entry at **http://www.courts.mo.gov/courts/ClerkHandbooksP2 RulesOnly.nsf/0/7db1c05900034fdc86256ca60052152c?OpenDocument**, last accessed November 15, 2011.

Montana
Montana Rule of Civil Procedure 4.2(c) No disclosure necessary.

Rule 4.3(a), Rule 4.3(b), Rule 11 at **http://data.opi.mt.gov/bills/mca_toc/ 25_20.htm**, last accessed November 15, 2011.

Nebraska
Nebraska Rules of Professional Conduct 501.2(c) and 501.2(d) at **http://www.supremecourt.ne.gov/rules/html/Ch3/art5/3-501.2.shtml**, last accessed November 14, 2011.

Nevada
Nevada Opinion 34 (revised 6/24/09) at **http://64.77.93.72/sites/default/ files/opinion_34.pdf** and Rules of Practice of the Eighth Judicial District Court of the State of Nevada Rule 5.28(a) at **http://www.leg.state.nv.us/ courtrules/EighthDCR.html**, last accessed November 15, 2011. Requires disclosure.

New Hampshire
New Hampshire Bar Association Ethics Committee, *Unbundled Services— Assisting the Pro se Litigant* (1999), at **http://www.nhbar.org/pdfs/PEA5- 99.pdf**, New Hampshire Rules of Civil Procedure 3, 17(c), and 17(g) at **http://www.nhbar.org/uploads/pdf/RulesCivilProcedureDraft011807.pdf**, last accessed November 15, 2011. Lawyer does not have to sign the ghost-

written document, but must include on the document "This pleading was prepared with the assistance of a New Hampshire attorney."

New Mexico
New Mexico Rule of Professional Conduct 16-303(E) at **http://www .conwaygreene.com/nmsu/lpext.dll?f=templates&fn=main-h.htm&2.0**, last accessed November 14, 2011. Disclosure required.

New Mexico Rules of Civil Procedure 1-089(A)(1), 2-107(C), and 3-107(C) at **http://www.conwaygreene.com/nmsu/lpext.dll?f=templates&fn= main-h.htm&2.0**, last accessed November 15, 2011.

New York
Association of the Bar of the City of New York Committee on Professional and Judicial Ethics Opinion 1987-2 (1987) and New York State Bar Association Committee on Professional Ethics Opinion 613 (1990) at **http://www .nysba.org/AM/Template.cfm?Section=Ethics_Opinions&template=/CM/ ContentDisplay.cfm&ContentID=49272**, last accessed November 15, 2011. Finding ghostwriting unethical and requiring disclosure.

New York County Law Association Committee on Professional Ethics Op. 742 (2010) at **http://www.nycla.org/siteFiles/Publications/Publications 1348_0.pdf**, last accessed December 11, 2011.

In re Fengling Liu, U.S. Ct. Appeals 2nd Cir., November 22, 2011, Docket No. 09-90006-am, finding that an attorney could not be disciplined for ghost-writing because of the lack of rules expressly prohibiting the practice.

North Carolina
North Carolina Opinion 2008-3 (2008) at **http://www.ncbar.com/ethics/ ethics.asp?id=792**, last accessed November 15, 2011. No disclosure required.

North Dakota
North Dakota Rule of Civil Procedure 11(e) at **http://www.ndcourts.gov/ court/rules/CIVIL/rule11.htm**, last accessed November 15, 2011. Requires disclosure and notice of both the scope of representation and when it is terminated.

Oregon
Oregon Uniform Trial Court Rule 2.010(7) at **http://courts.oregon.gov/ OJD/docs/programs/utcr/2010_UTCR_ch02.pdf**, last accessed November 15, 2011. Requires disclosure and, if no attorney authorship, the pro se lit-

igant must file a Certificate of Document Preparation. This form (2.010.7) may be viewed at **http://courts.oregon.gov/OJD/docs/programs/utcr/ 2011_UTCR_Appendix_of_Forms.pdf**, last accessed November 15, 2011.

Utah

Utah State Bar Ethics Advisory Opinion Committee Formal Opinion 08-01 (2008) at **http://www.utahbar.org/rules_ops_pols/ethics_opinions/ op_08_01.html**, last accessed November 14, 2011. No disclosure required.

Utah Rule of Professional Conduct 4.2(b) at **http://www.utcourts.gov/ resources/rules/ucja/ch13/4_2.htm**, Rule 4.3(b) at **http://www.utcourts .gov/resources/rules/ucja/ch13/4_3.htm**, last accessed November 14, 2011.

Utah Rule of Civil Procedure 75 at **http://www.utcourts.gov/resources/ rules/urcp/urcp075.html**, last accessed November 14, 2011.

Vermont

Vermont Rule of Civil Procedure 79.1 at **http://michie.lexisnexis.com/ vermont/lpext.dll?f=templates&fn=main-h.htm&cp**, last accessed November 14, 2011.

Vermont Rule of Family Proceedings 15(h)(1) and (h)(2) at **http://www .michie.com/vermont/lpext.dll?f=templates&fn=tools-contents.htm& cp=vtrules&2.0**, last accessed November 14, 2011.

Virginia

Virginia Legal Ethics Opinion 1761 (Jan. 6, 2002) No disclosure, not accessible online.

Virginia Legal Ethics Opinion 1592 (Sept. 14, 1994).

Washington

Washington Civil Rule 4.2 at **http://www.courts.wa.gov/court_rules/?fa= court_rules.display&group=sup&set=CR&ruleid=supcr04.2**, last accessed November 14, 2011.

Washington Civil Rule of Limited Jurisdiction 4.2 at **http://www.courts .wa.gov/court_rules/?fa=court_rules.display&group=clj&set=CRLJ&rule id=cljcrlj04.2**, last accessed November 14, 2011.

Washington Civil Rule 11 at **http://www.courts.wa.gov/court_rules/?fa= court_rules.display&group=sup&set=CR&ruleid=supcr11**, last accessed November 14, 2011.

Washington Civil Rule of Limited Jurisdiction 11 at **http://www.courts.wa .gov/court_rules/?fa=court_rules.display&group=clj&set=CRLJ&ruleid= cljcrlj11**, last accessed November 14, 2011.

Washington Civil Rule 70.1 at **http://www.courts.wa.gov/court_rules/ ?fa=court_rules.display&group=sup&set=CR&ruleid=supcr70.1**, last accessed November 14, 2011.

Washington Civil Rule of Limited Jurisdiction 70.1 at **http://www.courts .wa.gov/court_rules/?fa=court_rules.display&group=clj&set=CRLJ&rule id=cljcrlj70.1**, last accessed November 14, 2011.

West Virginia

West Virginia Lawyer Disciplinary Board Ethics Opinion 2010-01 at **http://www.wvodc.org/pdf/lei/ghostwriting.pdf**, last accessed November 12, 2011. Requires disclosure of any ghostwritten documents filed with the court.

Wisconsin

Milwaukee County Family Division Rule 5.6(c) at **http://www.wisbar.org/ AM/Template.cfm?Section=Rules_for_the_Family_Division**, last accessed November 14, 2011.

Wyoming

Wyoming Rule of Professional Conduct 1.2[7] at **http://courts.state.wy .us/CourtRules_Entities.aspx?RulesPage=AttorneysConduct.xml**, last accessed November 14, 2011.

Uniform Rules of the District Court of the State of Wyoming 102(a)(1)(B) and 102(a)(1)(C) at **http://www.courts.state.wy.us/CourtRules_Entities .aspx?RulesPage=DistrictCourt.xml**, last accessed November 15, 2011.

Contents

The Lawyer's Guide to Collaboration Tools and Technologies: Smart Ways to Work Together
By Dennis Kennedy and Tom Mighell

Product Code: 5110589 / LPM Price: $59.95 / Regular Price: $89.95

This first-of-its-kind guide for the legal profession shows you how to use standard technology you already have and the latest "Web 2.0" resources and other tech tools, like Google Docs, Microsoft Office and Share-Point, and Adobe Acrobat, to work more effectively on projects with colleagues, clients, co-counsel and even opposing counsel. In *The Lawyer's Guide to Collaboration Tools and Technologies: Smart Ways to Work Together*, well-known legal technology authorities Dennis Kennedy and Tom Mighell provides a wealth of information useful to lawyers who are just beginning to try these tools, as well as tips and techniques for those lawyers with intermediate and advanced collaboration experience.

Google for Lawyers: Essential Search Tips and Productivity Tools
By Carole A. Levitt and Mark E. Rosch

Product Code: 5110704 / LPM Price: $47.95 / Regular Price: $79.95

This book introduces novice Internet searchers to the diverse collection of information locatable through Google. The book discusses the importance of including effective Google searching as part of a lawyer's due diligence, and cites case law that mandates that lawyers should use Google and other resources available on the Internet, where applicable. For intermediate and advanced users, the book unlocks the power of various advanced search strategies and hidden search features they might not be aware of.

The Lawyer's Guide to Adobe Acrobat, Third Edition
By David L. Masters

Product Code: 5110588 / LPM Price: $49.95 / Regular Price: $79.95

This book was written to help lawyers increase productivity, decrease costs, and improve client services by moving from paper-based files to digital records. This updated and revised edition focuses on the ways lawyers can benefit from using the most current software, Adobe® Acrobat 8, to create Portable Document Format (PDF) files.

PDF files are reliable, easy-to-use, electronic files for sharing, reviewing, filing, and archiving documents across diverse applications, business processes, and platforms. The format is so reliable that the federal courts' Case Management/Electronic Case Files (CM/ECF) program and state courts that use Lexis-Nexis File & Serve have settled on PDF as the standard.

You'll learn how to:

- Create PDF files from a number of programs, including Microsoft Office
- Use PDF files the smart way
- Markup text and add comments
- Digitally, and securely, sign documents
- Extract content from PDF files
- Create electronic briefs and forms

The Electronic Evidence and Discovery Handbook: Forms, Checklists, and Guidelines
By Sharon D. Nelson, Bruce A. Olson, and John W. Simek

Product Code: 5110569 / LPM Price: $99.95 / Regular Price: $129.95

The use of electronic evidence has increased dramatically over the past few years, but many lawyers still struggle with the complexities of electronic discovery. This substantial book provides lawyers with the templates they need to frame their discovery requests and provides helpful advice on what they can subpoena. In addition to the ready-made forms, the authors also supply explanations to bring you up to speed on the electronic discovery field. The accompanying CD-ROM features over 70 forms, including, Motions for Protective Orders, Preservation and Spoliation Documents, Motions to Compel, Electronic Evidence Protocol Agreements, Requests for Production, Internet Services Agreements, and more. Also included is a full electronic evidence case digest with over 300 cases detailed!

The Lawyer's Guide to Microsoft Word 2010
By Ben M. Schorr

Product Code: 5110721 / LPM Price: $41.95 / Regular Price: $69.95

Microsoft® Word is one of the most used applications in the Microsoft® Office suite. This handy reference includes clear explanations, legal-specific descriptions, and time-saving tips for getting the most out of Microsoft Word®—and customizing it for the needs of today's legal professional. Focusing on the tools and features that are essential for lawyers in their everyday practice, this book explains in detail the key components to help make you more effective, more efficient, and more successful.

The Lawyer's Guide to LexisNexis CaseMap
By Daniel J. Siegel

Product Code: 5110715 / LPM Price: $47.95 / Regular Price: $79.95

LexisNexis CaseMap is a computer program that makes analyzing cases easier and allows lawyers to do a better job for their clients in less time. Many consider this an essential law office tool. If you are interested in learning more about LexisNexis CaseMap, this book will help you:

- Analyze the strengths and weaknesses of your cases quickly and easily;
- Learn how to create files for people, organizations and issues, while avoiding duplication;
- Customize CaseMap so that you can get the most out of your data;
- Enter data so that you can easily prepare for trial, hearings, depositions, and motions for summary judgment;
- Import data from a wide range of programs, including Microsoft Outlook;
- Understand CaseMap's many Reports and ReportBooks;
- Use the Adobe DocPreviewer to import PDFs and quickly create facts and objects; and
- Learn how to perform advanced searches plus how to save and update your results.

Virtual Law Practice:
How to Deliver Legal Services Online
By Stephanie L. Kimbro

Product Code: 5110707 / LPM Price: $47.95 / Regular Price: $79.95

The legal market has recently experienced a dramatic shift as lawyers seek out alternative methods of practicing law and providing more affordable legal services. Virtual law practice is revolutionizing the way the public receives legal services and how legal professionals work with clients. If you are interested in this form of practicing law, *Virtual Law Practice* will help you:

- *Responsibly deliver legal services online to* your clients
- Successfully set up and operate a virtual law office
- Establish a virtual law practice online through a secure, client-specific portal
- Manage and market your virtual law practice
- Understand state ethics and advisory opinions
- Find more flexibility and work/life balance in the legal profession

The Lawyer's Essential Guide to Writing
By Marie Buckley

Product Code: 5110726 / LPM Price: $47.95 / Regular Price: $79.95

This is a readable, concrete guide to contemporary legal writing. Based on Marie Buckley's years of experience coaching lawyers, this book provides a systematic approach to all forms of written communication, from memoranda and briefs to e-mail and blogs. The book sets forth three principles for powerful writing and shows how to apply those principles to develop a clean and confident style.

iPad in One Hour for Lawyers
By Tom Mighell

Product Code: 5110719 / LPM Price: $19.95 / Regular Price: $34.95

Whether you are a new or a more advanced iPad user, *iPad in One Hour for Lawyers* takes a great deal of the mystery and confusion out of using your iPad. Ideal for lawyers who want to get up to speed swiftly, this book presents the essentials so you don't get bogged down in technical jargon and extraneous features and apps. In just six, short lessons, you'll learn how to:

- Quickly Navigate and Use the iPad User Interface
- Set Up Mail, Calendar, and Contacts
- Create and Use Folders to Multitask and Manage Apps
- Add Files to Your iPad, and Sync Them
- View and Manage Pleadings, Case Law, Contracts, and other Legal Documents
- Use Your iPad to Take Notes and Create Documents
- Use Legal-Specific Apps at Trial or in Doing Research

Find Info Like a Pro, Volume 1: Mining the Internet's Publicly Available Resources for Investigative Research
By Carole A. Levitt and Mark E. Rosch

Product Code: 5110708 / LPM Price: $47.95 / Regular Price: $79.95

This complete hands-on guide shares the secrets, shortcuts, and realities of conducting investigative and background research using the sources of publicly available information available on the Internet. Written for legal professionals, this comprehensive desk book lists, categorizes, and describes hundreds of free and fee-based Internet sites. The resources and techniques in this book are useful for investigations; depositions; locating missing witnesses, clients, or heirs; and trial preparation, among other research challenges facing legal professionals. In addition, a CD-ROM is included, which features clickable links to all of the sites contained in the book.

How to Start and Build a Law Practice, Platinum Fifth Edition
By Jay G Foonberg

Product Code: 5110508 / LPM Price: $57.95 / Regular Price: $69.95

This classic ABA bestseller has been used by tens of thousands of lawyers as the comprehensive guide to planning, launching, and growing a successful practice. It's packed with over 600 pages of guidance on identifying the right location, finding clients, setting fees, managing your office, maintaining an ethical and responsible practice, maximizing available resources, upholding your standards, and much more. You'll find the information you need to successfully launch your practice, run it at maximum efficiency, and avoid potential pitfalls along the way. If you're committed to starting—and growing—your own practice, this one book will give you the expert advice you need to make it succeed for years to come.

Social Media for Lawyers: The Next Frontier
By Carolyn Elefant and Nicole Black

Product Code: 5110710 / LPM Price: $47.95 / Regular Price: $79.95

The world of legal marketing has changed with the rise of social media sites such as Linkedin, Twitter, and Facebook. Law firms are seeking their companies attention with tweets, videos, blog posts, pictures, and online content. Social media is fast and delivers news at record pace. This book provides you with a practical, goal-centric approach to using social media in your law practice that will enable you to identify social media platforms and tools that fit your practice and implement them easily, efficiently, and ethically.

30-DAY RISK-FREE ORDER FORM

ABA **LawPracticeManagementSection**
MARKETING • MANAGEMENT • TECHNOLOGY • FINANCE

Please print or type. To ship UPS, we must have your street address. If you list a P.O. Box, we will ship by U.S. Mail.

Name _____

Member ID _____

Firm/Organization _____

Street Address _____

City/State/Zip _____

Area Code/Phone (In case we have a question about your order) _____

E-mail _____

Method of Payment:
❏ Check enclosed, payable to American Bar Association
❏ MasterCard   ❏ Visa   ❏ American Express

_____
Card Number   Expiration Date

_____
Signature Required

MAIL THIS FORM TO:
American Bar Association, Publication Orders
P.O. Box 10892, Chicago, IL 60610

ORDER BY PHONE:
24 hours a day, 7 days a week:
Call 1-800-285-2221 to place a credit card order.
We accept Visa, MasterCard, and
American Express.

EMAIL ORDERS: orders@americanbar.org
FAX: 1-312-988-5568

VISIT OUR WEB SITE: www.ShopABA.org
Allow 7-10 days for regular UPS delivery. Need it sooner? Ask about our overnight delivery options. Call the ABA Service Center at 1-800-285-2221 for more information.

GUARANTEE:
If–for any reason–you are not satisfied with your purchase, you may return it within 30 days of receipt for a refund of the price of the book(s). No questions asked.

Thank You For Your Order.

Join the ABA Law Practice Management Section today and receive a substantial discount on Section publications!

Product Code:	Description:	Quantity:	Price:	Total Price:
				$
				$
				$
				$
				$
			Subtotal:	$
			*Tax:	$
			**Shipping/Handling:	$
			Yes, I am an ABA member and would like to join the Law Practice Management Section today! (Add $50.00)	$
			Total:	$

**Shipping/Handling:

$0.00 to $9.99	add $0.00
$10.00 to $49.99	add $5.95
$50.00 to $99.99	add $7.95
$100.00 to $199.99	add $9.95
$200.00 to $499.99	add $12.95

*Tax:
IL residents add 9.5%
DC residents add 6%

Join the ABA Law Practice Management Section Today!

Value is . . .

Resources that help you become a better lawyer:
- Up to 40% off LPM publications
- Six Issues of *Law Practice* magazine, both print and electronic versions
- Twelve issues of our monthly Webzine, *Law Practice Today*
- Your connection to Section news and events through *LawPractice.news*
- Discounted registration on "Third Thursday" CLE Teleconference Series and LPM conferences

Networking with industry experts while improving your skills at:
- ABA TECHSHOW
- ABA Law Firm Marketing Strategies Conference
- ABA Women Rainmakers Mid-Career Workshop
- LPM Quarterly Meetings

Opportunity given exclusively to our members:
- Writing for LPM periodicals and publications
- Joining ABA Women Rainmakers
- Becoming a better leader through committee involvement
- Listing your expertise in the LPM Speakerbase

Members of LPM get up to 40% off publications like this one. Join today and start saving!

www.lawpractice.org • 1.800.285.2221